T0287011

The Cult of Creativity

THE CULT OF
Creativity

A Surprisingly Recent History

SAMUEL W. FRANKLIN

The University of Chicago Press

Chicago and London

The University of Chicago Press, Chicago 60637
The University of Chicago Press, Ltd., London
© 2023 by Samuel Weil Franklin
All rights reserved. No part of this book may be used or reproduced in any manner
whatsoever without written permission, except in the case of brief quotations in critical
articles and reviews. For more information, contact the University of Chicago Press,
1427 E. 60th St., Chicago, IL 60637.
Published 2023
Printed in the United States of America

32 31 30 29 28 27 26 25 24 23   1 2 3 4 5

ISBN-13: 978-0-226-65785-1 (cloth)
ISBN-13: 978-0-226-65799-8 (e-book)
DOI: https://doi.org/10.7208/chicago/9780226657998.001.0001

Library of Congress Cataloging-in-Publication Data

Names: Franklin, Samuel Weil, author.
Title: The cult of creativity : a surprisingly recent history / Samuel W. Franklin.
Description: Chicago : The University of Chicago Press, 2023. | Includes bibliographical
    references and index.
Identifiers: LCCN 2022037344 | ISBN 9780226657851 (cloth) | ISBN 9780226657998
    (e-book)
Subjects: LCSH: Creative ability—United States. | Creation (Literary, artistic, etc.)
Classification: LCC BF408.F68 2023 | DDC 153.3/5—dc23/eng/20220825
LC record available at https://lccn.loc.gov/2022037344

♾ This paper meets the requirements of ANSI/NISO Z39.48-1992 (Permanence of
Paper).

CONTENTS

Introduction

By the time I reached adulthood I was pretty sure I was creative, and I considered this a good thing. I grew up in the 1980s in a milieu in which creativity was encouraged. My parents signed me up for pottery and music lessons and something called Odyssey of the Mind, where kids competed against students from other schools in skits and in quickly listing responses to prompts such as "unusual uses for a red brick." Though I only realized it later, being creative became an implicit part of my identity, and it seemed to fit. I doodled in class. When assigned an essay, I built a diorama instead. I took up the saxophone and played in bands, which made me creative almost by definition. Being creative even seemed to impart a positive spin on my less attractive attributes. Disruptive in class? Bad at math? Bad at sports and maybe a tad fey? Creative.

Lucky for me, by the time I graduated college the conventional wisdom among those who loved to reject conventional wisdom was not only that being creative was a good thing, but that creative people were going to inherit the earth. A recent crop of cocktail-party nonfiction about Right-Brainers and Bourgeoise Bohemians and something called the Creative Class said the age of rule-loving "organization men" had passed, leaving the field to those who rebelled against the status quo. As factories left American shores and computers automated more and more white-collar brain work, the raw material of our increasingly "weightless" postindustrial economy was no longer steel and coal, but rather ideas. In this "weightless" and "increasingly complex world," the creatives, long confined to garrets and bohemian cafes, would finally take their places as the leaders of a bright new future. The MFA was the new MBA.[1]

These turn-of-the-millennium prophesies soon became dogma. From its new nexus in Silicon Valley, corporate America introduced flex hours, free lunch, and Ping-Pong tables, supposedly to cater to the peripatetic workings of the creative process. Cities competed to attract creative workers, promising funky cultural amenities like live music and live/work studio apartments. Casually dressed and increasingly tattooed architects, designers, and musicians began to populate our advertisements and other aspirational media. In 2010, a poll of 1,500 CEOs ranked creativity as "the most important leadership quality for success in business," beating out such virtues as integrity and global thinking.[2] The Partnership for 21st Century Skills, a committee representing the National Education Association, the Department of Education, and a handful of top tech companies including Apple, Microsoft, and Cisco, listed creativity as one of the "4 Cs" along with Communication, Collaboration, and Critical Thinking. And in 2020 the World Economic Forum declared creativity "the one skill that will future-proof you for the jobs market."[3] We apparently already knew that: back in 2011, "creative" was already the most common adjective job applicants used to describe themselves on LinkedIn.

And all of this was treated as basically good news; the new economy was aligning with our deeper need for meaningful work, self-expression, and liberation from social constraints. But there were also new anxieties. In the most-watched TED Talk of all time, "Do Schools Kill Creativity?" Sir Kenneth Robinson mourned the fact that the Western education system was based on an industrial model that left little room for free expression and the experimentation necessary for the future of work. As the eminent psychologist Mihalyi Csikszentmihalyi wrote in his 1997 bestseller *Creativity*, where historically it had been "a luxury for the few," creativity was "now a necessity for all."[4]

An ever-proliferating genre of books, blogs, articles, workshops, and even master's degrees has emerged to address these fears. They promise to help us "harness," "unleash," "unlock," "pump up," or "jump start" our creativity. Business schools offer standing-room-only courses on creativity. The e-education service Coursera has dozens of offerings on the topic. Books like Jonah Lehrer's *Imagine: How Creativity Works* or Scott Barry Kaufman and Carolyn Gregoire's *Wired to Create* "unravel the mysteries of the creative mind," using a mix of cutting-edge neuroscience, psychology, and anecdotes from the lives of Leonardo, Picasso, Martin Luther King Jr., Bob Dylan, and Steve Jobs, to reveal the "ten attributes and habits of highly creative people."[5] These texts invariably insist that, contrary to popular belief, creativity is not the sole province of geniuses and artists but the birthright of every one of us. It is not mysterious, but can be understood and applied deliberately.

But creativity is more than just a job skill. Even the most business-focused, how-to, airport bookstore fare treats creativity as a key to personal happiness and self-actualization, a humane good in and of itself. The American Psychological Association's manual of *Character Strengths and Virtues*, described as the "DSM of the sanities," gives creativity first billing.[6] Much of the creativity literature is distinctly spiritual, such as in Julia Cameron's hugely popular *The Artist's Way*, which fuses Buddhist mindfulness practices with the Alcoholics Anonymous twelve-step program, and which sees creativity as our connection to the divine. We often hear that creativity is not really about work at all, but a form of play, "intelligence having fun."[7] Even as it tops the wish lists of prospective employers, we also can't help but feel like creativity originates in a realm outside of the practical and commercial, and that it is sullied and compromised when forced to do business. It is, as Csikszentmihalyi writes, "a central source of meaning in our lives," and the thing that fundamentally sets us apart as humans from the rest of the animal kingdom.[8]

Even so, creativity is much more than just a personal or a professional good. It's also said to be the thing that's going to save the world. "It is only with creativity that we can hope to address the myriad problems facing our schools and medical facilities, our cities and towns, our economy, our nation, and the world," write two preeminent psychologists; "creativity is one of the key factors that drive civilization forward."[9] Perhaps the best articulation of how we feel about creativity comes from the slogan of a 2018 Adidas ad campaign featuring the likes of the soccer superstar Lionel Messi and the music producer Pharrell Williams: "Creativity Is the Answer." What creativity is the answer *to* is left tantalizingly vague, but the implication is *everything*—from outwitting a defenseman to producing a new banger to the biggest of social problems.

All of these claims about creativity—that it is a cure-all for business, self, humanity, the planet—can feel irrefutable, unobjectionable, even self-evident. But also, when taken together, a bit grandiose, and confusing. Were Picasso, Einstein, Gandhi, Steve Jobs, and ten-year-old me coming up with strange uses for a brick really all running on the same stuff? Will learning to dance actually help kids thrive in the maelstrom of late capitalism? How can creativity be both a sacred and inalienable personal experience and an engine of economic growth? If creativity is really what it takes to make it these days, and everyone is at least potentially creative, how come inequality is compounding along the same old lines of race and class? And considering how many of our modern problems come from having too much new stuff too quickly, what reason do we have to believe that we lack creativity in the first place, or that encouraging more of it will solve any of those problems?

Such questions inevitably lead us to the conclusion that creativity is quite a fuzzy concept. Sometimes it is treated as a learnable skill, other times as an innate personality trait. In some cases it refers specifically to the arts or the "creative" side of business, such as design and marketing, while in others it extends to every corner of society. It can invoke the masterworks of great geniuses as well as the everyday doings of third-graders. And most confusing of all, these sometimes contrary meanings are often found side by side within any given text.[10]

Despite all this, we still believe in creativity. In its many splendors—playful yet profitable, extraordinary yet universally human, the driver of human progress and the thing that will save us from it—creativity is something of a cult object, something we project all of our desires and anxieties onto, imbued with almost mystical powers, and beyond rebuke. In our divided times, one of the most amazing things about creativity is that nobody ever says anything bad about it. Virtually all of us are members of this cult of creativity. Kindergarten teachers, mayors, CEOs, designers, engineers, activists, and starving artists, we all basically agree creativity is a good thing and that we should have more of it.

The Big Bang

The creativity literature tells us that, even though we're just now beginning to appreciate the importance of creativity in everyday life, it is a topic pondered by poets and philosophers since time immemorial. In fact, creativity has only been a regular part of our vocabulary since the middle of the twentieth century. Its first known written occurrence was in 1875, making it an infant as far as words go.[11] "Creativeness" goes back a bit further, and was more common than creativity until about 1940, but both were used rarely and in an ad hoc kind of way. Strikingly, before about 1950 there were approximately zero articles, books, essays, treatises, odes, classes, encyclopedia entries, or anything of the sort dealing explicitly with the subject of "creativity." (The earliest dictionary entry I found was from 1966.)[12] It is not, it turns out, in Plato or Aristotle (even in translation). It's not in Kant (ditto). It's not in Wordsworth or Shelley, or in the Americans Emerson, William James, or John Dewey. As the intellectual historian Paul Oskar Kristeller finds, creativity, though we tend to assume it is a timeless concept, is a term with "poor philosophical and historical credentials."[13]

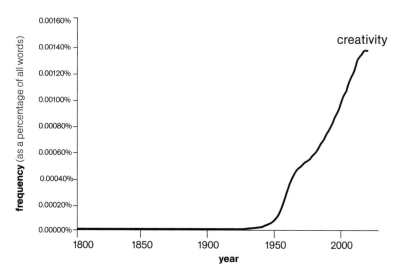

Figure 0.1 The relative frequency of the term "creativity" in books in English between 1800 and 2019. Google Books.

Yet, just around the end of World War II, the use of creativity shot upward—the Big Bang of creativity.[14]

How did we so quickly go from never talking about creativity to constantly talking about, it, and even anointing it as the reigning value of our time? And why? What was it about the dawn of the postwar era that demanded this new Swiss army knife of a term? Did it bubble up everywhere all at once, or did it emerge from specific corners of society? How did it fit with larger social and cultural transformations of the time? And whom did it serve?

This book is about how we came to believe in creativity—in the sense that we tend to think it is the answer to nearly all our problems, and in the sense that we believe in the phenomenon of something called creativity to begin with. This is not a book about how creativity works or how to be more creative. Nor is it a survey of how we've thought about art and invention and the like through the long sweep of history.[15] Instead, it is a history of how and why in the United States after World War II something called creativity became a topic, an object of academic study and debate, an official personality trait, a goal of educational and economic policy, an ideal of personal transformation. You could say it's about how creativity became, in more than one sense, a thing.

The story the book tells is unexpected. When I began researching creativity's Big Bang, I imagined finding its roots in the burgeoning youthful counterculture—the spirit of self-expression, experimentation, and rebelliousness that would crest in the 1960s and give that decade its distinctive mark. Instead, I found that the creativity craze began somewhat earlier, in the 1950s, an era we associate with conformity, bureaucracy, and suburbanization. And it didn't come from artists or the bohemian fringe in that era, either. As Dorothy Parker quipped in 1958, the high-water mark of the postwar creativity craze, the more a writer actually sits down to write, "the less he will get into small clusters bandying about the word 'creativity.'"[16] Despite the fact that many in the postwar American art world embraced self-expression and experimentation, it turns out the efforts to really get under the hood of something called creativity—which also encompassed ideas like "creative ability," "the creative personality," and "the creative process"—were primarily driven by a concern not for art *per se* but for inventiveness in science, technology, consumer products, and advertising. At the same time, the artsy connotations were not incidental: the postwar cult of creativity was driven by a desire to impart on science, technology, and consumer culture some of the qualities widely seen to be possessed by artists, such as nonconformity, passion for work, and a humane, even moral sensibility, in addition to, of course, a penchant for the new.[17]

This book follows an assorted cluster of academic psychologists, management gurus, advertising executives, and engineers who together, in collaboration, constructed the concept of creativity as we know it today. In their various attempts to quantify, explain, and methodically reproduce some human capacity called creativity, they imbued it with their particular, often conflicting desires: to reconcile fundamental tensions between the individual and mass society, the extraordinary and the everyday, the spiritual and the crassly material, the rebellious and the status quo. Making a master term to hold these tensions together was not easy; the concept was constantly falling apart on them. But in the aggregate, they were successful—if not in truly resolving the essential paradoxes of their time, then in generating a blueprint for doing so that continues to inform how we think about technology, consumerism, and capitalism up to the present day.[18]

What Did We Call It Before?

When I tell people the term "creativity" is new, I invariably get the question, "what did we call it before?" And my response, annoying but sincere, is always "what do you mean by 'it'?" There are two assumptions behind the first question, both correct. The first is that words and concepts are not the same thing; the arrival or popularization of a new word does not necessarily mean the arrival of a totally new concept. The alcoholic and the drunkard, for example, are two different eras' ways for describing the same person—one who habitually drinks to excess. The second assumption is that people have always been talking about the kind of stuff we talk about when we talk about creativity—in the way that people have always talked about excessive drinking. It's not totally wrong to say that creativity is, or at least can be in certain instances, a new term for old concepts, such as imagination, inspiration, fantasy, genius, originality, and even phrases like creative imagination and creative power, which long predated creativity itself.

Yet the modern concept of creativity does not perfectly trace back to any one of these older words. *Ingenuity* or *inventiveness* are too utilitarian; they lack the artsy vibe. Creativity may invoke monumental achievements in art and science, but as a synonym the term *genius* somehow feels too exclusive and grandiose—kids can be creative—while *cleverness* is a little too pedestrian, something you might attribute to a pig that finds its way out of its pen. *Originality* hits closer to the mark, but it's somehow not as soulful— nobody ever says "originality" is the key to a fulfilling life. *Imagination*, perhaps the term most often used interchangeably with creativity, lacks a sense of productivity. Like fantasy, it doesn't have to leave your head, and it can be utterly preposterous. The prevailing idea among creativity experts is that creativity is "the ability to produce something new and useful."[19] (That phrasing is taken—not coincidentally, we'll see—from US patent law). The term *creativity*, in other words, allows us to think and say things previous terms don't. It is not a new word for old ideas but a way of expressing thoughts that were previously inexpressible. When people in the postwar era increasingly chose the word "creativity," then, they were subtly distinguishing their meaning from those other, almost universally older concepts. The term may not be precise, but it is vague in precise and meaningful ways. Just as light can be both particle and wave, creativity somehow manages to exist as simultaneously mental and material, playful and practical, artsy and technological, exceptional and pedestrian. This contradictory constellation of meanings and connotations, more than any one definition or theory, is what explains its appeal in postwar America, in which the balance between those very things seemed gravely at stake. The slipperiness was a feature, not a bug.

If you go back to the Big Bang of creativity and read as many essays and books and talks on creativity as you possibly can—and dear reader, I have—you will immediately notice that within the first few lines there is almost always something like this:

Creativity must be seen in the work of the scientist as well as in that of the artist, in the thinker as well as in the aesthetician; and one must not rule out the extent to which it is present in captains of modern technology as well as in a mother's normal relationship with her child.[20]

There is no fundamental difference in the creative process as it is evidenced in painting a picture, composing a symphony, devising new instruments of killing, developing a scientific theory, discovering new procedures in human relationships, or creating new formings of one's own personality.[21]

[Creativity] in the arts and in science are analogous and characterized by the same fundamental psychic process.[22]

Presumably, the process of creativity, whatever it is, is essentially the same in all its branches and varieties, so that the evolution of a new art form, a new gadget, a new scientific principle, all involve common factors.[23]

Men can be creative not only in painting, writing poetry or discovering scientific theories, but also in cooking, carpentering, playing football or making love.[24]

This trope, repeated with the regularity of a daily prayer, was, as we'll see, never an empirical finding. It was, rather, a starting point, an assumption, a wish. To begin to understand why creativity has become such a salient topic in the last seventy-five years is to ask what is useful about a concept both so general that it can explain art and technology, the extraordinary and the everyday, yet so narrow that it can distill all of those down to a personal, as opposed to a social, phenomenon. To answer that we must understand the unruly mix of ideological and practical imperatives at the heart of postwar America.

Mass Society and the Permanent Revolution

America emerged from World War II as the most powerful nation on Earth, politically as well as economically. Yet triumph begot anxieties about how to wield so much newfound power and what doing so would mean for the country. With the Great Depression a vivid memory and communist Russia mounting its world-historical challenge, American policy makers, labor leaders, and businessmen developed a plan for continuous economic growth and broad prosperity driven by consumerism, peace between industry and labor, and military spending. It would be, as *Fortune* said in 1951, a "Permanent Revolution," a system of steady improvements to the standard of living such as only American capitalism could provide.[25] By delivering high wages, high profits, and a steady stream of both dazzling new consumer products and military technologies, the postwar architects would ward off socialism at home and abroad and fully realize the tremendous promise of modernity.[26]

The postwar economy represented a kind of high point for American blue-collar labor: the unionized workers of the steel mills, construction sites, and auto plants. But it also witnessed the terrific expansion of the white-collar world, as large corporations hired college-trained men (and sometimes women) to manage the factory floor, to oversee supply chains, to engineer new products, and to advertise and market those goods to the emergent middle class. With help from the GI Bill and monumental government investment in higher education, between 1940 and 1964 the number of people with professional and technical degrees more than doubled, growing at twice the rate of the general labor force. Scientists and engineers were the fastest growing among these: between 1930 and 1955, the number of scientists increased fivefold, and the lion's share of them were employed by the military or industry. By 1956, the number of white-collar workers exceeded that of blue-collar workers for the first time in American history.[27]

This new postwar world of engineers, ad men, and massive organizations in turn produced a national panic over the arrival of a "mass society." There were murmurs, rising to a chorus by the mid-1960s, that this rising standard of living was a devil's bargain. One could hear it in the cocktail party chatter about David Riesman's *The Lonely Crowd*, Vance Packard's takedowns of Madison Avenue and auto industry deceptions, or Herbert Marcuse's *One-Dimensional Man*. In the light of the Holocaust, Hiroshima, and Stalin's gulags, modern institutions took on sinister casts. Where the prewar generation had seen bureaucracy and technocracy as fixes to free-market madness, postwar critics cast them as examples of modern rationality out of control. The drive for efficiency was turning life itself into a soulless machine. The absolute faith in "science" was eclipsing spirituality and morality. This "affluent society," despite its comforts, was built on mass alienation at work, passive consumption at home, and an erosion of any sense of the social good. There was a strong sense that all of this supposed progress was essentially meaningless, or even immoral. As the sociologist Theodore Roszak put it, modern society had abolished all "traditional transcendent ends of life," and replaced them with a "proficiency of technical means that now oscillates absurdly between the production of frivolous abundance and the production of genocidal munitions."[28]

The worst of the ills of mass society—or, at least, the one everyone could agree on—was "conformity." "The trend of the age is towards a *herd state* of which the essence is the denial of the supreme value of the individual," warned psychologist O. Hobart Mowrer.[29] William Whyte, the editor of *Fortune* magazine, warned of the decline of an American tradition of individualism going back to the days of the yeoman farmer. "In a country where 'individualism'— independence and self-reliance—was the watchword for three centuries," he wrote, "the view is now coming to be accepted that the individual himself has no meaning."[30] David Riesman wrote that "inner-directed" individualists were being replaced by "other-directed" social beings. Those on the right blamed the New Deal and its collectivist intellectual champions. Those on the left, including many recent European arrivals with their fresh memories of totalitarianism, tended to blame corporate capitalism, with its deadening bureaucracies and mass media–driven consumerism and ceaseless utilitarianism. For the broad liberal center, conformity was poison for democracy, the domestic mirror of foreign communism. All across American society, from the right to the left, from sociologists to novelists to feminists to black liberationists, postwar thinkers were united in a quest to recover the autonomous self from the morass of mass society.[31]

Even those at the helm of mass society worried about the effects of conformity on innovation itself. The "dilemma that daily confronts today's managers of large-scale enterprises," wrote McKinsey director John Corson, was "how to maintain order, stability, and predictability . . . and, at the same time, stimulate and nourish to fruition the innovations on which all enterprises depend." William Whyte wrote that a "social ethic" was making American capitalism uninventive and uninspired. Economic progress of the past, he said, echoing the Austrian economist Joseph Schumpeter, had been driven by lone geniuses. Schumpeter had warned, in the 1940s, that corporatism was bad for innovation, having turned all the would-be inventors into salaried employees and killing the entrepreneurial incentive that powered capitalist growth. Now, Whyte observed, the "administrator," not the "creative individual," was in charge. The former, indoctrinated in "order, objective goals, agreement," was hostile to "the messiness of intuition, the aimless thoughts, the unpractical questions" of the process of invention. Echoing Whyte, Corson asserted that "ideas come from people," not organizations, and in particular from "the nonconformist innovator, rather than the 'organization man.'"[32]

This corporate critique of conformity had a particular Cold War resonance. The USSR, it was said, was achieving its technological edge by pressing its citizens into service, essentially "commandeering talent." By contrast, "the free society," according to the classified NSC-68, a 1950 Cold War policy manifesto, "attempts to create and maintain an environment in which every individual has the opportunity to realize his creative powers." Even after the launch of Sputnik in 1957, as hawks were calling for more emphasis on math and science, liberal education reformers insisted on a progressive approach that included arts and letters and allowed students to find their own paths. In the Soviet Union, it was often said, the ends justified the means. America's greatness, by contrast, would have to be built on a respect for the individual. Technical prowess must be backed by cultural purpose. American hegemony would have to appear consistent with the liberal values it was touting to the world. Put simply, the question was: how do we defeat the Communists without becoming like them?

Yet despite all the hand-wringing about the fate of the individual, virtually everyone agreed mass society was here to stay. "The interlocking complexities of modern society are an inescapable part of our future," concluded a 1961 Rockefeller Brothers Fund report. If the American spirit of individualism were to have a place in this world, "we shall have to learn to preserve it in a context of organization. . . . How may we rescue talented individuals from the lowered aspirations, the boredom, and the habits of mediocrity so often induced by life in a large and complex organization?"[33] The challenge of the postwar era, then, seemed to be how to unleash individualism within order. How to revive the spirit of the lone inventor within the maze of the modern corporation?

Moreover, the needs of industry were changing. Having achieved a productive capacity far beyond that necessary to meet everyone's basic needs, management was suddenly less worried about efficiency than about marketing, innovation, and adaptability. As Peter Drucker said, not manufacturing, but "innovation and marketing" were the new managerial priorities. Particularly as computers began to assume some of the more menial office tasks, managers began to fret that a whole half century of inculcating in workers the values of rationality and order, and encouraging specialization, was leaving the workforce ill equipped for this new reality. Just as the wartime factories had to be retooled to meet the demands of a consumer economy, so did the white-collar worker need to be retooled.

The concept of creativity, typically defined as a kind of trait or process vaguely associated with artists and geniuses but theoretically possessed by anyone and applicable to any field, emerged as a psychological cure for these structural and political contradictions of the postwar order. Psychologists developed tests to identify "creative people" based largely on the needs of military and corporate R&D, but they were also motivated by a larger desire to save individuals from the psychic oppression of modernity. Likewise, in industry, the first creative thinking methods, such as brainstorming, were initially geared toward industrial improvement and new product development, but they did so by addressing alienation on the job. Advertising professionals touted "creative advertising" as both a cure for lagging sales and a way to bring individual vision back into their field. And many corporations embraced creativity not only to help spur innovation but also because it made them look more humane amid backlash against the military-industrial complex. In all of these cases, the practical matters of staffing R&D labs, coming up with new product ideas, or selling said products coexisted with larger concerns about conformity, alienation, and the morality of work.

Creativity could, for one thing, ease a nagging tension between the utilitarian and the humane or transcendent. In 1962, the distinguished psychologist Jerome Bruner noted "a shrillness to our contemporary concern with creativity." Psychologists were being asked to dissect the nature of "the creative" not purely as scientists, "but as adjutants to the moralist." Bruner suspected that what really lay behind the sudden interest in research on creativity was an anxiety about the nature of white-collar work, particularly among scientists and technicians. These workers had been inculcated with the dogma of professionalism and efficiency, seeing themselves as part of a great social machine. But, he said, "to pattern one's function on the machine provides no measure for dignity. The machine is useful, the system . . . is efficient, but what is man?"[34] The idea that commercial, technological, or scientific work was an act of creation, Bruner felt, "endows the process with dignity." And so, "There is creative advertising, creative engineering, creative problem solving—all lively entries in the struggle for dignity in our time." For an engineer or an advertising professional to be creative was not simply to be *productive*, though it was that, but also to model oneself not on the machine but on the artist or poet. It was to pursue work with an intrinsic motivation, a passion for the act of creation. It was to be more *human*. Though this didn't necessarily change anything about the actual products these workers were employed to invent, design, and sell, it did implicitly add a moral aura to their work by shifting the emphasis from product to the process itself, creativity.

The development of the concept of creativity by psychologists and creative thinking experts allowed for the emergence of a new form of subjectivity, the creative person. The creative person was a producer in a world of consumers. No impotent Babbitt or parasitic pencil-pusher, the creative person was a rebel and freethinker. They lived to create. This person, generally assumed to be male, was nonetheless construed as more emotionally sensitive than the old model. And while generally assumed to be White, this new creative person was also more in touch with his "primitive" side than were his "over-civilized" peers. As reductive as they were, these tweaks to the middle-class self did broaden the view of whose mental labor might be valuable.[35] It should be no surprise that in the liberation movements of the 1960s, arguments for the right to participate in national life were sometimes made in the language of creativity. For instance, when Betty Friedan wrote in 1963 that women could achieve self-realization only through "creative work," she meant work that was traditionally male, such as journalism, the sort recognized as worthy of remuneration and renown.[36]

Friedan embodies an additional key theme—a tension between optimism and pessimism. She was deeply critical of the way the world was, but also very hopeful for what it could be. Focusing on creativity, which spoke of excellence, excitement, even joy, was for many an act of hope. Many psychologists, for example, contrasted their creativity research with the focus on mental illness and dysfunction that had preoccupied their field, while creativity management consultants imagined they were leading the charge in forming a more humane workplace. These people hoped that automation and affluence would provide more opportunities for human flourishing, even a transcendence of traditional capitalist relations.[37] Could we be headed, as Thomas Watson of IBM put it, for "a new age of Pericles," our material needs met and our minds free to partake in higher artistic and intellectual pursuits? Or would it all lead to opulence and stagnation, dooming America, as the historian Arnold Toynbee had warned, to the fate of fallen civilizations past? For all the optimism that gathered around creativity, the very need to name, and so to begin to understand and master, this thing, some individual font of dynamism, betrayed a deep fear that it was already sorely lacking.

Finally, besides the overarching tension between the individual and mass society, and between optimism and pessimism, creativity also mediated between elitist and egalitarian tendencies. On one hand, the postwar era was a profoundly democratic age, characterized by a strong welfare state, expanding minority rights, and widely shared prosperity. Americans were constantly reminded that it was in the name of democracy that they fought wars and now aggressively patrolled the globe, and the figure of the "common man" still had some heroic charm from the Depression years. On the other hand, particularly after the Russian launch of Sputnik, the fear of "mediocrity" brought on a new, often reactionary focus on "excellence." Toynbee lamented that America was neglecting its "creative minority" and so risking the kind of decline that befell every great empire before it. The question was, as the title of the 1961 John W. Gardner book put it, "can we be equal and excellent too?" It's no coincidence that Gardner, as an officer of the Carnegie Corporation, funded some of the earliest and most influential psychological research on creativity. Creativity was a topic capacious enough to apply to Great Men as well as elementary school children and rank-and-file engineers. Unlike genius, creativity could be said to exist in everyone, and in that sense was both more democratic and (more importantly, perhaps) more useful for managers overseeing scores or hundreds or thousands of employees. It satisfied a nostalgia for an earlier age of the genius inventor and entrepreneur, but in a form befitting the ideological and pragmatic realities of the mass society.

Over the next eight chapters we will see these dynamics in action through some of the people who most ardently championed the cause of creativity in the postwar era. Chapter 9 brings the story up to our own time. We will alternate back and forth between people who attempted to study creativity empirically and those who were more interested in putting creativity into practice. The first group includes psychologists who went in search of the nature of creativity in a variety of ways, from probing the minds of famous writers to testing Navy cadets on (what else?) their ability to come up with uses for a brick. Some of these psychologists were essentially after a better test to identify top scientific talent, while others aspired to create a "new type of human" equipped to deal with modern life. The second group includes the advertising-man-turned-creativity-guru who invented brainstorming, an interdisciplinary team of product developers who started the world's first creativity consultancy, and Madison Avenue people engaged in a war for the soul of advertising. These two broad groups, representing academia and industry, were always intertwined. They cited one another's work, spoke at one another's conferences, and appeared side by side in all sorts of books, magazines, and exhibitions on creativity. In the exchanges between these groups of actors—and the life-projects to which many of them devoted themselves—we see how desperately they sought to resolve the tensions of their age through the concept of creativity. Such resolutions were as difficult to sustain as any coherent definition of creativity that would satisfy all the criteria they heaped on it.

Excavating this history overturns many assumptions we have about creativity, including that it's always been with us, or that it was once a term reserved for gods, artists, and geniuses. To understand how recently creativity arrived, and the messy, practical world from which it arose, is to understand how we got to our own situation. Not only does this book reveal the roots of today's creativity expertise (at the very least we've all been in a brainstorming session); in a larger sense it helps illuminate the broad sweep of recent cultural history. As chapter 9 will tell, today's breathless talk of entrepreneurialism and the liberating, disruptive promise of the "gig economy"; our dogged determination to "do what you love" and our disdain for the 9-to-5; the fact that to think outside the box, color outside the lines, and go against the grain are now practically moral imperatives; the very fact that we now have a class of people known simply as "creatives" or even "creators"; and the persistence of optimism despite so many cruel realities of modern capitalism—all of these can in some way trace their origins to the immediate postwar cult of creativity. The fact that we are still in many ways dealing with the same contradictions helps explain why we continue to be so enamored of the idea, and why so many of us want so desperately to be creative.

Between the Commonplace and the Sublime

"I got the loveliest invitation," recalled the San Francisco rebel poet and essayist Kenneth Rexroth, with more than a hint of sarcasm. As he explained to readers of *The Nation*, earlier that year, 1957, he had been summoned, along with a handful of other literary luminaries including Truman Capote and William Carlos Williams, to a place called the Institute for Personality Assessment and Research (IPAR), located in a former fraternity house at the University of California, Berkeley, to participate in a study on "the creative personality." Over the course of three days, Rexroth submitted to a thorough psychological examination. The first evening he and the other guests were greeted with cocktails and dinner, after which "everybody paired off for Rorschachs." The next day they made pictures using colored tiles, "interpreted symbols," "sorted things," and shared preferences for paintings, followed by "long, chummy, deep-speaking-to-deep sort of talk" with the psychologists.[1]

Rexroth had found himself swept up in the postwar creativity research boom. At the 1950 conference of the American Psychological Association (APA), its president, Joy Paul Guilford, used his address to decry the "appalling" neglect of research on creativity. According to him, only 0.2 percent of articles and books in psychology had dealt with "creative behavior" (including "such activities as inventing, designing, contriving, composing, and planning"), and he found it nowhere in the textbooks used to train psychologists. Guilford implored his colleagues to remedy the situation, and they did. Over the next ten years the number of new books and articles on creativity matched that since the advent of the psychological profession. That number doubled again by 1965, and once more the following year.[2] The major psychological journals were flooded with study after study on "creative ability," "creative behavior," and "creativity," fed by money pouring in from the National Science Foundation, every branch of the military—Guilford's own research was funded by the Office of Naval Research—and education agencies and philanthropic foundations like the Carnegie Corporation (which, Rexroth noted, had granted IPAR "a bucketful of gold"). An audience quickly formed among fellow psychologists, military and industrial research directors, and educators, plus millions of ordinary Americans who could now read about how creativity worked through coverage in the glossy magazines. By the end of the 1960s a *Journal of Creative Behavior* had been launched, several research centers established, and dozens of conferences and symposia held—most notably a series of biennial conferences at the University of Utah starting in 1955. These nodes occasionally attracted well-known or soon-to-be well-known thinkers such as Margaret Mead, Herbert Simon, and Timothy Leary, but more importantly they provided an academic home for a number of researchers who would devote their careers to the study of creativity and establish a field that thrives to this day.

When psychologists take up a concept, be it hysteria, homosexuality, or depression, they give it a kind of social weight. Because they are nominally scientists, armed with tools of empirical observation, their embrace of a term tends to solidify it, make it seem like more than just a descriptive word, like something that actually exists out there in the world—typically, inside other people's

Figure 1.1 Frank Barron (right) and John A. Starkweather simulating ink blot and figure preference tests, 1954. "Creative" subjects were found to prefer abstract art and asymmetrical images, a fact attributed to their "tolerance for ambiguity" rather than their education or background. Copyright University of California, Berkeley. Image reproduced with permission.

heads. This process is called reification. Psychologists were central to constructing, promoting, and to some extent reifying the concept of creativity—even outside of psychology. We can't say they invented it—indeed, the word already felt self-explanatory enough to appear to them as a concept stable enough to study—but before Guilford's speech creativity was not a psychological term of art. These researchers were the first to systematically produce knowledge about creativity, define it, and quantify it, and in doing so they helped make it into the "thing" it is today.

It's therefore crucial to see how psychologists constructed this thing they called "creativity." What did it mean to them? How did they define it, both explicitly and operationally, in the design of their experiments and the selection of criteria for what counted as creativity in the first place? Should only clear instances of genius be considered? Or lesser instances of everyday problem solving? When considering a creative product, how new or different does it have to be? Can creativity be identified even if nothing has been created? One's answers to these questions might depend in part on what one understood the purpose of creativity research to be in the first place. As the founders creativity research would soon find, in creativity they had chosen an exceedingly slippery concept, one that easily defied attempts to find common ground.

But there is a second-order question, too: Why ask? What was it about the hard-to-pin-down and problematic concept that made it so appealing to psychologists? The answer lies in how creativity occupied a new space between older concepts that already had established psychological traditions, such as *genius, intelligence, imagination, and inventiveness.* Creativity, heroic yet democratic, romantic yet practical, seemed to be the answer to problems in society and, as it happened, within the field of psychology itself.

Ultimately, the question of *how* they constructed creativity and *why* go hand in hand. Creativity psychologists were in many ways working on extremely specific problems of the scientific and technological establishment—such as how to identify promising engineers—but they also believed they were working for individual happiness, and on behalf of liberal society against conformity and mediocrity. These several purposes were reflected in the specific theories and methods they devised. When they added these things together they ended up with a new creature, the "creative person": a somewhat unstable mix of particular cognitive abilities and personality traits that, while putatively universal—that is to say, potentially distributed across the population and not tied to any particular racial, gender, or class markers—nonetheless ended up reflecting the assumptions and interests of the psychologists themselves and their major benefactors.

The State of Psychology

The motivations for this sudden blossoming of creativity research reflected tensions in the field of psychology that in many ways mirrored those in American society writ large. Like the nation as a whole, American psychology at the end of World War II was at the very peak of its power. As members of the fastest growing profession after engineering, psychologists cropped up in nearly every corner of national life, from helping returning GIs adjust to civilian life to staffing large corporations to explaining juvenile delinquency. The postwar era was in many ways a deeply psychological age; one of the cultural effects of the red scare was a preference for psychological explanations over structural ones, the latter of which reeked of materialism and thus of communism. To see the root of social and even political problems in terms of psychology—alienation, anxiety, authoritarian personality types—meant those problems might also be solvable on a therapeutic rather than a structural level. As a result, psychologists held a great deal of power, both culturally and in the administration of daily life.

At the same time, there were new and sometimes conflicting pressures on the field. One was the need to make psychology ever more useful to funders in industry and the state. As the social sciences found themselves increasingly dependent on government dollars tied to the promise of defeating communism, they were increasingly at pains to prove themselves as "real," and applicable, sciences. One of the key ways psychologists did this was by helping to address the problem of identifying and fostering "talent." Calvin Taylor, organizer of the Utah conferences, appealed to his funders at the National Science Foundation on precisely these grounds. "If we are to survive in international competition," he explained, specific attention must be paid to identifying and developing "the highly creative person," for "even a few such persons can keep our scientific movement vigorously in front" (and, he added, reasoning that creative people were more resourceful and efficient at generating new ideas, at much less expense).[3] Guilford later acknowledged these utilitarian roots of creativity studies, saying that the Cold War "called for ever-accelerating efforts in a contest of intellects. Inventive brains were at a premium, and there were never enough."[4] Guilford's putting creativity at the top of the profession's agenda was also likely a bid to prove psychology's empirical bona fides: he hailed creativity research as a scientific incursion into territory no less mysterious and awe-inspiring than outer space, an area on which past psychologists had "feared to tread."[5] With sophisticated statistical methods and large datasets, they would clear away the obfuscating thicket of romantic thinking and "focus the scientific method upon" creativity, as Taylor put it, so as to "accumulate and implement detailed knowledge to aid in development of man's creative talents."[6]

But creativity research also responded to a countervailing tendency in postwar psychology, a determination to make psychology serve more than just utilitarian ends. This manifested itself foremost in the revolt against "behaviorism." Behaviorism, the reigning paradigm since the 1920s, attempted to rid psychology of ideology and metaphysics by rooting it in the study of empirically observable behavior, typically using rats. Behaviorists preferred not to speculate on issues of meaning and spirituality, instead building up an almost mechanical model of human behavior as a series of predictable and even programmable "stimulus responses." For behaviorists like B. F. Skinner, the author of the 1948 utopian novel *Walden Two*, the idea that people were malleable was proof that they were capable of progress and social harmony. But in the shadow of the war, as people looked around for moral certainty, many critics accused behaviorism of reducing humans to animals, implicating it in the kind of instrumentalism that had led to the Holocaust and the gulags, and even blamed it for producing techniques of mass persuasion and "brainwashing" purportedly used on American prisoners of war in Korea. The major new postwar movements in psychology, cognitive science, and humanistic psychology—which will be covered more in chapter 3—were largely attempts to elevate psychology's model of the human being above the bestial and to return to "man" a degree of dignity, complexity, and free will that behaviorism seemed to deny.[7]

Many creativity researchers understood their work as a direct rebuke of behaviorism, which Taylor said "descended like a plague" on psychology, making it hard to do credible research on anything so lofty and "elusive" as creativity.[8] Decrying how narrow and rational their profession had become, they were eager to reclaim the larger existential questions psychologists had ceded to philosophers at the beginning of the century: What is it that makes humans uniquely human? What is the source of art, of the higher human achievements, of human flourishing in general? Though the race for technological dominance was the direct stimulus for creativity research and a key reason it remained so well funded through the 1950s and 1960s, that research was also driven by a sense that in a society so oriented toward technological and material goals psychology should come to the rescue of individual well-being for its own sake.

Because it addressed these various currents in the profession, creativity research appealed to a wide swath of the psychologists. At the Utah Conferences, for example, probably the most important node of creativity research in the postwar decades, one could sense "a spirit of speculation, and of co-operation between one discipline and another."[9] Taylor made "a deliberate attempt to invite researchers representing various behavioral sciences, education, the physical and biological sciences, and the arts."[10] From the beginning he brought on as a key collaborator Brewster Ghiselin, a University of Utah English professor. Other attendees included humanities professors, child psychologists, testing experts, psychoanalysts, Pentagon officials, research managers from major manufacturers, and more. They probed topics ranging from the drawings of schoolchildren to patent production by engineers, from anal retentiveness in top mathematicians to verbal fluency in college freshmen. Creativity research was to be a big tent. Creativity, as Guilford had acknowledged, was surely a complex and multifaceted phenomenon that would need all hands on deck to properly apprehend.

Creativity research was so attractive as a big-tent project because it promised to make psychologists indispensable to the Cold War patronage system while also providing a broader agenda for social reform that jibed with the humane current of the era, returning agency to the individual while also ensuring that material progress continued apace. Such a unity of purpose was crucial during the Cold War, during which American leaders stressed individuality, not centralized power. To win the Cold War, America would need to balance technological progress with individual freedom. Creativity was the answer.

Creativity versus Intelligence

Creativity research began with a remarkably utilitarian goal: to devise a better test. Guilford was himself a psychometrician, an expert in mental assessment, and the genesis of the Utah Conferences (though they would come to encompass much more) was a 1950 grant to Dr. Calvin Taylor from the newly established National Science Foundation to help formulate assessment criteria for its graduate student scholarship program. The standard tools at the time for that sort of thing were tests of so-called general intelligence. But Taylor had reason to believe those, and the scientific theories they were based on, were deeply flawed.

The concept of "general intelligence" dated to the early 1900s, when the American psychologist Charles Spearman, using sophisticated statistical methods, purportedly demonstrated that all mental abilities, from spatial reasoning to verbal acuity to mathematical computation, were subordinate to a kind of underlying mental power, represented as g. There had been objectors who doubted any such *ur*-intelligence really existed, but by 1950 Spearman and his acolytes had largely been successful, not least because believing in unitary g made the problem of testing and sorting large numbers of people incredibly easy—a standard intelligence test could assign any individual an IQ number corresponding to categories such as "feeble minded," "dull," "normal," or "superior." To many, intelligence tests felt progressive, a scientific and democratic alternative to traditional class-bound measures of merit like family name and connections.[11] But such tests also, in the kind of circular logic that often attends psychological concepts, helped constrain and reify the very notion of "intelligence," powerfully shaping the terrain of opportunity for millions of Americans and giving a quantitative, putatively objective basis for what it meant to be mentally valuable to society. In any case, because of their utility as an all-purpose assessment for use in military, industry, government, and education, intelligence tests proliferated in lock-step with industrial society and made psychometric research into the modern field Guilford and Taylor inherited.

But Guilford and Taylor were among a growing chorus of psy-chometricians who disputed the theory of general intelligence, preferring instead a more variegated and multi-factor view of the human intellect. (Guilford was at the time working out a sixteen-factor model of the intellect.) They were particularly concerned that standard models of intelligence, and the tests those models produced, left out inventive abilities. As Guilford put it in his 1950 speech, "creativity and creative productivity extend well beyond the domain of intelligence."[12]

Early psychometricians like Lewis Terman had, in fact, rec-ognized abilities such as "originality" and "ingenuity," and by the 1910s several tests for such abilities were in use. However, by the 1920s, when intelligence tests were standardized and put into mass use, such assessments were not generally included, and Terman himself decided that such abilities were not essential to the model of general intelligence.[13] One reason seems to have been purely pragmatic: the difficulty of standardizing the scoring of such open-ended tests necessarily involved subjective judgment and so made the tests impractical for use in large organizations. But creativity researchers saw something ideological lurking behind this omis-sion, that abilities such as ingenuity and originality were seen by psychologists, modern organizations, and the culture at large with suspicion and dismissiveness.

Given the dire national need for scientific and technological progress, they reasoned, this attitude was gravely mistaken. Taylor figured such abilities were exactly what his NSF sponsors should be interested in, and, no doubt seeing an opportunity in Guilford's call to arms, soon decided what was needed was more research on specifically "creative" ability. Taylor asked the NSF for signifi-cantly more money—and patience—for a series of major biennial conferences, and the Utah Conferences on the Identification of Creative Scientific Talent were born.

Creativity research seemed like a perfect chance to prove how oversimplified *g* was. If creativity was merely a sub-phenomenon of general intelligence, then existing intelligence tests should be able to identify the most creative people, and therefore there would be no need for a new set of tests and thus no need for further psychometric research. But if Guilford and Taylor were right, psychologists faced a new frontier, a whole world of new research to isolate the specific traits that made creativity its own thing.

Creativity versus Genius

In taking aim at intelligence tests, creativity researchers were criticizing one of the key achievements of modern psychology and one of the exemplary technologies of mass society. But they were also, in a sense, trying to perfect it. For their most basic aim was still to provide organizations with tools that would help them identify and manage desirable individuals. To perfect these testing tools, or rather to adapt them to the new pressures of the Cold War and the Permanent Revolution, these researchers in some respects returned to the roots of psychometric science: the study of genius.

As it happens, the empirical study of genius and the field of psychometrics both go back to the same man, the British psychologist (and Spearman's teacher) Sir Francis Galton. Eager to wrest psychology from the wishy-washy speculation of metaphysics and philosophy, Galton pioneered the use of statistical methods to observe psychological phenomena across populations (a technique he also famously applied to forensic fingerprinting). He was also deeply worried about the fate of European civilization, and set himself to the study of the "grand human animals, of natures preeminently noble, born to be kings of men."[14] In 1869's *Hereditary Genius*, Galton selected three hundred "men of genius," including "the most illustrious Commanders, men of Literature and of Science, Poets, Painters, and Musicians, of whom history speaks."[15] He then studied their personal biographies and mapped their family trees to find out what they had in common. Observing that many geniuses also had eminent relatives, he concluded that genius was hereditary. Strikingly, he did not seriously consider that the family clusters might indicate the importance of connections, wealth, or family culture, nor did he think the absence of women from his list was due to a lack of opportunity. Nor (even though he selected his subjects based on reputation—awards, accolades, and the total number of words dedicated to them in reference books) did he consider confounding factors like cultural fashions or the whims of fame. For Galton everything had a biological explanation, a bias that would get baked into the science of mental ability from then on, all the way up through and including creativity research.

What Galton really dreamed about was a test to identify living geniuses at an early age, so they could be encouraged to interbreed with one another in the hopes of offsetting the deleterious effects of industrialization and globalization on European stock. (In addition to everything else Galton is also remembered as the father of the eugenics movement.) Galton's heirs invented such a test. In 1904 Alfred Binet, using some of Galton's statistical methods, developed a test for the French Ministry of Education to weed out the "feebleminded" from military and civil service by assigning each test taker a "mental age," which later researchers evolved into the Intelligence Quotient (IQ). Binet saw his tests as blunt instruments capable of making only very rough groupings, but American testers led by Stanford professor Lewis Terman eagerly used IQ tests during World War I to select officers, cementing the close relationship between psychometrics and the military and legitimating IQ tests' power. In 1925 Terman, who like Galton was deeply concerned with the weakening of the White race, published his first *Genetic Studies of Genius*, explicitly holding that modern psychological methods had "furnished conclusive proof that native differences in endowment are a universal phenomenon and that it is possible to evaluate them." The following year his student, Catherine Cox, calculated the IQs of "Three Hundred Geniuses" posthumously, in homage to Galton's landmark study. Terman's own work centered on a longitudinal study begun in 1921 of high-IQ Palo Alto children (nicknamed the "Termites"), which set out to prove that IQ tests could accurately predict the geniuses of the future, again so they might be encouraged to mate with one another.

By 1950, however, Guilford, for one, thought Terman's experiments were proving the exact opposite: while the Termites had seemingly passed into adulthood exceptionally well educated, socially adjusted, and professionally successful, their numbers contained "little promise of a Darwin, an Edison, or a Eugene O'Neill." In other words, no true geniuses. Guilford pointed out that the very term "genius" was originally meant to describe those "who distinguish themselves because of creative productivity," but had now, thanks to Terman and his followers, simply come to mean "the child with exceptionally high IQ."[16] The cart, in other words, was now before the horse. What would happen to American scientific and technological prowess if the tools psychologists had developed were causing the best and brightest to be systematically skipped over, their applications for college or a job denied, their inventive potential untapped? Identifying top talent was clearly a noble goal, Guilford thought, but it needed to be refocused on the ability that ultimately mattered—"creative" ability.

Creativity research diverged from previous genius studies in a number of ways. For one thing, it largely set aside any focus on heredity or race. This was in line with the broader field of psychology. In the wake of the Holocaust, research on the hereditary basis of intellectual abilities virtually ground to a halt. Previously, psychometrics had been massively important to the virulent racism of the interwar era. Early twentieth-century research showing low IQ in southern and eastern Europeans provided the intellectual scaffolding for anti-immigration legislation in the 1920s, and low IQ scores in Blacks were continually used to justify Jim Crow segregation and racist policy nationwide. But by the 1940s, thanks to the work of Franz Boas, W. E. B. DuBois, and others, psychologists had largely landed on a more moderate view, seeing innate individual differences within groups as more significant than differences between groups, and recognizing that environmental factors were largely to blame for any discrepancies between racial groups.[17] The banishment of scientific racism from mainstream social thought was further aided by scholars such as Ashley Montagu, author of the 1945 *Man's Most Dangerous Myth: The Fallacy of Race*, and Allison Davis, who showed that class, rather than race (and thus environment, rather than biology), was the primary determinant of IQ score.[18] By the eve of World War II many mainstream psychologists still assumed the existence of innate racial differences in intelligence, but the experience of fighting a war against a frankly racist and eugenicist regime (one inspired in no small part by America's own Jim Crow system) finally sent eugenicists to the shadows.

In that moment of stigma and confusion in the psychometric field, it's possible that many psychometricians may have found in creativity research a convenient pivot to a less racially fraught topic than intelligence that would nonetheless allow them to continue their quest for the talent that the Cold War demanded. Race and heredity were not really topics of discussion in creativity research. A few unrepentant eugenicists were welcomed into the creativity discussion, notably the highly influential factor analyst Raymond Cattell, who published a number of articles on creativity, and the Nobel laureate William Shockley, co-inventor of the semiconductor and Silicon Valley pioneer. Both presented at the Utah Conferences, though not on heredity.[19] Moreover, creativity psychologists took no pains to distance themselves from Galton. In fact, they embraced him as a sort of spiritual father. Calvin Taylor said it was Galton who "initiated the modern method of study of individual variation in imagination."[20] When Guilford penned a history of creativity research in 1967, he started with Galton and characterized himself as a standard-bearer.[21] (To this day there is an award for outstanding research in creativity named after Sir Francis Galton.) So, while we don't see in early creativity research any blatantly racist ideas, we also don't see an effort to purge psychometrics of its frankly racist foundations.

If not terribly interested in heredity, early creativity research was still thoroughly biological, sharing Galton's assumption that abilities were more or less inborn, and bracketing environmental factors. As Galton had, many studies relied on reputation to select their subjects. Guilford, for example, acknowledged the role of "inequality of stimulus or opportunity," but believed that "if environmental occasions were equal, there would still be great differences in creative productivity among individuals."[22] And although they quibbled with Galton's successors on the equivalence of genius with superior IQ, they eagerly took up the original spirit and aim of his psychometric research: to save a mental elite from the forces of modern mediocrity.

Yet there's a more important reason creativity researchers didn't say they were researching genius, and didn't call their field "genius studies." For "genius" did not really capture what they were after. Genius was, by all definitions, rare, but "creativity" seemed to denote something more widespread. "Creative acts," Guilford said, can be expected, "no matter how feeble or how infrequent, of almost all individuals."[23] As L. L. Thurstone, Calvin Taylor's graduate advisor, put it, creative ability was "qualitatively the same at all levels: in the trades and in the professions, as well as in the rare and extreme forms that we call genius."[24] The difference between a moderately inventive corporate engineer and Galileo was not in kind but in degree. The guiding assumption behind creativity research was, as Guilford put it, that "whatever the nature of creative talent may be, those persons who are recognized as creative merely have more of what all of us have."[25]

This assumption that creativity was distributed among the population produced a paradox. If, on one hand, there were assumed to be "kinships between the creativity of everyday life and that of a great scientist or artist," as two scholars wrote, then "the study of creativity need not limit itself to the eminent, the extraordinary." Yet how, as investigators went down the scale of distinction, could they be sure they knew creativity when they saw it? "If we include 'everyday creativity' in our study," they feared, "we may be in danger of making our conception of it meaningless," indistinguishable from imaginative, clever, resourceful, wacky, or even just lucky. "It is only at the extreme," the truly superior, they wrote, "that we can be reasonably sure that we are talking about it." Yet on the other hand, if they only considered major scientific discoveries and un-disputed artistic masterworks, they were right back to the genius paradigm, trapped "in a 'great-man theory' that leaves us no way of moving between the commonplace and the sublime."[26]

There were also practical considerations. The complex statistical methodology psychometricians used to isolate mental aptitudes, known as factor analysis, depended on large numbers of test subjects. As Guilford admitted, because "true creative accomplishment" was relatively rare, researchers might just have to "revise our standards, accepting examples of lower degrees of distinction."[27] If creativity research was ever going to challenge the concept of unitary *g*, considering only acts of genius would not do. Creativity was, then, in being more democratic than genius, not only more ideologically palatable, but also easier to study, and so made the findings of those studies potentially more valuable to users of psychological tests in education, industry, and the military.

Divergent Thinking

The most exciting direction in the early years was the hypothesis that a key to creative ability was a fairly pedestrian cognitive ability called "divergent thinking." The crux of the complaint about intelligence tests was that they contained only questions with right or wrong answers, whereas invention required an answer that, by definition, was not yet known. Calvin Taylor inherited this critique of IQ tests from L. L. Thurstone, perhaps the most prominent critic of the theory of general intelligence going back to the 1930s (he was the APA's president in 1933). Thurstone's interest in psychology arose while he was working as an engineer in the laboratory of Thomas Edison, where he began to wonder why certain employees seemed to be more inventive—he didn't use the word "creative"—than others. In a series of studies in the 1930s and 1940s, Thurstone concluded that while most scientists tended to arrive quickly at the answer to a problem, those who generated many possible solutions ended up with the most patents. Thurstone called this skill "divergent thinking."

Creativity researchers eagerly embraced divergent thinking as a possible key factor for creativity. Thurstone's inventiveness test was to present subjects with an ordinary object—typically a brick—and have them list as many different uses for it as possible in a limited time. Responses—which might range from the fairly common doorstop to something more unusual, like a meat tenderizer—were scored on fluency (the total number of responses), originality (relative to typical responses), and feasibility (as judged by the researchers). Guilford took Thurstone's brick test and elaborated it into a signature battery of open-ended tasks such as listing anagrams, interpreting ink blots, and coming up with a story based on a picture of a dramatic situation, all tallied on some combination of fluency, originality, and (Guilford's addition) "cleverness."

Technically, before these tests could be used to actually identify creative people, they first had to be validated. It had to be shown, in other words, that people who were already known to be creative (typically based on reputation or an assessment of output) also scored higher than the general population on divergent thinking tests. Then, researchers would compare creativity test scores of people with higher and lower IQ scores, to see if the creative population overlapped closely with the high-IQ population. If there was daylight between the two it would mean creativity was distinct from intelligence. Several studies over the course of the 1950s and 1960s claimed to have found just that. Though these studies would soon come in for questioning, for the time being they provided the key footnote upon which a flood of creativity research would proceed, seeming to have confirmed the founding hypothesis of the field of creativity research and thereby justifying its existence and continued funding.

By the late 1950s Guilford's battery was the gold standard for research on creativity, used any time one needed to isolate "creative" test populations. Even though Guilford and other test designers maintained that divergent thinking was only one of many possible contributors to overall creative ability—along with cognitive abilities and personality, as well as motivational and even environmental factors—the relative ease of both understanding and quantifying it caused divergent thinking to become nearly synonymous with creativity itself. Divergent thinking gave psychologists a controlled, replicable method for testing the creative potential in just about any subject, and in large numbers; this in turn allowed it to be subjected to the kind of statistical analysis by which others—including government funders—could be convinced that creativity was a discrete phenomenon worthy of continued research.

Identifying the Creative Person

Researchers understood that to say anything general about the nature of creativity, or to devise a test to pick out creative people who had not done anything creative yet, would require two steps: first, identify unambiguously creative people to study; and second, determine what they all had in common. Though it might at first glance seem the simplest, the first step proved in many ways the most difficult. Though most researchers felt confident they knew it when they saw it, when it came down to really defining what creativity was—to simply agreeing on what they were talking about in the first place—a series of paradoxes emerged.

One approach to identifying creative people to study was to go by reputation. Some proceeded as Galton had, by tabulating critical approval, while others asked for nominations from teachers, bosses, classmates, or expert panels. The IPAR studies that Rexroth participated in, for example, used a combination of press and peer questionnaires to determine reputation in fields the researchers deemed creative.

Donald McKinnon, who founded IPAR in 1949 with the mission of "developing techniques to identify the personality characteristics which make for successful and happy adjustment to modern industrial society," was used to identifying high performers.[28] MacKinnon had spent the war years selecting spies for the Office of Strategic Services; after the war, with grants from the Rockefeller Brothers Fund and the Department of Defense, he continued studies on "highly effective people," including high-ranking military personnel. The shift to "highly creative people" around 1955 was more of a nudge, a suggestion by John Gardner, also a former OSS psychologist on his way from Rockefeller to the Carnegie Corporation, who saw the growth potential in creativity research. McKinnon applied to Carnegie and was promptly awarded a major five-year grant to study "highly creative people."[29]

McKinnon's method was called "depth assessment": a combination of intelligence and personality assessments including the Myers-Briggs Type Indicator, interviews about their biographies and values, and observations of casual group situations. For the creativity studies he added "measures of originality, creativity, aesthetic sensitivity, and artistic reactiveness," including the newly available Guilford Creativity Tests and the Barron-Welsh Art Scale, which asked respondents to state their preference for abstract versus figurative images, and asymmetrical versus symmetrical figures.[30] The researchers gave these tests first to a group they deemed creative, then to one they felt was less creative, and compared the results.

And how did they determine the creative group? The difference between the "highly effective people" of their previous research and "highly creative people" essentially came down to occupation. The investigators identified three professions that together triangulated their idea of creativity and would allow them to make comparisons between creativity in different fields. In one corner were poets, novelists, and playwrights. Like all true artists, their products were supposedly irreducible to objective measures of success and functioned only in the realm of human-to-human expression. Across from the writers were mathematicians, who, though not creative in the "artistic" sense, were assumed to exhibit an unusual caliber of imaginative power, especially at the highest levels, where new theorems were the coin of the realm. Both the creative writers and the academic mathematicians seemed to dwell in the realm of pure ideas.

Then there were the architects. Triangulating between the aesthetic sensibility of the writers and the logical rigor of the mathematicians, architects seemed to encompass the spirit of creativity in its fullest sense. They sought beauty but also structural soundness, "creating" the human world in tangible and consequential ways. Architects' work life vacillated between the solitary labor of the studio artist and the teamwork and salesmanship of the businessman. Fiercely independent but not above their clients' needs, architects were the very ideal balance of the humanistic and the utilitarian, the individual thriving in modern mass society.

The theory behind choosing three such different professions was to test the hypothesis that creativity was a general trait. Comparing across occupations would rule out factors specific to any one of them. If spatial reasoning was high among architects but not writers, it would not be deemed specific to creativity, but if all three preferred asymmetrical figures, that surely was a trait of the creative person. The intention was to find not what makes a good architect, writer, or mathematician, but rather what makes the best in each field so creative.

The researchers acknowledged that simply working in a "creative" field did not make one highly creative; one must also be excellent. Thus, the researchers also compared those at the top of their fields with those in the middle and the bottom. This, echoing Galton's technique nearly a century earlier, was ascertained mainly from publishing and citation records, awards and honors, and press coverage, which the researchers assumed were fairly accurate indicators of talent. To account for undeserved renown and compensate for the researchers' lack of expertise, they consulted panels of experts in each field to nominate the most creative practitioners.

Here a problem arose: how would the expert panels define "creative?" The architecture critics and professors were told nominees should demonstrate the following traits: "originality of thinking and freshness of approach to architectural problems; constructive ingenuity; ability to set aside established conventions and procedures when appropriate; [and] a flair for devising effective and original fulfillments of the major demands of architecture." It is not clear those criteria were enforced, however: the rating form used to score nominees included only four so-called "major demands of architecture": "firmness," "delight," "commodity," and "social purpose." As a result, the nominees seem to have been ultimately chosen more on general architectural merit (the first three of those "demands" dated to a 1624 treatise) than on qualities such as "originality," "freshness," or "ingenuity."[31]

Given the preponderance of modernists among both the architects and their judges, it might have been reasonable to assume that originality was to be guaranteed in any architect deemed excellent by his peers. But there would have been no particular reason to believe the nominees represented the *most* original or innovative practitioners. Likewise, when it came to selecting control groups of less creative subjects, the researchers chose them based on their lower standing in the eyes of the press and their peers. (The Bay Area architect Henry Hill, one of the highly creative group, wondered how the researchers explained the selection of control group participants, "on the basis of being no good??")

The IPAR researchers were fairly typical in taking eminence as proof of creativity. A set of early-1950s studies by Anne Roe on the biographical and characterological similarities among eminent people in various professions, mostly in the sciences, were often cited as creativity research, even though they did not claim to be about "creativity" specifically, and did not include any qualitative evaluation of the accomplishments themselves.[32] Calvin Taylor, surveying the growing field of creativity studies, acknowledged the slippage between "creative" meaning a type of work and "creative" as a quality of work, noting that, for example, it was often unclear "whether a creative scientist, or merely a scientist in general, is being studied and described." He cautioned consumers of creativity research that "descriptions of *typical* persons involved in the more creative fields of endeavor do not necessarily apply to the *creative* persons in those fields. . . . It is important to review such studies to determine whether *creative* performance, or *overall* performance, is the factor under investigation."[33]

Class, Race, Gender, and the Creative Person

The IPAR researchers' willingness to take eminence as a proxy for high creative ability had its pitfalls. For one thing, they were

naive about the active role many top architects played in cultivating their own reputations, so their reliance on press coverage
and critical acclaim caused them to overlook architects outside
the critical canon.[34] Their faith that a reliable meritocracy was at
work, moreover, ensured that social factors, including class, race,
and gender, would be ignored. Pragmatically leaving the criteria
of creativity up to the communities in which it was defined, this
method in some ways reinforced the existing ideas about what
"creative" meant rather than separating reality from perception,
as it purported to do.

Predictably, many of the conclusions the researchers eventually reached about the creative personality reflected the momentary tastes of the intellectual class of the subjects and themselves
alike.[35] The researchers interpreted the apparent preference of
creative people for abstract art, for example, not as an artifact of a
historically- and class-specific acculturation to mid-century high-
brow taste, but rather as a manifestation of a more fundamentally
psychological "tolerance for ambiguity" and "momentary disorder."[36] This was one of the ways in which class, gender, race, and
the conditions of labor were naturalized and universalized as innate personality traits, and creativity subtly transformed from an
effect (an accomplishment or a behavior) into a cause (a psychological state).

Barron eventually acknowledged this process of self-flattering
prophesy. As he recalled:

> It came to me that the effectively functioning person had had
> two other rather locally determined restrictions imposed upon
> him; namely, like each and every staff member of the Institute,
> he was a man rather than a woman, and rather closer to middle
> age than to adolescence. At the end of those first comfortable
> discussions, then, we had arrived at an excellent picture of an
> effectively functioning and notably virtuous man in his middle
> years in late summer at Berkeley, California. . . . It turned out that
> individual staff members were using quite different adjectives to
> describe the same person, but with great consistency they were

describing highly effective people by exactly the adjectives . . .
they would use to describe themselves. . . . Each of us, in brief,
saw his own image in what he judged to be good.[37]

The IPAR studies illustrate the tangle of descriptive and norma-
tive claims that animated creativity research. Like all the human
sciences, the business of personality psychology is rife with subjectivity, and in retrospect can often be seen to reflect the biases
of those carrying it out. In the case of creativity research it is clear
in retrospect that even though the experts thought they were objectively uncovering an eternal human trait, they were in fact constructing the concept of creativity itself as their own ideal, and in
many ways in their own self-image.[38]

The result was to link the image of creativity to success in
high-skill, high-education professions, making creativity paradoxically universal and rare—anyone could be creative in theory,
but only those in occupations recognized as creative could prove
it. No matter how many times they insisted housewives could
be creative, psychologists rarely if ever studied creativity among
housewives. The operative sense of "creative" that really mattered
to most researchers and their funders had to do with productive
labor outside the household, particularly highly educated "brain
work" that was at the time virtually off limits to everyone except
for White men. This was, consequently, the sense of creativity embraced by many women as they sought workplace equality. Ever
since women entered office work in great numbers in the 1920s,
they were subjected to a division of labor supported by notions of
mental difference: women were good at tasks such as filing, typing, and directing calls, requiring consistency and attention to detail, while men excelled at higher "creative, judicial, and executive"
jobs.[39] In 1935 *Fortune* praised the "feminization of the American
office" which allowed a "synchronization of man's creative ability with woman's efficiency with detail [that] made the wheels of
commerce turn more smoothly."[40] But as women gradually fought
their way into universities and the professions, cracks began to appear in the myth of female intellectual inferiority.

The influx of women into the home front workforce during World War II, meanwhile, gave many women an appetite for the financial independence and sense of meaning that work outside the home could provide. For working-class women, of course, working outside the home was nothing new, but they were now joined by millions of middle-class women resisting a campaign to re-domesticate women and restore "traditional" gender roles at the war's end. These so-called second-wave feminists saw in the emerging white-collar order an opportunity to make inroads precisely because they possessed mental ability equal to men's. In the National Organization for Women's 1966 "Statement of Purpose," Betty Friedan wrote, "today's technology has virtually eliminated the quality of muscular strength as a criterion for filling most jobs, while intensifying American industry's need for creative intelligence."[41] For Friedan there was no question that women possessed this creative intelligence.

The concept of genius was, from its Roman origins to the modern era, strongly gendered male, often associated with a "vital force," personified, as Darrin McMahon writes, in "male charisma and power, often in explicitly sexualized terms."[42] (For centuries women's bodies were seen as empty vessels, with all the generative material coming from the male.) Though there was occasional debate, the broad consensus among both the Romantics and the empirical psychometricians after Galton was that only men could be geniuses.[43] To the extent creativity resembled the prior concept it carried with it masculinist baggage, but in other respects it was open to women's inclusion. The concept of creativity, just as it may have given psychologists an opportunity to shed the racist baggage of the concept of genius, might have opened up new horizons in conceptions of gender.

The question of gender difference was on the agenda of the Utah Conferences from the beginning.[44] Many psychologists, including Barron at one point, purported to have discovered that women were less creative than men.[45] In one staggeringly sexist example from 1962, an Arizona school psychologist named Robert Fahey tested 248 seventh- and eighth-graders using a modified form of a creative thinking battery Guilford had developed for his research, and found that in the span of two years the boys moved significantly ahead of the girls. "There is no question about it in my mind," he concluded, "the male is the creative sex mentally. As a matter of fact, creativity is what makes him male." "It's in the nature of the female to be a conformist," he went on, "to find the facts and regurgitate them." "Women, of course, have their own creativity—the highest of all in giving birth to children. But a woman probably has to pervert her nature to create ideas." This explained, he reasoned, why "all the great creative thinkers have been men." Fahey editorialized that the modern world, starting with hostile female teachers and extending to the corporate workplace, exerted a "feminizing process" on creative males, posing a fundamental threat to civilization.[46]

But for the most part, creativity research backed Friedan up. A few studies, including one by Guilford in 1967, found that women were the more creative sex, but most found no difference. In 1974 the *Journal of Creative Behavior* reported—"with a sigh of relief," given the charged atmosphere around the women's liberation movement—that the preponderance of the research since 1950 showed no difference in creativity between the sexes.[47] Particularly when creativity was measured by performance on divergent thinking tests, women performed as well as men, though they appeared to be more easily influenced by the social setting.[48] The tendency of girls and women to be socialized away from the kind of bold, competitive, or contrarian habits of mind that might aid invention was a common explanation for why they sometimes underperformed creatively. If the creative accomplishments of female artists and scientists were "far below that to which we are entitled," wrote the psychologist Jerome Kagan, it was simply because "the girl is taught from the earliest age to covet similarity to her peer and to flee from disagreement."[49] As second-wave feminism began to name its oppressions, researchers began to point to more fundamental systemic barriers. "Genuine creative accomplishment requires a single-minded dedication," wrote the *Journal of Creative Behavior* author. "To the degree that an individual is distracted from such pursuits by the social context," such as the peripatetic rhythms of childcare and domestic labor, "the effect is bound to be lessened creativity."[50]

Access to work, particularly white-collar brain work, was for Friedan a matter of not only economic justice but self-actualization. "The only way for a woman, as for a man, to find herself, to know herself as a person, is by creative work of her own," she wrote.[51] The antifeminist Phyllis Schlafly had the opposite take. Technological progress had liberated women not to join the workforce, but to enjoy domesticity. "Modern technology and opportunity have not discovered any nobler or more satisfying or more creative career for a woman than marriage and motherhood," she wrote in 1972. Not shy about embracing the Great Man theory of history, she continued, "the real liberation of women from the backbreaking drudgery of centuries is the American free enterprise system which stimulated inventive geniuses to pursue their talents . . . the great heroes of women's liberation are not the straggly-haired women on television talk shows and picket lines," but the Edisons and Howes.[52] Celebrity parenting authority Dr. Benjamin Spock likewise thought society should "get it through its noodle that rearing children is exciting and creative work." Fretting that if all the women went to college and got jobs nobody would be there to raise the children, Spock found it "absurd" that "men go into pediatrics and obstetrics because they find them interesting and creative, and American women shun child-bearing and child-rearing because they don't."[53] Even the leftist Paul Goodman wrote with a hint of jealousy in 1960 that a "girl does not have to, and she is not expected to, 'make something' of herself. Her career does not have to be self-justifying, for she will have children, which is absolutely self-justifying, like any other natural or creative act."[54] The radical feminist Shulamith Firestone had heard enough of this double-talk when in 1970 she mocked the refrain, "'why, my dear, what could be more creative than raising a child?'"[55]

All this haggling over the meaning of "creative work" marks an interesting moment in the evolution of the term "creative." Antifeminists like Schlafly and Spock were appealing to the sense of the word meaning generative or constructive, while Friedan was using the word to describe the mental experience of autonomous professional work outside the home—"the more advanced work of society"—a meaning much more aligned with that of the creativity psychologists.[56] This of course was presumably what Spock's male colleagues meant when they called their work "creative"—an experience very different from that of the child-bearing women in labor in front of them.

Though Friedan was a journalist and author, what she meant by "creative work" was not just the arts and letters. (In fact, she considered the image of the "happy housewife . . . painting, sculpting, or writing at home . . . one of the semi-delusions of the feminine mystique.")[57] "Creative work" for Friedan could also include social or political work: anything that served "a human purpose larger than" the women themselves, and, apparently, their immediate families.[58] In this sense the term *creative* retained the spirit of that older meaning—constructive, positive—but also reflected her belief that work outside the home was, or could be, fundamentally more "human" than housework. What was really creative about creative work was for Friedan not necessarily a certain kind of output (though it tended to involve some kind of result that would be recognized by society), but rather it being mentally and personally stimulating, using the highest of the individual's abilities, and being a vehicle for "identity" or "self-actualization." "There is something less than fully human in those who have never known a commitment to an idea, who have never risked an exploration of the unknown, who have never attempted the kind of creativity of which men and women are potentially capable," she wrote.[59] Later critics would justifiably criticize Friedan for her dismissive attitude toward working-class women for whom a job was "just a job," or working-class feminists who wanted to make mothering economically feasible. But Friedan, like Abraham Maslow, on whose writings she heavily relied, had a vision of a white-collar society in which brains, not brawn, would prevail, and of an affluent society in which self-actualization could be achieved through meaningful work. Rather than settling for the notion of a separate feminine, biological creativeness, Friedan wanted in on the kind of creativity the men were talking about.

The Criteria Question

Some researchers thought it was patently unscientific, in fact a tautology, to identify creative people based on their reputations as "creative." Speaking to the Utah Conference on behalf of the applied science community, Hubert E. Brogden of the US Army Personnel Research Office and Thomas B. Sprecher of the Western Electric Company insisted that the "ultimate criterion" must be the product itself. A person could truly be called creative only if they had demonstrably produced something, be it a drawing, a model, an article, or even a theory or technique, which has "an existence separate from the person who produced it."[60] Brogden and Sprecher suggested a system for rating products on their creativity. Dow Chemical research director Joe McPherson proposed a metric called "inventivelevel," based on the number and quality of patents an employee produced.

But this product-first criterion brought its own set of problems. What makes a product creative? Everyone agreed it had to be "new," for starters. But how new? New enough to please a patent court? New enough to surprise a panel of experts? Most agreed that if the law of conservation of mass was true, absolute novelty was an impossibility, so novelty was ultimately relative, and therefore, unfortunately, subjective. Thus, researchers had to clarify a fundamental question: "Does the outcome involve recognition by society or by others that the product is unique," as the educational psychologist John E. Anderson put it, "or does the uniqueness apply only to the individual?" Morris Stein, another prominent creativity researcher, thought the latter. "The child who fixes the bell on his tricycle for the first time may go through stages that are structurally similar to those which characterize the work of the genius," he wrote. Even though "his finished product . . . is a return to a previously existing state of affairs," and thus not recognizably new to the world, he argued that it deserved to be considered an act of creativity because of the process involved.[61] But if creativity meant anything that was new to the individual, Anderson objected, then "each act of learning is a creative process and all living is creative." This, for Anderson, was going too far. The "customary" meaning of the word creativity, and, as far as he was concerned, the whole point of creativity research, was about the production of something "accepted by society as an original product of value and as such to receive social acclaim."[62] Ghiselin, the English professor, concurred, proposing any given creative product be rated on "the extent to which it restructures our universe of understanding." Robert Lacklen, NASA's personnel director, likewise thought creativity should be measured by "the extent of the area of science that the contribution underlies."[63]

But insisting on social impact as a criterion, besides dramatically narrowing the pool of subjects, was terribly subjective. Researchers were fond of pointing out that many of the most creative people throughout history were unappreciated in their lifetimes. Anne Roe, whose psychobiographical studies of prominent scientists were often cited in creativity research, declared, "the process itself, that is, what goes on in the individual, is not directly related to any value which may . . . be placed upon the product. . . . There are artistic productions and scientific theories which were rejected when they were first offered, only to be acclaimed by later generations; there are others which were acclaimed and since have been rejected; but the process within the individual was as creative in one instance as the other."[64] Surely the man who invented the typewriter hundreds of years too early wasn't uncreative, just ahead of his time. But then again, wouldn't some degree of intelligibility in the present be necessary to tell the potentially valuable from the merely bizarre?

The paradoxes only piled up. Even if one could agree on what defines a creative product, how was one to know it was the result of "creativity," rather than dumb luck, better equipment, or superior education? Would it matter if the person took a long time, or many attempts, to arrive at the creative product? Did it matter if it was that person's only creation? Maybe not; they were interested in *creativity*, not *productivity*, and some of the greatest creative minds of the past had only one or two significant works to their name. Then again, if the idea was to identify those most likely to make good use of government research dollars, surely efficiency and productivity were germane. Recognizing this, the ever practical Brogden and Sprecher wondered how researchers might control for what they called "opportunity variables," in order to avoid overlooking "those who work under difficult circumstances, or of qualifying the success of those particularly favored (through no effort of their own) by ample resources, a stimulating environment, or an easy and new set of problems."[65]

Others argued that products should not be considered at all. Abraham Maslow said researchers' focus should be not on "the finished work of art or science which is socially useful," but the moment of "inspiration," which he called "Primary Creativeness," as opposed to the often mundane secondary process of actually completing a product. Maslow believed using "the finished product as a criterion introduces too many confusions with good work habits, with stubbornness, discipline, patience, with good editing abilities, and other characteristics which have nothing directly to do with creativeness, or at least are not unique to it." For those like Brogden and Sprecher who were interested in understanding on-the-job success, such attributes may well have been relevant. But Maslow, as we'll see, was uninterested in such practicalities.[66]

The "criteria problem," as it became known, was so troublesome that the Utah Conferences almost immediately set up a special working group dedicated to it. Brogden and Sprecher, who served on this committee, were frustrated that the insistence on including nearly everything and everyone in creativity research seemed to be making common ground impossible, and in the end they suggested that everyone go their own way. "'Creativity,' a controversial and nebulous word," they concluded, "has different meanings to different people."[67] Those looking for inventive engineers should develop their own practical criteria, while those interested in creativity in children should develop theirs, and so on. Deciding on one common criterion for the field, though "fundamental to all research" and essential to legitimating the field of creativity, seemed a lost cause.

Ghiselin too was frustrated, writing that "investigation of creativity has been hampered by a most crucial difficulty: the very subject of investigation is ill-defined and elusive. . . . [J]udgment has been guided by impressions, and by rationalizations of impressions, mainly proximate criteria, thoughtfully developed and employed, yet uncorrected by those ultimate criteria which alone could assure their validity. In short, discrimination of the creative from the uncreative, and of the more creative from the less, remains hardly better than guesswork."[68]

The criteria problem was ultimately one of creativity researchers' own making. In insisting that creativity included acts of both genius and everyday ingenuity, and works of art as well as scientific discoveries, they then had to deal with the significant differences between those things. Likewise, by insisting on a psychological cause for creative accomplishment and bracketing all social factors, they deprived themselves of some of the most obvious explanations for creative accomplishment, trapping themselves instead in a tautological spiral that left them bewildered and frustrated.

:::

The notion of the creativity that emerged out of postwar psychology was, with all its troubles, a reflection of the mixed priorities of the psychological profession. There was little question that the thing creativity researchers were after, at least in its pure and archetypal form, would manifest in works of great genius. Yet their refusal to settle for a "great man theory" of social change, in which a talented few push society forward, reflects their practical and ideological position as postwar psychologists. As intellectuals in a democratic age, they could not condone such an elitist view of society, and as handmaidens of the bureaucratic apparatus, they found the figure of the genius at best not very useful and at worst anathema. Creativity, by contrast, was a concept that at least conceptually allowed them to, as they put it, "move between the commonplace and the sublime." It was distinguished from both intelligence and genius, but always retained key aspects of both: the administrative practicality of intelligence, and the romantic heroism of genius.

As a new psychological term of art, "creativity" drew a conceptual space that included the greatest accomplishments *but also* everyday acts of originality. This new concept served much of the function that genius had in the nineteenth and early twentieth centuries—that is, the thing imagined to be the engine of the progress of mankind. But it also implied that the essential quality of genius—the active ingredient—was far less rare and could be, like intelligence, subjected to population-wide research and intervention. As psychologists tried to recover the spirit of genius from the pall of behaviorism and industrial-age intelligence testing, they rediscovered it not in the one in a million, but distributed among the millions.

This democratic notion of creativity was well suited to bureaucratic settings. Everybody would have loved to find a genius or two, but you can't staff a whole laboratory or fill a graduate cohort with them. As the psychologist Taher A. Razik summarized, "genius might account for the basic ideas on which new developments were possible, but thousands of men were involved in the further innovations necessary to deliver that power as it reached the people. . . . In the presence of the Russian threat, 'creativity' could no longer be left to the chance occurrences of the genius; neither could it be left in the realm of the wholly mysterious and the untouchable. Men *had* to be able to do something about it; creativity *had* to be a property in many men; it *had* to be something identifiable; it *had* to be subject to the effects of efforts to gain more of it."[69]

As was clear to Razik, the efforts to understand creativity were always about the ability to increase it. And this was, at heart, a managerial concern. Creativity research had from the beginning been centrally concerned with the problems of industrial personnel, and major US manufacturers as well as military agencies participated closely in setting its agenda and applying its insights.[70]

The Dow Corporation's research director, Joe McPherson, for example, a key player at the Utah Conferences, distributed a periodic "Creativity Review" to colleagues, summarizing developments in the field. Similarly, the Industrial Research Institute, the trade organization representing R&D executives, established a Creativity Sub-Committee that periodically distributed to its members a bibliography of new research. By the late 1950s a handful of new books had come out summarizing the scientific findings.

In general, the psychological research had thus far focused on (to use the title of a McPherson paper) "How to Use Creative People Effectively."[71] From a manager's perspective the prognosis was grim. In 1962 the McKinsey Foundation of Management Research and the University of Chicago Business School convened a panel of experts including the psychologists Frank Barron, Morris Stein, and Jerome Bruner, as well as the advertising guru David Ogilvy and William Shockley, the eugenicist Silicon Valley pioneer who reportedly used creativity tests in hiring. Their consensus, as reported by the psychology professor Gary Steiner, was that highly creative people exhibited high "independence of judgment" and "less conventionality and conformity" than their less creative peers. Where uncreative people were apt to "offer unquestioning obedience" to authority, highly creative people were likely to "view present authority as temporary."[72] Noncreative employees were socially oriented, "likely to see their future largely within the boundaries of one organization, to be concerned chiefly with its problems and with their own rise within it, and to develop extensive ties and associations within the community." Creative people, by contrast, were said to be "cosmopolitan," and hence "less 'loyal' to any specific organization."[73] They were, in fact, loyal only to themselves, "driven more by interest and involvement in the task itself than by external incentives" like salary and status.[74] Motivated only by his own passions, a creative person was free from the influence of carrots and sticks deployed to direct his effort on behalf of corporate goals, "except in the rare and fortunate case."[75] Like Howard Roark, the protagonist architect in Ayn Rand's *The Fountainhead*, the creative person was more than just an "idea man"; he was an individualist heroically beating back the pressures of mass society. He insisted on the purity of his vision and had a natural disdain not for the capitalist, whose entrepreneurial spirit he shared, but for the bureaucratic administrator tasked with managing him.[76] Not only was the creative person hard to direct—he was hard to evaluate, because his activity "may be hard to distinguish from totally non-productive behavior: undisciplined disorder, aimless rambling, even total inactivity."[77] Managing creative people seemed to be, Steiner concluded, "an administrative enigma."[78]

Luckily, Steiner reported, there were people out there who had developed ways to harness creativity not by identifying and then catering to creative people, but by helping ordinary employees make the most of whatever creative talent they possessed. These techniques, the first of which we will meet in the next chapter, rejected the notion that creativity was a solitary or unpredictable affair, insisting instead that it could happen in groups, and on a schedule. These methods promoted a different vision of industrial progress, one that "will not depend solely on the contributions of a gifted few," as the General Electric Creative Thinking instructor Eugene Von Fange wrote in the book *Professional Creativity*, but rather on "the sum of the contributions of the thousands and tens of thousands."[79] As Von Fange said, the "greatest lesson" of creative thinking methods was that "we do not have to wait helplessly for ideas to occur. . . . We can deliberately plan and accomplish desired results as they are needed."[80] It was music to a manager's ears.

The Birth of Brainstorming

2

When Alexander Faickney Osborn heard about J. P. Guilford's 1950 speech heralding the new era of creativity research, he must have jumped out of his chair. Osborn was an idea man, meaning he thought a lot about how to come up with ideas. "Advertising is my day job," he liked to tell people, "but imagination is my hobby." As the chairman and cofounder of the powerhouse ad agency Batten, Barton, Durstine, and Osborn (BBDO), Osborn oversaw a portfolio that included General Electric, General Motors, Lucky Strike, Lever Brothers, and DuPont ("Better things for better living through chemistry").[1] Osborn was not known as a "creative man," the industry term for a copywriter or an artist, but he believed he had discovered the secrets of creative thinking.

In 1942, he had written a slim volume called *How to Think Up*, introducing a method called "brain-storming." Whenever BBDO execs were stumped for a new slogan or marketing concept, he explained, they would gather "about a dozen youngsters and a few 'brass hats'" in a conference room or a private residence after work. Supper, coffee, and dessert would be served by an "attractive dietician." Once everyone was comfortable and relaxed, an appointed "chairman" would pose the problem and ask the group to call out as many ideas as they could think up, rapid fire.[2] ("Brain-storming" was meant to invoke the way troops might storm a beach). For the duration of the session, the normal hierarchy was suspended—"all are equal"—but rules were strictly enforced: criticism or second-guessing was strictly forbidden, "freewheeling" encouraged—no idea was too silly or ambitious—and participants were encouraged to build off of or recombine the ideas of others. Above all, brainstorming was about quantity. As ideas came pouring out a secretary would jot them down and later pass the list, perhaps several pages long, to an executive, who would, in the light of a new day, sort the good from the bad. Osborn believed the mind, like the advertising agency itself, was made up of a "creative" or "imaginative" half and a "rational" or "judicial" half. Both were necessary but needed to get out of each other's way to do their jobs. The modern workplace, like the modern mind, had overdeveloped the judgmental half to the detriment of the creative, and brainstorming was just one way to compensate. In a series of books including *Your Creative Power: How to Use Your Imagination* (1948), *Wake Up Your Mind: 101 Ways to Develop Creativeness* (1952), and the book that would become the "bible" of creative thinking, *Applied Imagination* (1953), Osborn made the case that creative thinking was no mystery, and not reserved for the special few, but that coming up with ideas was a skill that anyone could develop and deliberately apply.

This approach was very different from that of Guilford and most other creativity psychologists, who were at first mainly focused on how to identify latent creative talent rather than how to develop it. Nonetheless, and even though he virtually never used the words "creativity" or "creativeness" before 1950, Osborn took Guilford's speech as a validation of his work and an occasion to position himself as a leader of a new "creativity movement," which he pursued with gusto and an adman's touch. In 1954, at the age of sixty-six, Osborn retired from BBDO and founded the Creative Education Foundation (CEF), to "enhance public awareness of the importance of creativity" by distributing literature, sending brainstorming trainers across the world, and hosting an annual week-long Creative Problem-Solving Institute (CPSI) in Buffalo. Though his main acolytes and early adopters came from the upper management of some of the largest corporate, government, and military organizations, Osborn aspired to nothing less than a revolution in American society. He believed that by helping Americans put knowledge about creativity to practical use he could help solve every kind of problem, from marital disputes to the Cold War.

Executives trying to dig up a name for a new product sometimes feel that the lode has been mined out by all the namers who preceded them.

Drawing by AJay.

Brand New Brand Names

The search for them gets harder all the time, forcing harassed industrialists to try such desperate measures as "mass creativity."

By EDITH EFRON

Figure 2.1 Brainstorming caught on partly in response to the consumer economy's need for new products, slogans, and brand names. From The New York Times. © 1957 The New York Times Company. All rights reserved. Used under license.

Some skeptics in academia and business would see brainstorming as at best another fad, like skateboarding or hula hoops, and at worst a false substitute for true creativity. But Osborn's blend of freewheeling, almost hedonistic methods with an unapologetically practical, old-school self-help message resonated in postwar America. Embodied in provocative oxymorons like "applied imagination," "planned inspiration," and "mass creativity," brainstorming and the other creative thinking methods it would spawn assuaged concerns about the loss of individual agency and inventiveness in mass society.[3]

"You're as Rich as Your Ideas"

In the fall of 1947 Osborn picked up a pencil and began to solo-brainstorm, as he called it, a list of potential titles for his second book. Scrawling in two neat columns he filled up several pages, 589 titles in all. The list began:

Idea Power
Your Idea Power
Your Creative Powerhouse
You Can Create Ideas
Live Creatively
Think-Up Power
Your Power of Imagination
Idea Ability
Your Power of Ideas
Power of Ideas
The Gold in Your Mind
You Are Rich in Ideas
Your Unused Endowment
Fuller Life through Ideas
What Ideas Can Do for You
How Ideas Can Make You Richer
Ideas Can Better Your Life
Full Yourself Up with Ideas
Think Up and Rise

You're as Rich as Your Ideas
Gainful Imagination

Osborn was, he often reminded his readers, not a psychologist; he was fundamentally a self-help author. He wrote in aphorism and anecdote and his titles promised uplift and riches. Even the titles he didn't use can tell us much about what he was up to. A few persistent themes emerge: ideas as currency, commodities, or precious minerals ("Dollars from Daydreaming," "Bushels of Ideas," "The Jewels in Your Crown"); thinking as a power or force of nature ("How to Harness Your Thoughts"). Many of the titles telegraphed his instructional angle ("How to Get Ideas") and many alerted the reader that they, too, were capable of coming up with ideas ("So You've Got an Imagination Too!"). Over a third of the titles contained the words "idea" or "ideas," one in four contained "imagination," and over half contained the words "you" or "your." Osborn's philosophy was simple: contrary to popular myth, everybody had at least some innate creative power, which could be improved and unleashed with deliberate and methodical practice.[4]

Osborn saw himself as an evangelist of good news. "It used to be supposed that creative imagination was possessed by only a few geniuses," he wrote, but no: "you were born with it." He made no claim that his methods "could turn a wheel-wright into a playwright."[5] He only promised to help people maximize whatever creative power lay dormant within them and "make it more and more productive."[6] Hand in hand with this democratic idea was a Protestant ethic: Osborn believed creative thinking was a matter of work. "There is no genius in me," he insisted, "but I have learned by experience that imagination, like muscle, can be built up by exercise." A lifelong business Republican and opponent of the New Deal, Osborn believed in hard work and initiative ("Ideas as Boot-Straps"). Despite a career pushing consumer comforts, he mourned the loss of a harder age, believing modern society had sapped the "imaginative vigor" on which America was built. But rather than argue for a return to pre-industrial time, Osborn offered a replacement: a technique by which modern man could "help fill the gap caused by the loss of those environmental influences which formerly forced us to keep creatively strong."[7] "You, yes you, can speed up your think-up," Osborn wrote in his typically punchy, ad-copy style, "but you have to try."[8]

In the tradition of self-help writers from Benjamin Franklin to Dale Carnegie and Norman Vincent Peale, whose aphorisms he was fond of quoting, Osborn was adapting traditional bourgeois values to a modern corporate reality. Through the decades, self-help authors had helped members of the growing urban white-collar class see themselves as independent smallholders despite feeling increasingly like slaves to a system they could neither control nor understand. Using rags-to-riches anecdotes to demonstrate that everyone is master of his own destiny, the genre is paradoxically democratic yet elitist, naturalizing systemic inequalities and narrowing the scope of critique to the level of individual conduct, casting any failures as personal ones. Osborn was in many ways perpetuating the republican ideal of the yeoman farmer, but instead of little plots of land people had their minds, and ideas were the crops. There was no room in this post-materialist worldview for factors like resources, time, power, and politics, nor even for things like education, hard work (in the traditional sense), tact, foresight, courage, or dumb luck. "Up the ladder of business, ideas can serve as rungs," he wrote. "Ideas, more than luck, will land the job you want."[9]

For Osborn, feats great and small came down to ideas: from the wheel to the atom bomb, from Churchill to Eli Whitney to Grant Wood to the urban planner Robert Moses, he wrote, "civilization itself is a product of creative thinking." It was a claim as uncontroversial as it was astonishing. By insisting that everything from scientific theories to battlefield maneuvers to consumer gadgets to parenting tricks were the results of "creative thinking," Osborn reduced each particular feat to an interchangeable unit called the "idea," which anyone could have. This was the dignifying sleight of hand, the flattering oversimplification behind Osborn's formula. By putting brainstorming in the same class as a Shakespearean sonnet, or rather, by implying that whatever Shakespeare was doing when he wrote a sonnet was essentially what one did while brainstorming, Osborn invited his readers to see their workaday problem solving and slogan finding as little steps in the grand march of civilization. This was essentially the same generalizing move the professional psychologists made when they theorized a trait called creativity. Like them, Osborn wanted to find the common ingredient in the commonplace and the sublime. For Osborn, however, the goal was not to find who had it and who didn't, but rather to teach everyone how to use it.

Osborn claimed creative thinking could help anyone with anything. The CEF pamphlet *The Gold Mine Between Your Ears* read:

> Surely you would like to:
>
>> . . . make more money by winning promotions.
>> . . . think up more cash-winning ideas.
>> . . . become a better parent and spouse.
>> . . . get more FUN out of life!
>
> Are there ways you can help yourself toward those goals?
> Yes there *are*—just as there are knacks to pitching a baseball or tossing a horseshoe.
> The key in this case is a gift you were born with—your ability to *think up ideas*. And this is an ability which you can utilize much more intelligently if you read this booklet.

Yet, despite claiming "women can think up ideas with the ablest of men!" the little cartoon figure pictured throughout the pamphlet is your typical man-in-a-suit, and the preponderance of the examples are from the world of work. As the *New York Times* noted in a review of *Your Creative Power*, despite Osborn's stated pretentions to universality, the author "confines himself to creative imagination in business," his copious examples of creativity skewing heavily toward consumer products, "from soap powders to Eskimo pie."[10]

In fact Osborn's whole idea of "an idea"—a line or two of text signifying an easily digested message or an easily executed course of action—bore the marks of its business-world templates: the Madison Avenue slogan mill and what were then known as corporate suggestion systems. Suggestion systems proliferated during World War II when, racing to fulfill ambitious production goals with shortages of materials and manpower, many companies began tapping the rank-and-file employees for ideas on how to speed up or improve production. With the coordination of the War Production Board, special boxes began to appear on factory floors in which workers could drop a slip of paper letting management know their ideas. Posters declared, "Uncle Sam Wants Your Ideas!" and CEOs insisted "for victory's sake, let us put our imaginations on overtime!"[11] Workers had generally jealously protected shop floor knowledge, knowing that whatever they ceded to management would likely be used against them in the form of speed-ups, routinization, or job elimination. Now, managers hoped, the temporary wartime unity might provide a rare moment of accord, and workers might be willing to give up some shop floor knowledge.[12]

Osborn excitedly pointed to suggestion systems as evidence that ideas could be a source of extra cash or even a leg up to the middle class. General Motors was offering a $1,000 war bond for every useful idea (those already being paid for their ideas, such as engineers, designers, and managers, were not eligible), and within five months they were reportedly receiving two hundred suggestions a day. Osborn reported that a number of factory workers— "amateurs," not "professional thinker-uppers"—had already benefited. A Goodyear plant worker from Akron paid for a medical operation from his suggestion earnings. A group of women, though "not . . . so skillful as men at describing their ideas," had discovered a better method for painting aircraft hoses. Others were rumored to have won promotions to supervision and design. Though these ordinary men and women would never have their name on the company, Osborn reassured his readers that by using their "unsuspected ability and talent" they were joining the Goodyears and Edisons in the great tradition of American ingenuity.

Some readers may have felt something patronizing and patrician about this recent "discovery" that common people could have good ideas too—overlooking the hundred-plus years of strong-armed de-skilling by capitalists and their hired managers that reduced workers to mere operators in the first place.[13] Though it's hard to imagine many were genuinely surprised to learn they were capable of original thought, it may have been a while since they had been asked to have a good idea, at least on the job, and there must have been something surprising, or at least encouraging, about Osborn's pitch that he had a system for getting the rust off the old imagination.

But Osborn was writing as much for employers as for employees. "Employers are hungry for ideas from the rank and file," Osborn wrote. "But they are not good bosses unless they try hard to draw out, and know how to draw out, the imaginative talent of every man and woman on the pay roll."[14] Ultimately it would not be with the blue-collar rank and file that Osborn's ideas took off, but with white-collar workers, and especially with those in charge of them.

Brainstorming Takes Off

Between late 1955 and 1958 brainstorming was everywhere. A front-page story in the *Wall Street Journal* on December 5, 1955 read, "Brainstorming: More Concerns Set Up Free-Wheeling 'Think' Panels to Mine Ideas—Ethyl Gets 71 Ideas in 45 Minutes: Reynolds Metals Develops Marketing Plans." One executive was quoted as saying, "Our experience definitely proved you can use this method to get profitable ideas from the lower ranks of your organization."[15] In May 1956, the *New York Times*, *Newsweek*, the *New Yorker*, and *Life* all reported that the Navy had brought in Charles H. Clark of the Ethyl Corporation, a close Osborn associate and one of brainstorming's most avid evangelists, to generate "more Washington imagination in meeting the new Communist tactics." "Federal 'Brains' Brace for Storm: Apostle of Madison Avenue Technique to Try to Stir Up Sluggish Thinkers," ran the *Time* headline. In January 1958 the ladies' magazine *McCall's* convened a panel of sixteen women to "try a technique called 'brain-storming,'" facilitated by a CEF representative, to come up with ways to find a husband. The women came up with a whopping 404 suggestions, including "have your car break down at strategic locations," "get a job in a medical, dental, or law school," and "don't be afraid to associate with more attractive girls; they may have some leftovers."[16]

Such articles often read like press releases. Behind the scenes the CEF was hard at work, pursuing Osborn's mission with a salesman's doggedness and an adman's knack for the well-placed pitch. They solicited friends in the press, wrote guest columns, and even lobbied to have "brainstorming" added to the dictionary (in 1962 they succeeded, with a note from Merriam-Webster assuring them that their suggested language would be taken into account).[17] CEF associates scattered across the map conducting demonstrations for audiences such as the Passaic Township Public Schools, the Atomic Energy Division of the Babcock & Wilcox Company, the Cornell University Psychology Department, and the Church of Latter-Day Saints. One ambassador reported from the field that he had run brainstorming demos for "a high school student council, four Federal Management Seminars, a number of professional associations, several groups of government officials from Pakistan, and various service clubs," and was on his way to an engagement with top city officials from Beverly Hills.[18]

The campaign evidently generated excitement. "My creative imagination is soaring and I owe it all to you," wrote Arthur J. Fettig of Battle Creek, Michigan, a railroad claims agent who had recently founded a group called the "Battle Creek Brainstormers," set to "revolutionize the railroad industry." SpeedeeMart/7 Eleven requested copies of "Principles and Procedures of Brainstorming" for prospective franchisees, and a seminary teacher wrote for a copy of *Applied Imagination* and a few supplementary materials, saying he was "very interested in creativity and am anxious to develop it among my students."[19]

Attending the annual Creative Problem-Solving Institute in Buffalo was a conversion experience for many people, including Sidney Parnes, who attended the first year and returned every year for the rest of his life, first as a facilitator then as its longtime, beloved director. Research executives from General Electric, General Motors, Firestone, B. F. Goodrich, and Goodyear were among the early CPSI attendees and incorporated what they learned into their companies' regular training programs.[20] Enrollment reached almost five hundred by the third year.[21] (The "Wives Club" did its own creative thinking exercises between catering duties. Women were invited to join CPSI a few years later.)[22] Motorola CEO Robert Galvin, a CPSI attendee, personally commissioned a new printing of Osborn's *Your Creative Power* and distributed it to every one of his employees. According to Osborn, by 1963 executives had ordered over a million copies of the CEF pamphlet "The Goldmine between Your Ears," an illustrated, twenty-four-page distillation of *Applied Imagination*. In his 1958 report on the progress of the creativity movement Osborn listed dozens of companies that had reportedly set up creative thinking programs, including Alcoa, Bristol Myers (Lee Bristol, a close Osborn friend, served as president of CEF), Carnation Milk, Chicago Tribune, Kraft, General Foods, Glenn Martin, H. J. Heinz, IBM, Hoover, Kroger, National Cash Register, Pitney-Bowes, Remington Arms, RCA, Reynolds Metals, Shell Oil, and Union Carbide.

Not all of these companies were using Osborn's methods exclusively. The Creative Engineering program at General Motors' AC Spark Plug division, for example, was formed in 1953 with the help of MIT professor John Arnold, who attended the first CPSI and taught brainstorming as well as his own techniques for "creative engineering." These included an exercise in which students were asked to design products for a race of aliens from the fictional planet Arcturus IV whose unusual physiology and culture would require designers to think creatively.[23] Many such methods for stimulating new ideas coexisted together at CPSI, which quickly became the center of gravity for a "creative thinking" or "creative problem-solving" trend. But by the late 1950s Osborn's name was practically synonymous with creative thinking. As one author wrote, "Until Osborn came on the scene, interest in the creative process was largely confined to a small group of philosophers, psy-

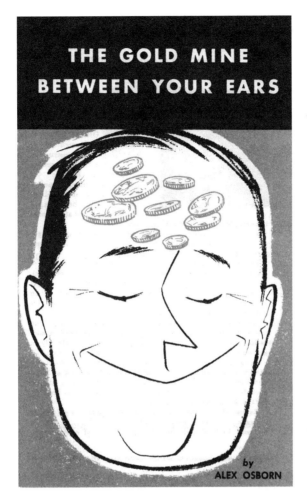

Figure 2.2 Pamphlet distributed by the Creative Education Foundation to hundreds of thousands of readers, mostly through their employers. Courtesy of the University Archives, University at Buffalo, The State University of New York.

chologists, and mathematicians." His "popular books on creativity have excited the imagination of a great many people," and he had "done more than any other man to draw attention to the subject of creative thinking."[24]

Whether brainstorming worked or not, however, would soon come into question.

Brainstorming at Work?

On September 13, 1956, Willard Pleuthner, Vice President and Co-ordinator of Brainstorming at BBDO, conducted a "fishbowl demonstration" at DuPont headquarters in Wilmington, Delaware, before what he called "the greatest collection of top management that has ever been assembled to hear about and see Brainstorming." The organizers, Virgil Simpson and James McCormick of DuPont's in-house advertising division, had attended CPSI a few months earlier after being asked to set up an in-house brainstorming task force. In addition to Pleuthner they invited representatives from GE, General Foods, and a handful of other companies, and they presented a new twenty-page booklet, "Brainstorming at DuPont." The task force would be responsible for educating DuPont's various departments about creative problem-solving, distributing copies of the booklet, and most importantly, conducting brainstorming sessions for specific projects by request. According to the historian Kyle VanHemert, any manager with a problem he wanted attacked could request one of the specially trained "chairmen" to gather a group of promising brainstormers, book a room, and facilitate a meeting.[25]

By October 1956, the group had conducted eleven brainstorming sessions. In June the textile division manager had requested a session for ideas on selling nylon safety belts (which were not yet mandatory in cars). The group came up with ninety-nine ideas, including fluorescent safety belts, safety belts with handy pockets for storing credit cards and cigarettes, and Mickey Mouse and Davy Crockett–themed safety belts for kids. In another, the group brainstormed a new name for brainstorming, to be used internally. The 175 suggestions included "Skull Session," "Cranial Congress," "Think-a-torium," "Idea Potpourri," "Thought Tackler," and "Thoughtacular," but in the end they decided to stick with "brainstorming."[26]

Momentum had picked up after Pleuthner's visit, but, McCormick wrote, "So far our brainstorming work may be likened to planting and cultivating a crop," he said. "We have yet to reap a harvest." By March 1957, when Sid Parnes wrote to see if DuPont might like to share its experience at that summer's CPSI, things seem to have fizzled somewhat. As McCormick confided to Simpson, "We could participate, and be on reasonably sound ground in discussing how we work and why. We'd be on less firm footing, however, if required to get into tangible results. Our story has been spotty—a few bright spots here and there, but no generally favorable picture." Simpson replied to Parnes that both he and McCormick would regrettably be unable to attend.[27] Instead, they sent Pleuthner a short list of a few brainstorming successes (e.g., "On how to advertise a new specialty product—152 ideas—33 screened ideas—7 used, adapted or under active consideration") which were a bit rosier than the reality, but which Pleuthner presented at CPSI anyway, touting DuPont's task force as one of brainstorming's great success stories.

DuPont's brainstorming chairmen had realized quite quickly that what was supposed to be a system for creativity within bureaucracy was often stymied by bureaucracy itself. It could take several months for lists of hundreds of ideas to be passed around, combed through, winnowed down, and reported back to the respective departments. And even then, quantity did not reliably lead to quality. As Kyle VanHemert writes, "The fastidious typewritten accounts of DuPont's brainstorming sessions in the 1950s may well constitute the best-kept record of bad ideas in business history."[28]

Doubts about brainstorming became widespread. The headlines from the fall of 1956 included "Brainstorming: Cure or Curse?" "Brainstorming—Bunk or Benefit?" and "Why Doesn't Brainstorming Always Work?" The following year the *Proceedings of the Institute of Radio Engineers* reported on "The Limits of Brainstorming."[29] Most damning, in June 1958 Yale professor Donald Taylor published the first detailed scientific study of brainstorming. He compared the quantity and quality of ideas brainstormed by teams of four Yale undergrads to those generated by four students working alone, and concluded emphatically that "group participation when using brainstorming inhibits creative thinking."[30] Attendance at that year's CPSI dropped to 200, from 500 the year before.[31]

The backlash was as ideological as it was practical. For many, the takeaway from the Yale study was not just about brainstorming in particular, but about the very idea that groups can be creative. "Yale Study Backs Individual" crowed the *New York Herald Tribune*, as if the deepest philosophical question was at stake.[32] An opinion writer in *Printers' Ink* insisted that "Groups Don't Create: Individuals Do," and that brainstorm sessions "tend to be superficial and mechanical because they subordinate the individual to the group."[33] In fact, even though he didn't mention it by name, William Whyte may have had brainstorming in mind when he wrote in *The Organization Man* that the most "misguided" belief of the social ethic was that "creative work" could be done "by committee." "People very rarely *think* in groups," he wrote, "they talk together, they exchange information, they adjudicate, they make compromises. But they do not think; they do not create."[34]

Some of brainstorming's harshest critics came from within the advertising world, where the method was born. David Ogilvy, the chief of BBDO rival Ogilvy and Mather, called brainstorming "the delight of sterile loafers who would rather fritter away their day in meetings than shut their doors and get down to work."[35] One particularly harsh pile-on occurred at a 1958 creativity conference at the swanky Waldorf Astoria hotel in New York. "Only an individual can have an idea. So much for brainstorming," said W. John Upjohn of the Upjohn Corporation. E. Finley Carter, director of the Stanford Research Institute, was "frankly skeptical" of such "gimmicks." Pointing explicitly to the Yale study, Paul Smith, the organizer, emcee, and president and creative director at the Calkins & Holden Agency, called brainstorming "a variety of 'groupthink' . . . with little or no basic understanding of the creative process." Even Walter J. Friess, director of the flagship AC Spark Plug creativity program, which Osborn constantly touted, hastened to point out that brainstorming was only one of several approaches his company used, insisting that although "some organizations consider brainstorming and creativity synonymous," one "must go beyond . . . brainstorming" for real creative results.[36]

Most hostile of all was the designer Saul Bass, known for his animated title sequences in motion pictures like *North by Northwest* and *The Man with the Golden Arm*, as well as countless movie posters and corporate logos. Bass agreed with the Schumpeter-Whyte consensus, and with Osborn, that in its drive for efficiency in mass production industry had "bred out" the very thing "necessary to maintain the vitality of that system . . . creativity."[37] But brainstorming, Bass thought, was an ersatz creativity. "The chief danger of brainstorming lies . . . not in the question of whether or not it produces more or less ideas . . . but in fact, that it distorts the creative process by dealing with it piecemeal and putting it on the production line. "Creativity is a total process," Bass insisted, echoing the psychologist Carl Rogers, from whose influential 1954 essay on creativity Bass plagiarized portions of his speech, "it cannot be isolated in the experience of individuals, and turned on and off like a faucet every Thursday afternoon. It cannot operate from nine to five every day and not at any other time." At the root of the problem was brainstorming's insistence on the group. "In the history of ideas not one significant contribution has come from a group of people," Bass said. "The great theories or points of view . . . and new philosophies setting the tenor of the day are the province of one mind." Brainstorming was Mickey Mouse business, "useful only in giving birth to gadgets or their visual and verbal equivalents."[38]

At that point in the conference Willard Pleuthner asked to say a few words. He had been "squirming on the front seat" for two days as one speaker after another sullied his work. Waving a copy of CEF reports full of hundreds of brainstorming success stories in all areas of industry, he insisted brainstorming was about far more than "gimmicks, gadgets, and twists," as Bass had alleged. The Yale study, and probably any company who had failed with brainstorming, he said, had not followed the exact procedure BBDO had worked out over nearly twenty years. (For example, brainstorming sessions were thirty minutes to an hour; Dr. Taylor had given his students only twelve minutes.) Anyway, Pleuthner added, Osborn only ever claimed that brainstorming was an "extra tool." Pleuthner offered to send Bass and anyone else materials to set the record straight.[39]

Bass, still on the dais, was unconvinced, and a bit riled. He assured Pleuthner, "I have a file about this high, on brainstorming," including his touted reports from, "what is it, the Creative Education Foundation, something of that sort?" The problem, Bass reiterated, was not the method itself, but the way in which it had become "a substitute and symbol of creativity." "Let's understand how minimal, how superficial, *this* method is for achieving the kind of fundamental creativity, excitement and vitality that we need," he implored. Of course their industry depended on "twists and gimmicks and gadgets. . . . But we need something more. This is only the froth."[40] Trying to steer Bass toward some practical advice, a member of the audience asked, "where can we look for new visual creativity in visual techniques and approaches?" Bass simply and somewhat unhelpfully reiterated, "where do we find new creativity? In individuals. I can't say more than that." The chairman Smith, possibly sensing the issue had exhausted itself, quickly wrapped things up.

Figure 2.3 Brainstorming session at the RAND corporation in Santa Monica, California. Brainstormers were encouraged to take relaxed postures while an assistant (on stairs) recorded the ideas. Leonard McCombe/The LIFE Picture Collection/Shutterstock.

The awkward exchange reveals how brainstorming had become a lightning rod in the big national conversation about individualism and the corporation. It also reveals competing notions of creativity. For Bass, true creativity was not simply any idea, it was a *great* idea, the kind of idea that might sometimes come up in an advertisement or a product but which was really the stuff of high thought. For Pleuthner, Osborn, and other brainstorming evangelists, though they insisted the method was for more than just gadgets, brainstorming was also for exactly the kind of everyday problem-solving and gadget-making that Bass admitted it was for. What they disagreed about, then, beyond whether it "worked," was—in a parallel to the criteria questions being hashed out in academia—what really counted as creativity.

The Solution of Almost Every Human Problem

In fact, there was no problem Osborn did not believe could be solved by deliberate creative effort, and his most ardent wish was for his methods to be embraced outside business. His early writings often focused on personal problems. On writing letters to your loved one in the army: "Instead of dashing off all that dullness, why not try to think up something brighter?" On keeping the peace between siblings: "We could ward off this bedlam if we could think up the right idea." With divorce rates soaring, Osborn wondered how many couples had "consciously applied *imagination* in search of ways to avoid the rocks?"[41] But as the creativity movement gained steam he became more ambitious. At the second CPSI, Osborn pitched the crowd of business executives and military brass:

> Only recently has it been realized that imagination can be the key to the solution of almost every kind of problem. . . . By becoming more creative, we can live better with ourselves and with each other. By becoming more creative, we can provide better goods and services for each other—to the result of a higher and higher standard of living. By becoming more creative, we may even find a way to bring permanent peace to all the world.[42]

Indeed, Osborn often claimed creative thinking could solve political impasses such as urban "race riots" or the Cuban Missile Crisis. When Osborn called the Cold War "a war of ideas," he did not mean a clash of ideologies, but rather an arms race of schemes. America should be "geared for idea-production," he said, proposing a secret government panel of brainstormers to come up with ideas for beating the Russians (which, he pointed out, would cost "peanuts" compared to the money being spent on weapons research).[43] As for winning hearts and minds, he wondered, "why not set up a group of creative people in the State Department . . . to suggest new ways and more ways to win the friendship of the rest of the world?"[44] For Osborn, every problem was a failure of imagination.

Osborn's ultimate goal, in fact the very mission of the Creative Education Foundation, was to get creative thinking into American schools. "Almost every campus has a French club, a Spanish club, even a German club. Why not an idea club?" he wrote.[45] Osborn believed that every school should offer classes in creative thinking, and that creative thinking techniques should be incorporated into the standard subjects. He imagined nothing less than a total reformation of American education—for every student to receive, as he put it, only half jokingly, "indoctrination in creativity."[46]

By 1957 Osborn was happy to report that thanks to the CEF's efforts an estimated two thousand classes incorporated the principles from *Applied Imagination* in some form, plus an increasing number of stand-alone creative thinking courses. Cornell University and Macalester College both required brainstorming training as part of freshman orientation, and Webber College, where Osborn was a board member, required all students to purchase and read *Applied Imagination* before taking a stand-alone course in creative problem-solving. The courses incorporating creative thinking ranged from animal husbandry to law to weapons systems, with strong uptake in military academies and the ROTC— where by 1960 an estimated 37,000 Air Force members had taken creative thinking courses—but the majority were in business and technical schools, especially marketing and engineering.[47]

Nevertheless, Osborn was frustrated by the "snail-like" progress in education, especially in the liberal arts, where "the majority of professors still spurn our offerings," insisting they already taught creative thinking.[48] (Unconvinced, Osborn delegated a colleague to survey college textbooks in philosophy and psychology, only to find that "creative imagination" was nowhere to be seen.) Osborn's frustration may have been a product of competing ideas of what creative thinking entailed. Recalcitrant professors perhaps had in mind what we might now call critical thinking: that reading and debating great works of art, literature, and science opened students' minds and prepared them to come up with their own interpretations. In contrast to the alternative approaches to higher education—technical, vocational, or classical—the liberal arts might in fact have seemed to its proponents the very epitome of a "creative education."[49]

Deliberate creative thinking methods, by contrast, seemed to these liberal arts professors to be, Osborn reported, "tainted with vocationalism." Osborn gladly admitted to being pragmatic. "Although I am a liberal arts graduate," he wrote, "I am not intelligent enough to understand why it is wrong to teach a type of thinking which can best help students to do better in their careers."[50] Osborn was proud of his hardheaded, results-oriented approach, which he contrasted with the overly deliberate style of academic psychologists and with the expert class in general. His mantra (attributed to Einstein, but who knows), which he had emblazoned on the CEF letterhead, was "imagination is more important than knowledge." He celebrated the massive new national expenditures on R&D but insisted that without "deliberate creative effort"—by which he meant, essentially, brainstorming—scientists would not be able to make the most of it. He railed against the "national habit of going all-out in fact-finding and then petering out when it comes to applying creative thinking to the facts as found." The very title of his creative thinking "bible," *Applied Imagination*, was apparently a riff on the term "applied science," then coming into use to differentiate industrial research (and a growing amount of Cold War academic research) from "basic" or "fundamental" science.

In choosing the term, Osborn was making it clear, as in everything he did, that ideas were about results. The fact that Osborn dedicated the later part of his career to convincing educators that every American child needed to be trained in his Madison Avenue–bred, industry-forged methods of creative thinking reflects a worldview in which commerce was, or should be, the model for society itself.

This anti-intellectualism echoed a larger culture war bubbling up in postwar America between liberal and leftist intellectuals and an emerging coalition of business and populist social conservatives who characterized the former as "eggheads" or "pointy-heads"—people who were lacking in common sense and the common touch, weak of heart and loin. The professoriate, technocrats, and "social engineers" responsible for the New Deal order tended to be social constructivists and cultural relativists who advocated government intervention in matters ranging from racial desegregation to consumer protections. Osborn favored individual approaches to social betterment and saw the reigning technocratic culture of "research" as stale and impotent.[51]

Osborn's supreme belief in "ideas"—particularly the kind that can fit on a suggestion card or a line of a secretary's notepad—often shaded into a shallow solutionism. Take for example a brainstorming demonstration at the second annual Creative Problem Solving Institute in 1956 that tackled the issue of juvenile delinquency. In just twenty-four minutes a panel of fifteen (thirteen men, two women, almost all in business, and all middle-aged) produced 125 ideas. The best of these, as determined by the organizers, included essay contests, campaigns to encourage church-going and club-joining, and, perhaps cheekily, the establishment of creative-thinking classes for youngsters to brainstorm ways to contribute to the community.

Juvenile delinquency was at that time a subject of intense national debate, occupying hundreds of social workers, psychologists, sociologists, and the sort, and dividing America over whether the causes were moral or social, psychological or economic, or whether the problem existed at all.[52] The brainstorming approach assumed the issue was simply that nobody had thought up a good solution yet. What's more, the very statement of the problem—"What could be done to make teen-agers feel contempt for juvenile delinquency and feel admiration for law-abiding behavior?"—constrained the possible answers to begin with, admitting no solutions that didn't already assume the problem was the attitudes of young people toward the law.

This narrowing of possibilities was, of course, a structural element of brainstorming. Both the initial framing of the problem and the eventual selection of the solution were typically decided by higher-ups. Brainstorming was not designed to produce truly revolutionary ideas; rather, it exemplifies what the philosopher and literary scholar Mikhail Bakhtin has called the carnivalesque, a special occasion in which the traditional order is temporary upended so that those at the bottom can get their resentments out of their system before the traditional order is finally restored. In a brainstorming session people are encouraged to be zany and speak out of turn for an hour or so before the workday returns to normal and the pecking order is restored. Brainstorming embodied the idea of a managed revolution, the promise that disorder, individualism, irrationality, play, and irreverence could be harnessed where it was least likely to thrive, and that corporate capitalism was not, contra its critics, inherently hostile to those fundamental and venerable human energies.[53]

Even as brainstorming was coming under attack in industry and meeting with stonewalling in the liberal arts, Osborn was attempting a foray into academic creativity research, which he hoped might legitimize and amplify his message. In 1956, he arranged to have Sidney J. Parnes hired as assistant professor in retailing at the University of Buffalo School of Business Administration, and simultaneously as Director of Creative Education at the University of Buffalo's extension program. (Osborn was vice chairman of the University of Buffalo board at the time.) Parnes, a young man with a degree in organizational psychology, had attended the first CPSI in 1955, and, having found his life's calling, returned to direct the conference the next year. In his new academic position, Parnes could also teach and test Osborn's methods. In 1955 the

CEF had commissioned a study by a Barnard College psychology professor on the efficacy of the methods in *Applied Imagination*, and although the results were inconclusive, the author acknowledged that Osborn's lay theory of "deferred judgment" had some correlation with academic theories of divergent thinking and tolerance of ambiguity.[54] This was heartening, but when the more negative (and somewhat more credible) Yale study landed, Parnes rebutted with a series of articles between 1959 and 1961, roundly supporting Osborn's methods. One found that students trained in brainstorming performed up to 94 percent better in subsequent brainstorming sessions.[55] Parnes also went after research money, in 1963 winning a $46,000 two-year grant from the US Office of Education to study the effects of creative thinking education. Despite the murky science, Osborn was convinced, touting the Parnes studies and declaring at every chance he got that research had conclusively "proved that creative ability can be deliberately and measurably developed."[56]

The mainstream creativity researchers tended to be more conservative with their pronouncements. The Yale study cast serious doubt on the efficacy of the methods, but on a more fundamental level researchers felt the kind of creativity Osborn and Parnes were talking about was a much thinner phenomenon than the kind of creativity they themselves had in mind. Showing that people could improve in brainstorming when they practiced brainstorming was not the same as saying creative ability can be developed, at least if by "creative ability" one meant something larger than brainstorming ability. Many researchers doubted that divergent thinking alone—which brainstorming approximated—was the full picture of creativity, while Osborn and Parnes went around talking as if they were one and the same.

While some academics saw Osborn as overeager and simplistic, Osborn himself was at times frustrated with the cautious pace of scientific research, chalking it up to needless complexity. At one point he suggested a kind of truce, where the CEF would teach "the arithmetic of deliberate creativity" to the masses and "let others delve into the calculus of our subject."[57] Indeed, Osborn and the credentialed scientists were generally chasing different beasts: while Osborn sought to improve the creative talent of "every Tom, Dick, and Harry," the majority of the psychology research was more interested in how to identify great and innate creative talent.

But perhaps Osborn was onto something: brainstorming certainly seemed to bear a strong resemblance to the "divergent thinking" tasks that were at the core of Guilford's and others' tests of creativity. If this one aspect of creativity was in fact mutable—and that was still a big "if"—then it might point the way to how creativity might be improved with education, which would obviously be a massive social benefit and major coup for creativity research. In 1959 Calvin Taylor put Parnes in charge of a new subgroup at the Utah Conference studying "development" of creative ability. Another addition to the program that year, the educational psychologist E. Paul Torrance, credited Osborn as an influence in his mission to show that creativity could be taught in schools. These new faces signaled the field's movement, within a decade of its founding, toward a qualified acceptance of Osborn's conviction that creative ability might be learnable.

The ties between Buffalo's school of "applied creativity" and the other nodes of academic creativity research only continued to tighten over the years. Around 1963 the institution, newly known as SUNY Buffalo, hired Gary Cooley, formerly a research assistant to Calvin Taylor, to join Parnes as a full-time research associate in "creative education."[58] Taylor, meanwhile, began to host a CPSI-like Summer Creativity Workshop at the University of Utah starting in 1962, using the CEF's *Sourcebook for Creative Thinking*, a compendium edited by Parnes in which research by Guilford, Barron, Taylor, Torrance, and Abraham Maslow sat cheek by jowl with how-to case studies by Osborn, John E. Arnold, and William J. J. Gordon, founder of the brainstorming competitor Synectics. Over the next several decades Buffalo would be a refuge and backbone for the creativity community, even after academic research began to contract in the 1970s. Guilford, MacKinnon, Barron, and Torrance were regulars at CPSI and served as CEF board members, some until the end of their lives, earning lifetime achievement awards and other accolades along the way. In 1967, the year after Osborn's death at the age of seventy-seven, Guilford himself, whom Osborn had credited with "sounding the alarm which started this movement" and whose research had "empowered the creative education movement with new-found truths," penned a retrospective of the field in which he heartily acknowledged the contributions of Osborn and Parnes to the larger understanding of creativity and cited the importance of "creative education" as part of "the solution of mankind's most serious problems."[59]

:::

Despite all the press attention, the rapid spread of his ideas in industry, and the somewhat less successful though still encouraging infiltration of the ivory tower, ten years into his "creativity movement" Osborn felt it was falling short of its transformative potential. He was not surprised that military and industry people would be on the vanguard of adopting his methods, but he lamented that when it came to solving "people problems," "there [was] no conscious creative effort at all comparable to what scientific research is doing to better the products we use."[60]

Osborn deeply believed he had the idea that would change the world. And that idea was more ideas. Lots of them. Spilling out from every Tom, Dick, and Harriet across the land. Though creative thinking methods were ultimately taken up most in industry, Osborn's claim that his brand of creative thinking was deep down more than just a vocational skill was key to its resonance. Just as it gave his life's work a larger social significance, it also allowed the hundreds of thousands of employees who received creative thinking training or participated in brainstorming sessions to feel like they were becoming active agents of change. For managers, meanwhile, creative thinking seemed a way around the Schumpeterian dilemma, that corporate employment necessarily shut down the flow of new ideas.

There was, at the same time, another way of looking at creativity—not as simply a skill, or a procedure that could be started and stopped at will, or even a way of thinking, but as a fundamental life force. The people who took this view, to whom we will turn next, came to the creativity conversation with a very different set of concerns that rubbed up against, and yet in other ways complemented, Osborn's hopes for the "creativity movement."

Creativity as Self-Actualization

3

In 1952, upon returning from an academic conference on creativity at Syracuse, the psychologist Carl Rogers penned "Toward a Theory of Creativity."

> The mainspring of creativity appears to be . . . man's tendency to actualize himself, to become his potentialities. By this I mean the directional trend which is evident in all organic and human life—the urge to expand, extend, develop, mature—the tendency to express and activate all the capacities of the organism, or the self. This tendency may become deeply buried under layer after layer of encrusted psychological defenses; it may be hidden behind elaborate façades which deny its existence; it is my belief however . . . that it exists in every individual, and awaits only the proper conditions to be released and expressed.[1]

This was a way of looking at creativity very different from most other researchers at the time. Where psychometricians like Guilford and Taylor were looking at creativity primarily as an intellectual ability, Rogers saw it as something much more expansive: the expression of human nature in its fullest flowering. This perspective reflected Rogers's particular disciplinary background as a psychoanalyst, interested not in sorting the population but rather in helping individuals achieve a sense of happiness and fulfillment. It also reflected his somewhat distinct motivations for caring about creativity in the first place. While Rogers nodded to the "talent" problem, that industry had "an ample supply of technicians" but few innovative thinkers, what scared Rogers more than the threat of falling behind the Russians was the pace of technological change itself. "In a time when knowledge, constructive and destructive, is advancing by the most incredible leaps and bounds into a fantastic atomic age," he wrote, "genuinely creative adaptation seems to represent the only possibility that man can keep abreast of the kaleidoscopic change in his world." This adaptation—social and cultural rather than technological—was the only thing that could save us. "International annihilation will be the price we pay for a lack of creativity."[2] Rogers also worried about the toll the Fordist order was taking on individuals' sense of meaning. "Creative work" was hoarded by those at the top, while the masses were bored at work and spent their leisure hours in "passive" and "regimented" activities. Industrial society produced a "tendency toward conformity," wherein "to be original, or different, is felt to be 'dangerous.'" And this, he felt, had repercussions far beyond military and economic concerns.

Despite his somewhat divergent perspective, Rogers's essay, published in 1954, would soon become a classic of both creativity literature and of a distinct movement known as humanistic psychology. As Rogers' comments indicate, humanistic psychologists were skeptical of modern society but also optimistic about the potential for human flourishing in a post-materialist age. They believed that traditional psychologists focused too much on dysfunction, and on trying to get people to be normal, and so, seeing normalcy as akin to conformity, they turned their attention to human thriving, expression and individuation.[3] The influence of Rogers, as well as Abraham Maslow and Rollo May, the three main exponents of that movement, was almost immediately felt in the larger field of creativity research, and permeates creativity literature to this day, quoted liberally in everything from education to management to spirituality and self-help.[4] Although military industrial concerns were the initial spur to creativity research, the interest these pioneering humanistic psychologists took in the notion of creativity, and their influence on the wider academic discourse, indicates that creativity became a key topic in postwar psychology for more than utilitarian reasons. In fact, creativity, connoting something more romantic than just inventiveness, arose due to a countervailing trend in the field and in society in general, a conviction that organized society was stifling the irrational, the artistic—in short, the cluster of attributes that were coming to be seen as "human." Many of the writings of humanistic psychologists originated as explicit challenges to the early creativity research, which they accused of being overly reductive, utilitarian, even sexist. Nevertheless, there was something in their message—that creativity and self-actualization were deeply linked, and that treating it as a quantifiable resource was a fool's errand—that somehow complimented, via contradiction, the technology-oriented elements of the field.

Maslow Against Creativity

On April 26, 1957, Abraham Maslow delivered a talk to the US Army Engineer School in Fort Belvoir, Virginia, titled "Emotional Blocks to Creativity." The year before, 150 Fort Belvoir engineers had participated in a brainstorming training by a Creative Education Foundation associate, and the leadership perhaps felt Maslow could give a different perspective. He began by confessing how "uneasy" he felt addressing such a crowd. "I've been amazed to be plucked at in the last couple of years by big industries of which I know nothing, or organizations like the U.S. Army Engineers," he said. Indeed, Maslow was not yet the management thinker he would be remembered as, and he did not come armed with hard data on how to identify creative engineers or increase the rate of innovation. He came instead with psychoanalytic, even romantic ideas about creativity. He cautioned that what he had to say might be useless for such an audience, for creative people were "precisely the ones that make trouble in an organization."[5]

This fish-out-of-water posture was typical Maslow; he often positioned himself as an antagonist and gadfly to the kind of tech-oriented creativity talk happening around the Utah Conferences, which he believed treated creativity in a strictly utilitarian light, as something to be instrumentalized, even weaponized. His ribbing of the Army engineers was part of his larger mission to "humanize" American society, starting with professional psychology itself, which he (like many others) believed had become far too rational.

Despite being remembered later as the "father of creativity" by one of his many acolytes, Maslow was not at first particularly interested in the specific problem of how people come up with ideas.[6] He was, however, interested in exceptional people, and in that sense he was very much on the same wavelength as other creativity researchers. Like them he believed psychology had at some point stopped wondering about human excellence, and instead only thought about dysfunction and disease. His watershed 1950 article "Self-Actualizing People: A Study in Psychological Health" examined the lives of eminent individuals such as Abraham Lincoln, Albert Einstein, Eleanor Roosevelt, Jane Addams, and Baruch Spinoza. This was not dissimilar from the IPAR studies of eminent people, and was even more in the spirit of Galton's studies of Great Men of Genius. Where earlier psychologists had attempted to assign such figures' posthumous IQ scores, Maslow put them on the virtual analyst's couch, plumbing their deepest psychological processes and personalities for the secrets to their singular successes. For Maslow their accomplishments were proof of inner flourishing.

When Maslow first began writing about creativity—or "creativeness," as he tended to call it—it was sometimes privately, in response to the studies coming out from Guilford and others, and sometimes when he was occasionally invited to address audiences like the Army Engineers. His skepticism was not about the possibility of understanding creativity, but about how psychologists and their tech-minded patrons were going about it. "I get the strong impression that industry keeps looking for some secret button to push, like switching a light on and off," he wrote in 1952 in a note to himself. "I half expect to hear someone ask soon 'Where is it localized?' or try implanting electrodes with which to turn it off or on." He found the prevailing approach to creativity "atomistic," reducing it to specific cognitive processes. At the seventh Utah Conference in 1966, Maslow attacked the field directly, claiming that despite the "accumulation of methods, of ingenious testing techniques, and of sheer quantity of information," actual knowledge about creativity hadn't advanced a bit.[7] Maslow rejected the idea that creative accomplishment could be explained by some cognitive ability like divergent thinking. Inspired by Gestalt psychology (Max Wertheimer had been a mentor to Maslow), he thought it was imperative to understand the "whole person." Maslow urged the Utah crowd to take a more "holistic, organismic, or systemic" approach, saying that "creating tends to be the act of a whole man, not added-to the organism like a coat of paint."[8] Rather than looking for a "secret button" to activate latent creativity, Maslow argued, society should instead try to create "a better *type* of person . . . who, incidentally, would be more creative."[9] "General creativeness, holistically conceived, emanates from the whole system, generally improved," Maslow wrote. A "more fully human, healthier person would then, epiphenomenally, generate and spark off dozens, hundreds, and millions of differences in behaving, experiencing, perceiving, communicating, teaching, working, etc., which would *all* be more 'creative.'"

For Maslow, the approach of people like Guilford was a perfect encapsulation of how narrow and utilitarian psychology had become. In 1954, Maslow declared that the field of psychology "too often pursues limited or trivial goals with limited methods and techniques under the guidance of limited vocabulary and concepts."[10] Maslow was originally trained as a behaviorist, studying monkey sexuality and writing a doctoral thesis on "learning, retention, and reproduction of verbal material." But like many other psychologists in the wake of World War II, Maslow came to see behaviorism as narrow, and sought to carve out a "larger jurisdiction for psychology" that could account for deeper philosophical questions about spirituality, the search for meaning, and transcendence. He also wanted psychology to be not just descriptive but also inspiring, something everyday people could use to find meaning and better themselves.[11]

Maslow therefore looked to Freudianism, which behaviorists had fought to banish from "empirical" social science, and which was experiencing a revival in the postwar era because it seemed to offer a thicker description of human nature in all its tangled and irrational glory. As psychoanalysts got to work adjusting returning GIs and newly re-domesticated housewives to the bewildering modern age, many postwar neo-Freudians, including the humanist psychologists, took a more critical approach. Suddenly acutely wary of mass society, they were less interested in adjusting individuals to potentially sick social norms than in helping them resist social pressures to conform. Where Freudianism traditionally focused on dysfunction, humanistic psychologists like Maslow and Rogers thought it was time to turn attention onto "positive" behaviors, like happiness, thriving, and creative accomplishment. As they did so they flipped old bourgeois ideals of psychological health on their head, drawing into question traits associated with getting along, while rinsing aspects once considered "beastly" or "evil" of their "taint of pathology."[12]

This was the guiding spirit behind Maslow's message for the Army Engineers. Drawing on his own research on self-actualizers as well as the recent IPAR studies on the creative personality, Maslow said that creative people were "unconventional," "a little bit queer." Their less creative colleagues often saw them as "unrealistic," "undisciplined," "unscientific," even "childish," "irresponsible," or "crazy." The creative person was one "who can live with his unconscious . . . his childishness, his fantasy, his imagination, his wish fulfillment, his femininity, his poetic quality, his crazy quality." Uncreative people, on the other hand, were "very orderly and very neat and very punctual and very systematic and very controlled." They made "excellent bookkeepers." The uncreative man, "rigid and tight," was "afraid of his emotions, or of his deepest instinctual urges, or his deepest self, which he desperately represses."[13]

There was something perverse in Maslow's decision to tout these values at Fort Belvoir, of all places. Rationality, punctuality, stoicism, and dependability were the kinds of values the engineers there likely picked up from their fathers, from Boy Scouts, from self-help books, from basic training, or indeed from engineering school. But this was just the beginning of a shift in the culture of the technical professions. For engineers and other white-collar professionals were increasingly being told by their superiors that creativity was a trait they should cultivate in order to thrive in their careers, to beat the communists, and, Maslow now told them, to be fully authentic and healthy human beings.

Against the Mad Genius Theory

Just as psychologists were drawn to the idea of creativity as a more democratic alternative to genius, so too did they find in creativity a replacement for the old myth of the mad genius. The early nineteenth-century Romantics saw genius as both a gift and an affliction, causing many a young man to descend into madness, tortured by ideas far ahead of their time and out of step with society. Early psychological science did little to dispel this notion. The nineteenth-century French psychiatrist Jacques Joseph Moreau claimed genius was an inherited pathology, interpreting "all engrossing passion for work and fits of enthusiasm" as morbid obsession, while his Italian follower Cesare Lombroso (the father of the debunked science of craniometry, the measuring of skulls) found that geniuses were "degenerates," afflicted with physical weakness, pallidness, and shortness of stature. Numerous "pathographies" circulated, diagnosing everyone from Socrates to Pascal with various psychological afflictions.[14] In the twentieth century, partly thanks to Galton, such ideas attenuated somewhat, but they persisted through Freud, who thought artists (but not scientists) were motivated by sublimated libido, and in no small part through the critical reputation of many modern artists themselves, for whom depression, drug abuse, and eccentricity were construed as markers of artistic authenticity.

Many postwar creativity researchers wanted to abolish such conceptions, chief among them Frank Barron. Barron joined Donald McKinnon at IPAR in its founding year, 1950, as a newly minted PhD in personality psychology, and would quickly become a rising star in creativity research. As IPAR's ambassador at the first Utah Conference in 1955, Barron presented an empirical paper on "the disposition toward originality" in Air Force captains (in which he used Guilford's new creativity battery in addition to personality tests), and thereafter became a co-organizer of the conference (and, with Calvin Taylor, a co-editor of the proceedings). Meanwhile, on the faculty at UC Santa Cruz, Barron became an early pioneer of psychedelic drug research (with his graduate school classmate Timothy Leary) and a founding board member of the Esalen Institute in Big Sur, where Maslow and Rogers were known to mingle with new-age and countercultural types.[15] At some point in this mix Barron came to identify as a humanistic psychologist, believing psychology could be, like art and poetry, a "sacred discipline devoted to the celebration of the human spirit."[16] In his 1963 book *Creativity and Psychological Health,* Barron explained his conviction that "psychology should take a look at the positive side of human nature and concern itself with unusual vitality in human beings rather than with disease."[17]

One of Barron's key claims was that creative people were not, as their stereotypes would suggest, crazy. From depth assessments of prominent writers, mathematicians, and architects, he and McKinnon reported that "the creative person seldom fits the layman's stereotype. . . . In our experience, he is not the emotionally unstable, sloppy, loose-jointed Bohemian," but rather "deliberate, reserved, industrious, and thorough." (MacKinnon jokingly called this "the briefcase syndrome of creativity.")[18] Creative subjects scored high in tests of self-confidence, independence, curiosity, and work ethic.[19] Rather than spilling over into blind arrogance, the creative person's high self-confidence was offset by a capacity for "honest self-assessment." Creative people tested high in "ego strength," yet still had access to the irrational and erotic energies that in lesser men might manifest in bizarre, hedonistic, and self-destructive behaviors. Borrowing the language of their contemporary David Riesman, Barron and McKinnon described the creative person as "inner directed"—a rare exception in that era of "other-directed" men—without being self-absorbed. The creative person was, as Barron put it, "both more primitive and more cultured, more destructive and more constructive, crazier and saner, than the average person."[20]

If genius had been defined by excess, creativity was, these researchers argued, a product of balance. The architect's skill at balancing his individual visions with those of his clients, the writer's ability to push forward the form in ways meaningful to his audience, and the mathematician's ability to imagine objectively provable truths all stemmed from this balancing act between irrational and rational, id and ego. Truly creative people understood how to channel their substantial imaginations into socially productive work. Thus, the image of the tempestuous, unstable, and inscrutable Romantic genius was replaced by the much less troublesome "creative person," and the "creative process" came to be seen, as Rollo May wrote, "not as the product of sickness, but as representing the highest degree of emotional health, as the expression of normal people in the act of actualizing themselves."

The notion of "self-actualization" or "self-realization" was the hinge by which humanistic psychologists joined creative behavior to psychological health. According to Kurt Goldstein, the German psychologist from whom Maslow borrowed the concept, self-actualization was a fundamental organismic desire to reach one's full potential. It was a concept that drew on various streams of twentieth-century Western theory: Jung's notion that every person naturally strives to "individuate"; the existentialist philosophy of Sartre, in which humans were the artists of their own lives; and Henri Bergson's notion of "creative evolution," a sort of primal life force driving every organism toward change. Creativity theorists like Barron took this one step further, linking the outward inventiveness of people such as artists, architects, and engineers to *the* fundamental human drive. It was not, as Freud had it, the "sexual drive" that powered the whole human circus, Barron declared, but rather "creativity." Not biological procreation but symbolic creation was "the peculiarly human energy, the triumphant form of energy in the living world."[21]

By 1963 Maslow noted, "my feeling is that the concept of creativeness and the concept of the healthy, self-actualizing, fully human person seem to be coming closer and closer together, and may perhaps turn out to be the same thing." It was perhaps a bit of self-fulfilling prophesy. At a moment when both concepts were still very much embryonic, Maslow, Rogers, May, Barron, and others fused creativity, in the sense of inventiveness, with self-actualization, rendering the search for one's true self and the search for outward novelty two sides of the same coin.[22]

Of Rebels and Romance

There was perhaps a tension between the domesticated version of the creative person as perfectly sane and the version of the creative person as a misfit or outsider. But to postwar thinkers trying to rescue the individual from modern society, perfect sanity and autonomy were one in the same. In the creative act, Maslow wrote, we become "free of other people, which in turn, means that we become much more ourselves, our Real Selves." This authentic self was not the social self that dominated interwar thought but the absolutely autonomous self, free of any entanglements or obligations. Like a modern-day Rousseau, Maslow celebrated the childlike "innocence" of the creative state, writing that creative people were able to become momentarily "guileless . . . without 'shoulds' or 'oughts,' without fashions, fads, dogmas, habits," or *a priori* notions of "what is proper, normal, 'right.'"[23] Even as they dispensed with the Romantic myth of the mad genius, humanistic psychologists, particularly Maslow, often traded in exactly the kind of Romantic notions that Guilford found so unhelpful. While the latter sought to reduce creativity to everyday cognitive processes, Maslow linked it to the kind of "peak experiences" he observed in his self-actualizers, moments of "bliss, ecstasy, rapture, exaltation." He wrote lyrically of the creative spirit as a muse, even a lover: "we let it flow in upon us. We let it wreak its will upon us. We let it have its way." To create was to be "lost in the present . . . to become timeless, selfless, outside of space, of society, of history."[24]

Frank Barron echoed this almost antisocial notion of the creative nonconformist:

> He rejects the demand of society that he should shun in himself the primitive, the uncultured, the naïve, the magical, the nonsensical; that he must be a "civilized" member of the community. Creative individuals reject this demand because they want to own themselves totally, and because they perceive a shortsightedness in the claim of society that all its members should adapt themselves to a norm for a given time and place.[25]

So there was this paradox. On one hand, to be creative was to reject the demands of society, a society that according to many postwar thinkers was probably mad; on the other, it was also to be utterly productive and useful, even or especially in a professional context.

There was also a typically postwar tension here between elitist and egalitarian sensibilities. If creativity was the result of self-actualization, then it could theoretically be accessible to anyone. Timothy Leary, in a paper somewhat incongruously titled "The Effects of Test Score Feedback on Creative Performance and of Drugs on Creative Experience," asserted, "creativity is not a function of lucky heritage or elite training. There are more visions in the cortex of each of us than in all the museums and libraries of the world. There is a limitless possibility of new combinations of the old symbols. A true democracy of creativity—experienced and performed—is possible and is, indeed, close at hand."[26] Maslow, for one, distinguished his more democratic theory of creativity from others by rejecting the "dichotomous separation of . . . creative from noncreative" on which psychometric studies relied. Maslow differentiated "secondary creativeness," the actual completion of works of value, from "primary creativeness," that initial moment of inspiration that he believed was "very probably a heritage of every human being . . . the kind of creativeness that any healthy child had and which is then lost by most people as they grow up."[27] For Maslow, the question was not how to identify creative people, but rather what had happened to this suppressed potential: "why in God's name isn't everyone creative?"[28] And so on this point the humanistic psychologists came into an unlikely agreement with the Osborns and Parneses of the world.

While they insisted creativity was a common inheritance, people like Maslow and Barron were also clearly infatuated with the exceptional, and they disdained the ordinary. Maslow wrote of the creative person as "a particular or special kind of human being, rather than just an old-fashioned, ordinary human being who now has acquired . . . a new skill like ice skating."[29] More strikingly, he noted, "no society can function very successfully unless there is a built-in arrangement whereby the aggridants"—the biologically superior members of a species—"innovators, geniuses, and trailblazers of all types and in all fields are admired and valued and are not torn apart by those seething with Nietzschean resentment, impotent envy, and weakling *counter-valuing*."[30] When Maslow wrote of the need to "develop a race of improvisers," in other words, it was unclear whether he was talking about the whole human race or a superior race. At the end of the day, for humanists as for the mental testers, the very concept of creativity depended on the maintenance of a hierarchy of human achievement against which all other behavior could be measured. And despite a few pokes at the edges of that hierarchy, it was left largely intact. The dream, as always, was inherently paradoxical: to alchemize the everyday and the sublime, to create a nation of people, as Maslow wrote, "who are different from the average kind of person."[31]

Creativity and Change

The humanistic psychologists were also somewhat in tension with the psychometric research over the question of science and technology. Where Guilford and Taylor tried to convince their sponsors that creativity research was crucial to speed up technological innovation, those of a humanistic bent were more likely to voice the opposite concern, wondering how social and cultural progress would keep pace. Brewster Ghiselin, the English professor at the Utah Conferences, similarly warned, in 1955, "the human mind is prepared to wrap the whole planet in a shroud." Saving us from nuclear holocaust—a problem he noted was created by human "ingenuity"—could only be solved "creatively—that is, by a profound and thorough alteration of our inner life," and a loosening of our "too-rigid patterns of current thought and feeling."[32]

The implication was that the technological iron cage humanity found itself in was not really the product of "creative" thinking, but of some other kind of thinking: rational, instrumental, narrow, specialized. For Ghiselin, as for humanist psychologists like Rogers and Maslow, creativity was clearly more than mere inventiveness or ingenuity. It was something wiser, more in touch with human nature, and was thus the antidote to machine-age thinking. Rollo May likewise saw creativity as a force for mindful and deliberate change:

> Frightened by the loss of our familiar mooring places, shall we become paralyzed and cover our inaction with apathy? If we do those things, we will have surrendered our chance to participate in the forming of the future. We will have forfeited the distinctive characteristic of human beings—namely, to influence our evolution through our own awareness. We will have capitulated to the blind juggernaut of history and lost the chance to mold the future into a society more equitable and humane.[33]

The mechanisms by which creative thinking would fix, rather than exacerbate, technology run amok were typically left vague. Rogers believed that although creativity was itself value neutral— "one man may be discovering a way of relieving pain, while another is devising a new and more subtle form of torture for political prisoners"—on balance fostering creativity was a positive social good because it would by definition go hand in hand with general psychological health, easing the anxieties that led to conflict. May, likewise, didn't explain why, if it is human nature to self-consciously change our "evolution," history should be seen as a "blind juggernaut." But the theme running through all of these men's work is that disruptive change was inevitable, the way of the world. Rather than standing athwart history yelling "stop," as the postwar conservative William F. Buckley urged, or questioning the whole system of constant growth and military one-upsmanship that drove such roiling change, they formulated a model of human nature consistent with it.

The role of psychologists, Maslow wrote, should be to "develop a race of improvisors, a different kind of human being to be able to live in a world which changes perpetually."[34] America needed to "make ourselves over into people who don't need to staticize the world, who don't need to freeze it and to make it stable, who don't need to do what their daddies did, who are able confidently to face tomorrow not knowing what's going to come . . . with confidence enough in ourselves that we will be able to improvise in that situation which has never existed before."[35] According to this psychological schema, change was natural, organic, healthy, and positive, whereas stasis—including even the comforts of stability and tradition that the previous generation so earnestly sought—was artificial, repressive, a sign of weakness and insufficient individuation. To be "creative" was, for Maslow, above all to be change-oriented, and thus was just as good for adapting to the dislocations of modern society as for contributing to them in the first place. Though they may have disagreed with some of the ends of their counterparts in the more quantitative realm of psychology, at least in the notion that creativity was a positive good, these humanistic psychologists found something they could all get behind.

The Democratic Personality

The framing of creativity as a kind of generally healthy personality trait regardless of its application gave it a larger political valence in the Cold War era. The "insistence on self-regulation" and "tendency to resist acculturation" that purportedly defined the creative person could be seen as antisocial traits, but they were exactly what postwar intellectuals thought made creative people ideal citizens in a complex and pluralistic liberal society.[36] During the early Cold War it became a common pastime among intellectuals to map political systems and preferences—liberalism, conservatism, democracy, totalitarianism—onto different personalities. *The Authoritarian Personality*, a massive 1950 study, put political tendencies in psychoanalytic terms, arguing that "authoritarians"—which included both racist conservatives and hardcore communists—were, among other things, "anal," "rigid," and "narrow-minded," and exhibited "conformity to externally imposed values," whereas the democratic personality, in addition to being less "ethnocentric," was "tolerant" and "flexible," and possessed "greater autonomy" and "an internalized conscience . . . oriented toward genuine, intrinsic values and standards rather than toward external authorities." As Jamie Cohen-Cole writes, according to liberal intellectuals "the bland and homogeneous American suburb and the totalitarian machine that was the USSR shared a common feature: they were both populated by a similar sort of subject . . . that kind of person who, devoid of a true self, could undermine American democracy."[37]

"Creativity" didn't come up in the first edition of *The Authoritarian Personality*, which was written before Guilford's speech, but the IPAR creativity studies borrowed both personnel and ideas from it, resulting in the creative personality being largely a new iteration of the democratic personality.[38] One study found that creative people and democratic people both preferred asymmetrical figures to symmetrical ones, and abstract art to representational or figurative images, which reportedly reflected their "tolerance for ambiguity."[38] According to this theory, the same thing that made democratic personalities tolerant of different races and nationalities apparently made creative people tolerant of foreign ideas, while an ability to live with "momentary disorder," which made the democratic person fit for the messiness of the democratic process, also made the creative person capable of resisting falling too quickly for hackneyed solutions. The fact that such aesthetic inclinations might be attributed to shared cultural preferences of the largely educated and professional class from which both democratic and creative people were selected, as opposed to their innate personalities, was hardly considered.[39]

The creative person was even a metonym of the democratic society itself. "Totalitarian states which depend upon suppression to achieve unity," Barron wrote, "are psychodynamically similar to the neurotic individual who suppresses his own impulses and emotions in order to maintain a semblance of stability."[40] On the other hand, he surmised, "the psychological conditions which make a society or an epoch creative and consistently original" were likely "analogous to those seen in individual creativity," including "freedom of expression . . . lack of fear of dissent and contradiction, a willingness to break with custom, a spirit of play as well as of dedication to work, (and) purpose on a grand scale." The creative person and the creative society were made in one another's image.

Despite the political resonance, creativity research clearly wasn't only about politics. That is to say, although freedom of thought and of expression were bedrock democratic values, for Barron and others who focused on creativity specifically, the benefit of free thought was not primarily a healthy body politic, but rather productivity. The ability to "resist acculturation" and an unwillingness to "surrender one's personal, unique, fundamental nature," which in the political sphere might inoculate a person against being swayed by demagogues, in the creative person resulted in bold innovations.[41] Tolerance, which in the democratic citizen might result in fair treatment of racial minorities or acceptance of the disorderly process of policy-making, could in the engineer aid in solving messy problems. In fact the creative person was by definition one who put their open-mindedness to work. "The creative individual not only respects the irrational in himself," Barron explained, "but courts it as the most promising source of novelty in his own thought."[42] The creative person, he wrote, is one who solves "problems external to himself" and *creates himself* at the same time."[43] In the creative personality individuation and invention were fused.

Art (Not) for Art's Sake

Though everyone agreed creativity was not the sole province of the arts, humanistic psychologists, generally skeptical of the postwar cult of science, were more likely to emphasize the arts. Their exemplars of creative individuals tended to be men and (occasionally) women of arts and letters, and their descriptions of the creative process were heavily drawn from the arts. Maslow even suggested that it was not to the scientist that researchers should look for the secrets of creativity, but rather to the artist and the child, for science was merely "a technique, social and institutionalized . . . whereby noncreative people can create."[44] (He said this, in his typical cheeky fashion, directly to the Utah Conference, which was after all specifically about creative scientific talent).

Indeed, many in the academic arts and humanities regarded the sudden enthusiasm for creativity among the science and technology set with a mix of pride and trepidation. The organizers of a Syracuse conference attended mostly by arts educators and Freudian psychologists wrote with a kind of bemused defensiveness, "where once creativity was greeted with derisive laughter, scorn, and suspicion, it is today considered a professional interest and treated with the respect it deserves, even among engineers, inventors and medical personnel." Their assumption was that, even though they had never really discussed anything called creativity in a systematic way, and thought they virtually all agreed that creativity, whatever it was, transcended the arts, that arts were somehow creativity's native home.[45]

To stress the significance of the arts was sometimes to align with non-instrumentalism. At the Syracuse conference Melvin Tumin (later famous for work on social stratification) chose to define creativity as "the esthetic experience . . . enjoyed for the actions which define and constitute the experience, whatever it may be, rather than for its instrumental results." That definition was a far cry from the one being hashed out at the Utah Conferences, which stressed novelty as well as utility. In 1964 the writer Arthur Koestler argued that the core characteristic of a creative act was the production of "surprise," a definition that nicely fit art and literature but was just broad enough to include technological novelty as well; neither Tumin's nor Koestler's ever became a standard definition. Arguing against the instrumentalism of much creativity research, Maslow likewise insisted that creativity was not about "problem-solving" and "product-making," but about self-expression. "Without purpose or design or even consciousness," he wrote, "creativeness is 'emitted,' or radiated, and hits all of life, regardless of problems . . . like sunshine."[46]

The arts focus gave humanistic theories of creativity a particular ideological shading, for art was traditionally understood as the antidote to the ills of industrial society. The Romantic artist was putatively (if never really actually) outside the realm of capitalist production, and as such represented an exception to modern alienation. "When Beethoven created the Ninth Symphony, the Ninth was Beethoven and Beethoven was the Ninth," said Viktor Lowenfeld, a prominent arts educator who had famously argued that children should never be taught to imitate the work of others. The creative process, he said, was defined by the ability "to identify with one's own work so closely that the distinction between the work and its creator almost ceases." This "ability to identify completely with one's own work" was, he lamented, "a rare ingredient at a materialistic time in which the job is mainly considered as a mere means by which to make money."[47] Likewise for Maslow, there was no distance between the artist and his work. "A musician must make music, an artist must paint, a poet must write, if he is to be ultimately at peace with himself." Even though Maslow elsewhere insisted that creativity was not essentially about art, it was still to the arts that he looked as the place where person and product became one.

Those who emphasized art may have cast a skeptical eye at the more science- and tech-oriented researchers, but even they were not talking about art for art's sake. In all of their cases, creativity was more fundamental than aesthetic production. The editors of the Syracuse conference's proceedings encouraged the reader to set aside their assumption that creativity was about aesthetic objects. "The creative process that one uses to paint a picture or to compose a poem or a ballad is the same process that integrates the mind," they wrote. Creativity was at its root "a positive self-integrating force." Maslow likewise advocated for art education—or, as he clarified, "Education-Through-Art"—"not so much for turning out artists or art products, as for turning out better people."[48] The artist, in other words, was a model of creativity, and the benefit of the artistic way of being was not art itself but something else. There was something paradoxical about this: It held art apart from the ordinary, the commercial, the technological. Yet it promoted art not for its own sake—that is, say, for the production of aesthetic objects—but rather as a manifestation of something called creativity, a capacity that could be applied to any field, including the technical and commercial. Indeed, Maslow, despite his own artistic bias, was keen to point out that creativity was not restricted to the arts. He recalled a housewife, "uneducated [and] poor," whose resourcefulness and good taste in furnishings revealed her to be so "original, novel, ingenious, unexpected, inventive [that] I just *had* to call her creative." Meanwhile, people went around calling classical cellists "creative," when all they did was reproduce notes written by others. Psychologists should check their assumptions, "that creativeness was the prerogative solely of certain professionals," for "cooking or parenthood or making a home could be creative while poetry need not be."[49] True creativity was not, clearly, about aesthetics per se, though there was something essentially artsy about it.

Gendering Creativity

In addition to demonstrating that creativity could manifest itself outside the arts, Maslow's creative housewife example also indicated his belief that creativity research was baking sexist assumptions into the very notion of creativity. "Practically all the definitions that we have been using of creativeness, and most of the examples of creativeness that we use are essentially male or masculine," he observed, so "we've left out of consideration almost entirely the creativeness of women by the simple semantic technique of defining only male products as creative."[50] Elsewhere, however, Maslow noticed that creativity was in some ways a feminized concept, and that its uptake by psychologists might herald a new openness if not to women, then to the "feminine" in men. "Feminine means practically everything that's creative," Maslow said: "Imagination, fantasy, color, poetry, music, tenderness, languishing, being romantic, in general, are walled off as dangerous to one's picture of one's own masculinity." Too many men, he said, even sometimes the creative ones, displayed "a horrible fear of anything that the person himself would call 'femininity,' 'femaleness,' which we immediately call 'homosexual.'"[51] But Maslow and other humanistic creativity researchers tended to believe that being in touch with one's feminine side was a sign of mental health, and in the case of the creative person, a productive characteristic. MacKinnon, finding that his creative samples scored higher "femininity" ratings, hypothesized that "cross-sex typing" individuals—effeminate males or masculine females—may be more creative than more gender-conforming individuals, as such people were less repressive in general, including potentially of new ideas.[52] (A reviewer found this theory "less than convincing.")[53]

The willingness of researchers to entertain the idea that mild effeminacy, if not necessarily homosexuality, was a good thing suggests how ideas about sexuality and gender were changing in the postwar era. It was a time in which American manhood was the subject of considerable anxiety, but also some flux. The recruitment effort during World War II had revealed the American male to be concerningly anemic (owing obviously to the Great Depression, but often interpreted as a deeper problem of modern society), while the newly massified white-collar suburban existence raised old fears of "overcivilization" and "feminization." All of this helped revive an earlier cult of masculinity (think John Wayne and all those ads for bodybuilding in *Boys Life* magazine), but also a new middle ground, an emerging sense that in the world of corporate work a softer, more emotionally attuned maleness was desirable. On television shows like *Father Knows Best*, America saw men struggling to avoid becoming their own authoritarian fathers without giving up their dominant position in the nuclear family structure. (Women, conversely, struggled to be "efficient" in household matters and firm with unruly kids without being "domineering.") In the world of arts and letters, swaggering figures like Jackson Pollock, Jack Kerouac, and Norman Mailer stood for the possibility that art could be both sensitive and "muscular." For some psychologists, the creative personality was a kind of exemplar of how being in tune with one's feminine side could be potent and productive.

For Maslow in particular, the gender-bendiness he saw in creativity mirrored his larger project of reforming psychology. In Maslow's highly gender-essentialistic worldview "science" was male and "art" female—the former the realm of "hard" and "muscular" reasoning, and the latter the realm of morality, "softness," and emotion. Maslow privately reflected that his desire for the new psychology to reconcile these spheres came from his own struggle to reconcile "the artist in me & the scientist."[54] But Maslow was also profoundly scared of becoming too feminine. His private diaries recall a boyhood tortured by the pressure to be physically strong and manly, a pressure that never really left him, according to the historian Ian A. M. Nicholson. As he became a celebrity of the counterculture and liberation movements of the 1960s, he fretted endlessly about "giving up [his] maleness," being perceived by real scientists as "soft-headed" because of his association with "the tender-minded ones, the existentialists, the Big Sur group, the religion people." Maslow projected this fear onto society. Though he was pleased when his ideas began to take off through the work of feminists like Betty Friedan, whose 1963 *The Feminine Mystique* was deeply Maslovian, Maslow privately felt that feminism was perverting women's subservient and domestic nature (of which he was convinced from his early career studying sexuality in monkeys, and briefly among human women at Bard

College).[55] Psychology, like the creative person, and like Maslow himself, should, he believed, remain essentially male, with just enough of the feminine to remain vital.

Back to Business

If in 1957 Maslow felt uncomfortable dispensing management advice, by the time of his death in 1970 he was becoming known as one of the foremost management thinkers in America. Maslow had long recognized that the need for creativity extended to executives, who must be "capable of coping with the inevitably rapid obsolescence of any new product"; but over the course of the 1960s the corporate workplace had moved to the center of his thinking. He first went to California in the summer of 1962, on a fellowship of sorts at a company called Non-Linear Systems in Del Mar, and began to read the new management theory of Peter Drucker and Douglas McGregor.[56] As he soaked in the baths at Esalen, he was introduced to a cohort of businessmen who took interest in his work. Over that period he compiled a "journal," eventually known as *Maslow on Management*, which would become his most read work and a staple of management thought. Finally, in 1968, the year he also became the president of the American Psychological Association, he moved to California full time, supported by a fellowship at a Menlo Park food service company whose board chairman was drawn to Maslow's ideas about human growth.[57]

In his "journal," Maslow introduced the idea of "Enlightened Management," which he defined as management that assumes employees want to be "prime movers" rather than simply follow orders, and which seeks to align individual goals with corporate goals—which he called "synergy"—to achieve employee self-actualization and profits at the same time. He argued that managers should give each employee a sense of being "autonomous, the determiner of his own fate." This could, Maslow believed, be nothing short of revolutionary, solving the deepest problem of modern capitalism as he saw it: alienation. It would also, in the process, make firms more lithe and innovative. "Since so much of the trouble with mechanical and authoritarian organization, and with old-fashioned treatment of the worker as an interchangeable part, seems to be the inability to shift and change," he wrote, "it seems to me that it would be basically quite important for the philosophy of democratic management to study more carefully the psychodynamics of creativeness."[58]

Maslow believed modern management was as pathologically rational as psychology had become, dominated by "the accountants" and "authoritarian organizational theorists" "who force upon the industrial situation the concern with numbers, with exchangeable money, with tangibles rather than intangibles, with exactness, with predictability, with control, with law and order." Those who sought to impose rules to stave off anarchy and chaos were not simply being smart businessmen, but were "possibly neurotic or irrational or deeply emotional." The "creative personality," on the other hand, was one who could go with the flow of business challenges, with the self-confidence to know they would be able to improvise solutions when the time came. It was this creative personality that employees, managers, and firms themselves should try to emulate.

Ultimately the humanistic insistence on a "holistic" approach to creativity, even though it was offered as a challenge to the frankly instrumentalist work of Guilford and others, fit in with the corporate milieu of Cold War creativity research. By naturalizing the human drive toward the new and different, it brought into alignment the humane good of psychological health, a liberal political philosophy, and the postwar innovation imperative. Postwar champions of creativity smashed productivity and personal growth together, with professional success serving as the proof of, and means to, a fully realized self. Despite sometimes challenging bourgeois values, this humane discourse of creativity was right in line with a long American republican tradition that sought to harmonize the economic and inner self.

At the same time, the humanistic discourse of creativity helped dramatically reconfigure the culture of capitalism. Maslow's move to California was emblematic of the general drift of American industry at the time, from the traditional WASP-y echelons of the Northeast and Midwest to the Sunbelt South and West—a move that, in the case of Silicon Valley, resulted in a new synthesis of countercultural, academic, and industrial trends in which Maslow himself was a guiding light. Maslow's ideas would underwrite a never-ending slate of corporate reforms, from "flat" hierarchies to sensitivity trainings to the work-play fantasylands of the twenty-first-century tech campus.

But what would it mean for the average white-collar worker to "own themselves totally," or to reject the demands of civilization? Beethoven may have been one with his Ninth, but what was the likelihood a rank-and-file engineer or adman, let alone a line worker at an electronics company, would happen to be one with whatever project landed on his desk? The kind of synergy Maslow and Barron had in mind was clearly an ideal in tension with the realities of modern work; but they believed these tensions were not intractable. Autonomy, for them, was not necessarily about the freedom to dictate projects or set wages. It was a feeling, a state of mind, a matter of personality. It was an innate and a portable thing, moving with its possessor whether in an artist's studio or a corporate office. And that made it a very useful thing indeed.

Synectics
at the Shoe

The Shoe was running out of ideas.

They had tried brainstorming, even hypnosis, but they still had not found a reliable method for generating new product ideas.

The United Shoe Machinery Corporation's story was typical of the American corporation in the postwar era. A manufacturer not of shoes but of shoe-making machinery, the USMC (or "the Shoe," as it was affectionately known) had, since its consolidation in 1899, become one of the Boston area's largest employers and, as *Fortune* put it, "the bluest of blue chip corporations." By 1950 the Shoe enjoyed 85 percent market share, essentially a monopoly. But by the early 1960s an ongoing antitrust battle with the US government plus increasing competition from abroad spurred it to aggressively diversify its product line. Management had read about "How to Unleash Your Creative Powers" in *Business Management*, and a "step-by-step approach . . . guaranteed to improve your idea output" in *Machine Design*. They knew that new creative thinking methods were already in use at Westinghouse, General Motors, General Electric, and Alcoa. They kept tabs on this new trend, saving articles, brochures, and business cards in a file folder called "Creativity Training." In 1963 the heads of the Research Department put together a list of forty-one "Objectives for Creative Thinking—Diversification Area," and began to think about hiring someone to come teach them the secrets of creativity.

In May and June of 1962 the pamphlet "Synectics: A New Method for Developing Creative Potential" made the rounds of the Shoe's senior executive and research management. As they learned from the pamphlet and from subsequent correspondence with Synectics founders, Synectics was based on analogical thinking. In a Synectics session a trained facilitator would guide a small group, eliciting analogies, getting further and further afield from the original problem, before guiding them back to (ideally) a workable solution. Like brainstorming, Synectics was based on the theory that "each man and woman is born a creative problem solver."[1] And, contrary to the hysterical handwringing of individualists like William Whyte, creativity need not be stifled by the group but could actually be enhanced by it. Ever since they discovered the inner workings of creativity, Synectics vice president Dean Gitter said, there was no longer a need for "scouting up a bunch of modern-day Edisons." "You probably have enough latent creativity right in your own organization."[2] The Synectics method was, Gitter said, "a kind of empirical recipe for creativity—a rigid ritual designed to . . . produce, almost mechanically, that ethereal state called inspiration."[3]

This paradoxical phraseology was Synectics's hallmark. The frontispiece of founder George Prince's book, *The Practice of Creativity*, read: "CREATIVITY: an arbitrary harmony, an expected astonishment, a habitual revelation, a familiar surprise, a generous selfishness, an unexpected certainty, a formable stubbornness, a vital triviality, a disciplined freedom, an intoxicating steadiness, a repeated initiation, a difficult delight, a predictable gamble, an ephemeral solidity, a unifying difference, a demanding satisfier, a miraculous expectation, an accustomed amazement."[4] This syntheticism was reflected in Synectics's method itself, which was

designed to unleash the irrational, playful, and poetic mind in order to achieve concrete corporate ends. According to the founders, it was the "ability to ignore the logical and suggest the combination of seemingly unconnected and irrelevant thoughts that
leads to new ideas." (The word Synectics itself was a neologism
from Greek roots meaning "the bringing together of disparate elements.") Everything about the company embodied this sensibility.
Their staff included a chemist who sculpted, a psychologist who
played jazz clarinet, and an engineer who painted on the side. It
was even in the way they dressed: Prince was famous for keeping a
collection of colored markers in his otherwise white shirt pocket,
in case an occasion to doodle came up.

If brainstorming had struck the business community as a bit
unconventional, Synectics sessions were downright bizarre. "To
the uninitiated," *Fortune* would later write, "a full-blown Synectics
session is a startling affair—like an LSD party . . . or an experiment in group psychotherapy." The company insisted there was a
method to the madness, but would a company like the Shoe spend
good money to find out?[5]

Using Scientific Management to Undo Scientific Management

Despite the stock Synectics put in irrational thought, its origins
were solidly rational. The company's founders, George Prince and
William J. J. Gordon, met as employees of the consulting giant
Arthur D. Little (ADL), at the time a bastion of scientific management. ADL's eponymous founder began his career in 1909
dispensing technical advice to the chemical industry, becoming
effectively America's first corporate consultant. On the presump-
tion that manufacturing processes and laboratories could be run
by the same basic principles of efficiency, the company was soon
helping companies start and run their own R&D labs; by the 1940s
ADL was engineering engineers all across the country as the largest consulting firm in America.

The postwar consumer economy brought new challenges that
overturned the old assumptions. As ADL's clients began to ag-

gressively pursue product diversification, they needed help with a new sort of problem: How to come up with products that had no market yet? How to leverage existing intellectual property for purposes that nobody has asked for? What, in other words, would be the mother of invention if not necessity? Around 1958 ADL formed an ad hoc Invention Design Group, comprising scientists and engineers from around the company, many of whom were known to have diverse interests. Gordon, for example, had studied mathematics, psychology, biochemistry, and physics, including at Harvard.[6] As "Invention Design" implied, the group was meant to bridge the worlds of engineering and design, a recognition that, to sell consumer products, non-utilitarian and aesthetic considerations could be just as important as the technical and pragmatic ones. Accordingly, they brought on Prince, a former creative director at an advertising firm and an expert in motivational research—the psychology of consumer desire.

Gordon and Prince came to believe, as they would soon tell clients, that the traditional R&D approach, the one so typified by ADL, was a "brute force" approach, labor intensive, costly, and inefficient.[7] Its capacity to produce results was "sporadic at best," just as "ten monkeys left long enough with ten typewriters will produce Shakespeare."[8] The bureaucratic approach to innovation, they said, was, ironically, based on a "Romantic view" that creativity was mysterious, capricious, and inborn, and so there was "no way of generating creativity in the individual."[9] Prince and Gordon pointed to the exciting new research being done on creativity as an indication that it was now possible to understand the creative process and, they hoped, actively improve it. To do this they reached for the oldest method in scientific management— empirical observation.

The early twentieth-century founders of the "scientific management" movement, Fredrick Winslow Taylor and Frank and Lillian Gilbreth, were engineers who used stopwatches, diagrams, and eventually film to make "motion studies" of people at work. They started in factories and later moved on to white-collar and even domestic workplaces, carefully breaking down each job into its constituent parts to eliminate inefficiencies and discover the "one best way" to do any given task. Prince and Gordon set up video and audio recorders around their meeting rooms and recorded thousands of hours of invention and problem-solving sessions "in vivo," as they put it, reviewing the tapes in scientific detail to isolate the productive elements and identify inefficiencies.[10] Through this research Prince and Gordon soon developed what they believed was a method—perhaps the one best way—to generate "dependable creativity."

They quickly made a splash in the creative thinking scene. They presented in 1958 at one of John E. Arnold's summer workshops at MIT along with brainstorming evangelist Charles Clark, and "the Gordon method" got mentions in several creative thinking books as a compelling alternative to brainstorming. In 1961 Gordon wrote up their findings as *Synectics: The Development of Creative Capacity*, and he and Prince and a few other members of the Invention Design group split from ADL to form Synectics, Inc., America's first boutique consultancy specializing in "creativity and innovation." From their downtown Cambridge office, they ran sessions for clients and soon began offering week-long trainings to send Synectics out into the world. The majority of their early clients came to them with specifically product-related problems, but the company gradually broadened its scope beyond product development, tackling everything from marketing plans to internal reorganizations. Their product was not just new products, it was "creativity" itself.

As the Shoe's internal discussions reveal, convincing budget-minded executives to spend good money on something as hazy as creativity consulting was a tough pitch. One executive confided that he found the whole idea "pretty nebulous" and suggested the significant cost—about $100,000 over three years—could be better spent on more practical trainings for traditional engineering competencies such as subject matter expertise and cost-cutting strategies.[11] Another supervisor, however, did some back-of-the-envelope math showing it could be a sound investment: "Five individuals each passing on what they learn to another five would amount to 30 individuals affected in the first year. Assuming

Figure 4.1 Synectics session with recording equipment in background. Tapes were studied to refine the method for dependable creativity. Used with permission of Synecticsworld®, Inc.

that are all [*sic*] worth their salaries, and improved an average of 5% each, the investment might return 10% the first year, and in increasing amount thereafter." Even if that didn't work out, he added, "one really good idea developing from the effort could more than recover the whole amount."[12] W. Clark Goodchild, Senior Engineer in the New Products Group, initially decided to pass on Synectics, telling the CEO that though he was still interested in pursuing "the general subject of creativity," he was "personally . . . not convinced of the value of this training."[13] Within a few years, however, Synectics had had a few high-profile features in *Fortune* and the *Wall Street Journal*, and its client list included Alcoa, GE, GM, Kimberly-Clark, Procter & Gamble, and Black & Decker. (Prince and Gordon had parted ways unamicably in 1964, with Gordon founding Synectics Education Systems, to apply the method to education.) Prince was persistent with the pitch letters, and his overtures eventually succeeded. In 1965 Goodchild decided Synectics was the best method for "stimulating and conditioning minds," and the Shoe decided to take a chance.

In June 1966 five of the Shoe's research managers traveled to Cambridge for a three-day workshop, and that November Goodchild returned for a week-long course to train up as the in-house Synectics facilitator to assist with problems throughout the corporation, not just in R&D. Also in attendance in June were the heads of research and new product development for Lever Brothers, General Foods, Western Electric, Esso, and Cincinnati Milling Machine. Over the course of an intense week the executives were pushed well beyond their comfort zones, and indoctrinated into the Synectics theory, jargon, and method. On one day the group attacked a sample problem: how to get a hammer head to stay on the handle. That was, in Synectics jargon, the PAG, the Problem as Given. The facilitator then asked them to articulate the PAU, the Problem as Understood, what they assumed to be the underlying challenge—in this case "bonding wood to steel." From there the group went on a number of "Excursions," during which the facilitator prompted them for Direct Analogies (DA), Symbolic Analogies (SA), and Personal Analogies (PA). What a long, strange trip it must have been, passing by fish spines and stomachs, "flexible tension" and "gutless hero," before the facilitator finally asked for a Force Fit (FF), where a solution would be squeezed out of the collection of seemingly irrelevant images, impressions, and phrases generated along the way. (There is no record of the group's eventual solution.)

The transcript of a session in which engineers from the Steel Products Engineering division of Kelsey-Hayes tackled the seemingly unexciting problem of "gear rounding" was even more bizarre:

> JACK: O.K., the date is March 4, 1965, the PAG is "How to make a finished gear round," the PAU is "How to grind gear without rounding." . . . O.K., start off with rounding as the key word. We need a direct analogy first.
>
> ALEX: How about pregnancy? Swelling abdomen—rounding?
>
> BILL: When I think of rounding, I think about the universe.
>
> HORACE: Marble.

JACK: Let's take a symbolic analogy of marble.

JIM: Well, let's see, I'm a very still lake—and I get tremendous enjoyment from reflecting all the objects that come over me—and I'm terribly upset when the wind blows and the ripples form so that the reflections can't be transmitted.

HORACE: Ripples destroy the reflections.

JIM: Yeah, ripples ruin me.

BILL: On that same lake, let me get in here. I have enjoyment from the knowledge . . . that the waters from me give birth to little streams but I'm especially proud when I realize that some of the waters which come from me leave me in evaporation . . . I see this beautiful colored rainbow. I realize this is a child of mine . . .[14]

Indeed, compared to the image of brainstorming, with its "chairmen" and panels of button-down military types, Synectics, as *Fortune* noted, seemed to be channeling something of the emerging counterculture. Previewing the laid-back office design later preferred by postindustrial creative industries, the Synectics office resembled "the loft studio of a Greenwich Village artist," with exposed brick, canvas lounge chairs, and a quirky spiral staircase that would become the company logo. But this was not just for fun. *Fortune* called Synectics "invention by the madness method," but execs insisted there *was* a method to the madness. The solicitation of irrelevant metaphors was meant to access the "pre-conscious," which, "in spite of its apparent non-rational and irresponsible behavior," was in fact "purposive," feeding the conscious mind from the "vast storehouse" of forgotten "impressions, information, and feelings" and pointing it in promising, ultimately marketable directions.

The comparison to group therapy was also quite apt. Prince and Gordon were heavily influenced by Carl Rogers, who in the late 1950s had begun experiments in group "encounter therapy," and they were also in the mix with new postwar management phenomena such as "T-groups" and "sensitivity training," which took a therapeutic approach to group dynamics. (In the 1970s Synectics executives dabbled in the new-age self-development movement EST—Erhard Seminars Training.) Much of what Gordon and Prince had learned from their recording sessions, in fact, bore not so much on the creative process *per se* as on how interpersonal dynamics—peoples' choice of language, posture, reactions, and so forth—affected a session.

Just as the Buffalo school of creative thinking had its synergy with academic psychology, so Prince and Gordon contributed presentations and articles to the research literature and were in turn influenced by the IPAR research on the creative personality and Maslow and Rogers's work on creativity and self-actualization, which they tried to reverse engineer for a corporate setting: if passion for work was the hallmark of the creative person, then by stimulating passion in the workplace they might be able to ignite creative energy no matter the particular problem or product. Though first and foremost a method for reliable invention, Synectics was simultaneously and necessarily a kind of therapy, a healing of the alienated corporate self, attending to the "whole person" to develop more products faster.

The Synectics method was indeed a kind of individual therapy: to heal a split in the American professional self, to reintegrate the "poetic," "artistic," "emotional," "naïve," "childlike," "playful," "irrelevant," and "irrational" aspects from which it had become alienated. Engineers, they said, were taught to be "ultra-rational in approach, conservative in drawing conclusions, and respectful of established bodies of knowledge." Industry, with its cult of "expertise," tended to ignore the "personal, the non-rational, the seemingly irrelevant, emotional aspects" that "make up the whole man (or woman)," and which were "*essential* to the generation of new ideas." To the postwar eye, the spectacle of "gruff and down-to-earth" mechanical engineers waxing poetic about placid mountain lakes and rainbows was as heartening as it was hilarious: it suggested someone had figured out how to make the Organization Man into a full human again.[15]

Art implicitly served as both a contrast and a model for Synectics's conception of invention. "The traditional . . . view of the nature of creativity places heavy emphasis on the fine arts and poetry as the 'only' creative enterprise," wrote Gordon.[16] To the contrary, the "phenomena of invention in the arts and in science are analogous and characterized by the same fundamental psychic process." As Prince clarified in a television interview, however, "This is not the kind of creativity that will land your work in museums—this is another animal."[17]

To be sure, Synectics was not designed to help artists make art. But why bring up art at all, if you really mean invention? Why choose the word creativity, which—as opposed to, say, inventiveness, originality, or ingenuity—constantly forces the clarification that one does *not* mean art or poetry? Art, as always in discussions of creativity, was a spectral presence in the Synectics cosmology— always referred to, never really discussed. To invoke art was to signal that Synectics's brand of creativity shared *something* with art— not in materials, technique, knowledge, or conditions of work, but in a supposed way of thinking, even a way of being in the world. Per Synectics theory, this meant thinking poetically. But it also meant being one with the work.

According to Synectics, all work could be fun and filled with passion. The modern "attitude" toward work held that it was inevitably boring and hard, and that it should be left at the office. Employees tended to be "socially motivated," rather than stimulated by the work itself. But Prince explained to the Shoe's research director, Homer Overly, that such attitudes were anathema to creativity, pointing to the studies that showed highly creative people were dedicated beyond "9 to 5, business as usual."[18] Synectics's goal was to forge a deeper connection to work by encouraging "hedonic" responses, or "what felt right," and by using the "whole person." Of course, most companies could not simply tell their employees to work on whatever made them want to stay late. But for Prince and Gordon the source of passion was not to be found in a product, but rather in the process. One happy CEO reported that after a Synectics session, "every member of the group thinks the product is his idea. Enthusiasm never seems to flag."[19] Synectics could apparently generate a *feeling* of ownership, alleviating corporate alienation in a psychological sense, if not necessarily an economic one.

In its attempt to align individual and corporate desires, Synectics was in tune with emerging management trends. The theorist Chris Argyris, in books like *Personality and Organization: The Conflict between System and the Individual* and *Integrating the Individual and the Organization*, and Douglas McGregor, in his *The Human Side of Enterprise*, sought to increase employees' productivity by harnessing their individuality.[20] Translating the new humanistic psychology of Abraham Maslow directly into management terms, Argyris and McGregor sought to replace the goal of "adjustment" to the corporate system with the "integration" of the deepest self with management goals.[21] According to McGregor the "traditional view," meaning Taylorism, or "Theory X" as he called it, assumed that workers fundamentally did not want to work and therefore had to be "coerced" through top-down management and subordination to the group. The new, more enlightened view, "Theory Y," understood the importance of bringing the goals of the corporation into line with "the satisfaction of higher-level ego and self-actualization needs."[22] For Synectics, creativity was the one goal the individual and the corporation naturally shared. "The human individual is always in search of his uniqueness," Gordon wrote, and the corporation was in search of unique products.[23] At least some saw Synectics as the next major development in management theory: in the corner of a page of notes he took in a meeting with Gordon and Prince, USMC director of research W. L. Abel scrawled, possibly transcribing a pithy bit of the sales pitch, "Theory X, Y, Now S."[24]

Synectics presumed that something about the process of creating, rather than the particular form or purpose of the thing being created, motivated people. It didn't matter whether they were tasked with designing a new hair dryer or a wheelchair or a marketing plan (all Synectics projects, at some point). All of them could, indeed should, engage the "whole person," thereby erasing the distinctions between product and producer, for it was only a non-alienated worker who could be truly creative.

Marketing and Innovation in the Same Room

In addition to boosting morale, Synectics may have worked (to the extent that it did) for a more pedestrian reason: the appropriate coordination of personnel. It is possible that the R&D system was not as dysfunctional as Gordon and Prince made it out to be, but rather that it was not up to the new tasks the consumer economy demanded. While much R&D was still focused on highly technical military or industrial problems, an increasing amount was oriented toward the consumer marketplace, and this, particularly in the context of the diversification drive, asked engineers to ramp up the invention of products nobody had asked for. In the context of product development, a "problem" was no longer the well-defined unit of work. Now it might be finding a new use for aluminum, to take an example Alcoa workshopped with Synectics, which had to "work" in the marketplace as well in the world of things, and which was only a "problem" insofar as Alcoa's profits were concerned. The constant slippage between "problem-solving" and "invention" in Synectics literature and in the larger discourse of creative engineering may reflect the fact that for many engineers the lines between the two were dissolving.

In a letter to the Shoe's research department, Prince wrote that most companies had problems with communication among the people responsible for conception, development, and marketing. The Synectics approach was to bring marketing in from the beginning.[25] One CEO who used Synectics concurred that product development "requires us to do things differently all the way up the line . . . now we have R&D people thinking up advertising slogans and marketing men coming into the labs."[26] This heralded a major trend, as many research-intensive corporations made similar organizational adjustments as part of their diversification efforts, including promoting marketing to key positions in strategy and planning and forming in-house design teams. The mixing of innovation and marketing—which Peter Drucker called the two true concerns of modern management—was in fact a common rationale behind the larger creative problem-solving movement. The creative engineering pioneer John E. Arnold—who, incidentally, had worked as an engineer at the Shoe in the early 1940s—wrote, "creativity provides a common meeting ground for diverse specialties, it supplies a common experience on which to base a language for communicating our ideas to one another. . . . Product Design provides an almost perfect vehicle for experimenting in the effectiveness of bringing people of diverse backgrounds together in a creative effort. The scientist, engineer, artist, philosopher, psychologist, sociologist, anthropologist, salesman, and advertising man must contribute their know-how to insure a successful product development."[27] In other words, Synectics sessions may have offered an approach to personnel coordination that befitted the new product development regime as the soft arts of persuasion seeped into the hard world of industrial science, just as Prince and Osborn had traveled from Madison Avenue to the R&D labs of industrial giants.

The prospect of retooling a purely technical organization for the consumer economy may be one reason the engineers at the Shoe found Synectics so attractive. Before the war they knew what they had to do: make their shoe manufacturing machinery faster and more reliable. After the war, it felt like incremental improvements were not good enough, and they needed to start thinking more entrepreneurially, finding opportunities in consumer and leisure sectors. In 1968, for example, Goodchild summoned ten members of the research staff to develop an improved ski-lift ticket system, inspired by two executives' recent trip to Maine. It was felt that with their expertise in fasteners the Shoe might be able to devise a better method for preventing skiers from sharing tickets. Some of the ideas that came out of the meeting included issuing skiers low-power radio transmitters or short-range supersonic frequency devices like TV remotes, attaching polaroid photos to tickets, applying beta ray–charged cement with a 24-hour half-life to ski tips, and stamping garments with a disappearing dye.

It is not clear whether any of these lift ticket ideas, or any of the ideas the Shoe generated in its in-house Synectics sessions, ever came to fruition. Whatever role Synectics played, the Shoe's product diversification strategy clearly worked in its own way. By 1972 the shoe industry, formerly its only market, now accounted for only one-third of its revenue. Now the Shoe manufactured hundreds of products in a wide range of industrial and consumer markets, including fasteners, adhesives, and other non-shoe-related machinery, designed, improved, produced, and sold by 26,000 employees in fifty-eight plants around the world.[28] Much of this was accomplished by the acquisition of over fifty smaller companies, but some of it was from in-house invention, and may have come out of Synectics sessions.

:::

Because much of its product development work was done for hire, Synectics, Inc. could not publicly take credit for the results, and because much of its work was to train others in its methods, it is difficult to identify many specific products that clearly resulted. Nevertheless, Synectics has taken credit for, at the very least, Pringles potato chips (attributed to a session Procter & Gamble held early on at Arthur D. Little wherein the concept of a tennis ball carton was applied to the problem of chips being crushed during transport) and the Swiffer mop. Both successfully applied existing proprietary technologies to something that had no previous demand. Executives, trainees, and session participants over the years have been effusive in their praise, and several creativity psychologists deemed it more sophisticated than the more popular brainstorming. IPAR's Donald McKinnon called it "the best of the methods" for creative thinking.[29] What's most significant is not how well Synectics "worked," but that in a world of straitlaced engineers, a technique like Synectics, promising the perfect salty-sweet combo of empiricism and romanticism, efficiency and whimsy, and group cohesion and individual liberation sounded like a rational use of R&D funds. As Dow Chemical's "Creativity Review" wrote approvingly, "with emphasis on the whole person (heart, hands and mind), Synectics has proved effective, and appears to give those who have used it more pleasure in their efforts."[30]

Synectics was, in some sense, another attempt to rescue the individual from mass society. "Fifty years ago," George Prince wrote in 1966, "the social scene looked much like the Kansas Prairie. Wherever you looked the individual was the highest, the tallest thing on it. If you look at this modern society of ours . . . it is a society of large organizations." Prince saw a direct connection between this new mass society and the youth rebellions popping up all around the country. "The only difference between students and the rest of us," he said, "is that they are young enough to rebel; we are just as lost in this world as they are, and just as hard put to make sense out of it." Synectics attempted to foster a sense of rebellion, and of new meaning, within a corporate context. As with brainstorming there was perhaps something carnivalesque in all of this; as fun as the process may be, it must always come back to someone else's bottom line, the session must always end. Its attempt to reunite the artistic and scientific, the poetic and the practical, was a therapy meant to make work less alienating; it also made practical sense in a consumer economy in which the boundary between design and engineering was increasingly blurred, and in which necessity was no longer an adequate mother of invention. In all of these ways Synectics was a harbinger of how business would reinvent itself in the coming decades. It also illustrates how powerfully the concept of creativity—a disciplined freedom, an intoxicating steadiness, a predictable gamble, an ephemeral solidity, as Prince put it—attempted to contain the paradoxes at the heart of postwar America.

The Creative Child

5

On November 4, 1957, the USSR successfully launched the first manmade satellite into orbit. The prospect of American technological inferiority, once mostly restricted to conversations among research directors and policy makers, suddenly became a matter of intense public scrutiny, with the brunt of the anxiety directed toward the nation's schools. A coalition of Cold War hawks, traditionalist conservatives, and opponents of the 1954 Supreme Court decision *Brown v. Board of Education* cast Sputnik as, according to the historian Diane Ravitch, "a symbol of the consequences of indifference to high standards," blaming the progressive education movement and the push for racial educational equality. Almost immediately there were urgent calls for more training in math and science, earlier specialization, stricter discipline, and a greater focus on the best and the brightest.[1]

The very next year a sizable government check landed on the desk of one Ellis Paul Torrance, a new professor of educational psychology at the University of Minnesota, for a multi-year study on "gifted" children. The son of a Georgia farmer who had worked his way from high school career counselor to Air Force psychologist studying jet aces, Torrance was convinced of the importance of talented individuals. But he also had a soft spot for the misfit—with whom he identified—and was no fan of discipline or specialization. These two interests came together for Torrance under the banner of creativity. Inspired by exciting new developments in creativity research, Torrance concluded the reigning conception of giftedness—and the tests that both reflected and reinforced it—favored unimaginative conformists, little organization men and women in the making. As Torrance told *Look* magazine in a 1961 feature on "the creative child," IQ tests rewarded only "children who accept yes-no, right-wrong question situations . . . the convergent-thinking, nonexperimental, memory-dependent types, instead of the truly productive, original minds." "If we were to identify children as gifted on the basis of intelligence or scholastic aptitude tests," he continued, "we would eliminate from consideration approximately 70 percent of the most creative."[2] That's why, almost immediately upon receiving his grant for the study of gifted children, Torrance decided to focus on the specific problem of how to identify and foster "creative talent." Childhood education had been a stated concern of creativity research since its inception, but almost a decade on, the field was still largely focused on high-level scientific personnel or accomplished professionals. Torrance would make it possible to study childhood creativity. Within only a few years he had developed the eponymous Torrance Tests for Creative Thinking, the first widely available pencil-and-paper test for creative ability and the gold standard on which much subsequent creativity research would proceed.[3]

In that moment of national crisis that followed the Sputnik launch, Torrance attempted to transcend the warring factions in American education, funneling into his concept of creativity an antipathy toward conformity and a progressive sensibility with practical Cold War prerogatives. For Torrance, as for other researchers, creativity occupied an ambiguous position between genius and something every child possessed, between a practical skill and a personal good in itself. Though these tensions would lead to significant challenges and even disappointments, Torrance nonetheless became one of the leading researchers in the field of creativity. As a prolific researcher and a lifelong advocate for creativity he helped redefine Americans' assumptions about the ideal child and the purpose of education, and was an inspiration to teachers and parents anxious about their children's future in an uncertain age.[4]

Getting to Creativity

Later called the "Father of Creativity," Torrance was actually a relative newcomer to creativity research in 1958, though he later said he felt like he had been studying it his whole career.[5] Prior to joining the Minnesota faculty Torrance had been a lead psychologist in the Air Force's Survival Training Program, established in the wake of reports that American Korean War POWs had been "brainwashed" to communism. (This was not, then, the first time Torrance had benefited from a national panic about America's mental integrity.) During that period Torrance produced a manual on "The Psychology of Interrogation," describing techniques for resisting torture, and a widely read study on jet aces.[6] These experiences attuned Torrance to the question of why some individuals thrived under adverse and unfamiliar conditions, which would become key to his definition of creativity. But Torrance also had experience with those who were not thriving. During the war his job had been to counsel dishonorably discharged veterans, and before that he had served as a career counselor at a school for troubled boys. Torrance himself identified as a misfit, having grown up bookish and physically unfit in a family of rural Georgia farmers, and he came to believe that some of those troubled boys shared many attributes with the jet aces—strong will, a capacity to think on their feet, a disregard for rules and preconceived notions. Those whom society considered failures, Torrance believed, were often gifted people stifled by arbitrary rules which their natures could not abide.

To Torrance's thinking, what educators traditionally considered good pupils were actually little conformists in the making, "those who can memorize considerable amounts of culturally approved data, and those who might be motivated by a desire to ingratiate themselves with authorities." These traditionally gifted students, *Look* bemoaned on behalf of Torrance, were treated with "reverent attention" by teachers and administrators and given all the opportunities for advancement, while the highly creative student, whose "sometimes bohemian ways" befuddled teachers, was more likely to be "[slapped] down" and humiliated in front of his peers. Calvin Taylor, also interviewed for the *Look* article, added that dropout rates among creative students were likely greater than the national average, while Torrance warned in distinctly psychoanalytic terms that the repression of the creative student often resulted in "destructive or incapacitating hostility" toward those in power.[7] Not only was this cruel to the student; it also represented an incalculable amount of wasted human potential. "Creative talent is *needlessly* killed by the coercive pressures of the peer group and of the institution of education itself," he wrote.[8]

Torrance was not alone in seeing the whole Western system of education as authoritarian. At a conference organized by Torrance, George Stoddard, the dean of New York University's School of Education, said that "inside the school, many teachers and textbooks (refrigerated versions of teachers stamped and sealed) pay homage to the same god of conformity," and that "three hundred years of standard instruction" had "produced populations whose chief reliance is on the conditioned response, the repetitive act, the voice of authority."[9] Advocates of progressive education had long rejected rote learning, seeing it as not only authoritarian but also ineffective. Now they feared the new focus on math and science might exacerbate the problem. At the same time, even some tech-focused reformers were now wary of the problem of static thinking, and so it was that the progressive animosity toward strict discipline resonated with the decidedly non-progressive emphasis on workforce development and gifted children. All agreed the imperative for educators was to salvage creativity from the discipline of modern schooling.

The task Torrance set for himself, then, was to redefine "gifted-ness" in terms of creative potential in a way educational bureau-cracies could understand: a test. Many researchers had doubted it would be possible to study creativity in children. It was hard enough to figure out how to assess creativity in college graduates or rank-and-file engineers, who hadn't yet had the opportunity to pro-duce the kind of unambiguously creative works characteristic of ac-knowledged geniuses. Schoolchildren, then, would be even harder to assess. For Torrance, though, this was not a problem, because for him creativity wasn't about product, but about process. While oth-ers defined creativity as the ability to produce something new and useful, his rather idiosyncratic definition read, "a process of becom-ing sensitive to problems, deficiencies, gaps in knowledge, miss-ing elements, disharmonies, and so on; identifying the difficulty; searching for solutions, making guesses, or formulating hypotheses about the deficiencies; testing and retesting these hypotheses and possibly modifying and retesting them; and finally communicating the results."[10] In his earlier work Torrance never described his topic as "creativity," nor would most psychologists at the time, seeing as it didn't really have to do with producing anything. But Torrance could look back and imagine, as he would later say in an oral history collected by the Creative Education Foundation, "I really think we were studying creativity then," because for him, as for Maslow in chapter 3, creativity was simply a way of thinking—it was never re-ally about the production of anything in particular.[11]

His procedural definition, elaborated from previous theories such as Wallas's about the stages of creative thought, made it pos-sible for Torrance to connect creativity research to educational psychology, because unlike the studies of top scientists, writers, or architects, it did not require subjects to have produced an ex-emplary accomplishment, but only to have "communicated" an idea, which could be as simple as an utterance or as complex as a finished work of art. In truth, Torrance's definition was not really a definition at all, but rather a theory of how creativity worked. To actually study this process or verify it, as he needed to do to ful-fill his research contract, it would still be necessary to have some kind of operational definition, some kind of output to prove who was being creative and who was not. Luckily for Torrance, by 1958 a few researchers had already developed some "tests of creative ability" that seemed to show promise. Torrance's job would be to adapt these to study children.

Torrance later quipped that he became a psychometrician by accident. With no significant experience in designing tests, he set out to study creativity in children only to realize that a test for creativity did not exist yet.[12] So he built one, largely by adapting for children the Guilford Battery of divergent thinking tasks. The Minnesota Tests of Creative Thinking, as they were initially called before Torrance decamped to the University of Georgia, after which they would be known as simply the Torrance Tests of Creative Thinking (TTCT), consisted of verbal and figural parts, and came with standard forms and detailed instructions for administrators with scripts for explaining each task and detailed rubrics for scoring. The verbal section consisted of tasks such as coming up with book titles based only on a blurb, while the figural section asked test-takers to complete a series of drawings based on incomplete figures. For example, one might open the test book to see a grid of twelve identical squares, each one containing a pair of vertical lines an inch apart, repeated for several pages. Using a pencil, one might turn the first pair into a pair of skis, the second into a skyscraper, the third into a long nose on a funny face, the fourth into a cop chasing a robber, and on and on for ten minutes.

The TTCT was scored on a combination of four factors, simplified (for ease of assessment at large numbers) from Guilford's sixteen-factor model of creativity: Fluency, for the raw number of different responses produced in the allotted time; Originality, for how uncommon each answer was compared to those of one's peers; Flexibility, for variation (did a student keep making the two parallel lines into stick figures, or did she also depict household objects, buildings, animals, action scenes, big things, little things, things from different perspectives, etc.?); and finally Elaboration, for the level of detail. The instructions for administrators provided guidance to eliminate as much subjectivity as possible—for the

Figure 5.1 E. Paul Torrance administering a creativity test in which children were asked to come up with ways to improve a toy, a variation on the red brick test. E. Paul Torrance Collection, Hargrett Rare Book & Manuscript Library, University of Georgia.

parallel lines section, turning the lines into the sides of a ladder or the walls of a house was not considered very creative, but adding a black cat sitting on the ladder got two points for elaboration (one for the cat, one for the color black), while a stick figure climbing to save another stick figure waving their hand from a burning brick house got even more. Since this was not meant to be a test of artistic or verbal ability, drawings and stories were not judged on artistic skill or composition, nor on totally subjective aspects like beauty, narrative depth, or poignancy, but rather on those qualities believed to reflect a generally creative mind: speed of ideation, cleverness, and imagination.

To test his tests—to prove they had predictive validity—Torrance set out on a massive longitudinal study of 215 Minnesota elementary school children, repeating testing at 7-, 12-, 22-, and 40-year intervals, to see if those who had done well as third graders went on to creative success. He would have to wait and see how his subjects did.

Torrance didn't really need a scientific study to know that schools killed creativity, but he found some support for that conviction in early testing results that revealed a "fourth-grade slump," when scores on tests of creative ability dipped suddenly. Educational psychologists already knew that children began to exhibit increased awareness of social conventions around fourth grade, resulting in more attention to rules and a decline in imaginative free play. This was generally considered a natural part of development toward adulthood, but Torrance hypothesized that it had a dark side. He admitted that socialization had its place, but thought excessive inhibition might lead to "future school dropouts, delinquency, and mental breakdown," three things that terrified observers of American youth.

To find out if creativity could be maintained over the fourth-grade gap, Torrance and his fellow researchers trained one set of students using such exercises adapted from the TTCT. In one activity based on the Unusual Uses task, students were given an object—a toy in place of the traditional brick—and challenged to come up with as many different uses for it as possible. In another, based on the TTCT's Product Improvement section (which Torrance intended to mimic the kind of on-the-job creativity students might be faced with in the white-collar world), students came up with improvements to a toy horse. Perhaps unsurprisingly, students who trained in these divergent thinking tasks showed more improvement on subsequent tests than those who did not. From these findings Torrance drew his optimistic thesis: that the loss of imaginative capacity was not simply "an inevitable and healthy part of human development," and that it was possible to achieve "development" without sacrificing "creativity," by deliberate means.

From Identification to Development

Armed with this research, Torrance became a vocal advocate for the promotion of creativity in American schools. He advocated art in the classroom, replacing right-or-wrong assignments with open-ended ones wherever possible, and concerted use of creative thinking exercises. He developed and distributed a series of classroom exercises, including a box set of record albums narrating stories of famous explorers and discoverers to illustrate the importance of taking risks and going against the crowd. These familiar figures in the story of Western progress were by no means all "creative" in the conventional sense, and no effort was made to argue that they would have been any good on the TTCT, but that was the implication anyway. Following each story, teachers would lead students through a series of divergent thinking exercises.

Throughout the 1950s and 1960s there had been a constant tension between those scientists who considered the main task of creativity research to be the recognition of creative ability, which they assumed to be largely innate and static, and those whose goal was to stimulate or develop creative ability. The latter were, according to one psychologist, nothing more than "enthusiasts who tend to rely on anecdotal evidence, or whose experiments are rather poorly controlled."[13] People such as Alex Osborn and Sidney Parnes, who taught techniques like "brainstorming" to ignite creativity in otherwise uncreative people, had come from the world of industry and gradually made inroads into the academic discourse, finding in Torrance one of their greatest allies. Torrance seemed to feel no tension between the projects of identification and development; working with children, whose creativity was innate and at risk of dying, and testing and developing creativity were naturally part of the same process. In 1959, the organizers of the third Utah Conference invited Torrance to head up a new subcommittee on the development of creative potential, marked by a renaming of the conference to the "Conference on the Identification *and Development* of Scientific Talent" (emphasis added). Calvin Taylor, whose original interest was in high-level scientific personnel, wrote in 1964 that despite the question of teachability still being very much unresolved, psychologists were now at least "convinced that all people are, to some degree, potentially creative . . . (across) all ages, all cultures, and all fields of human endeavor."[14] The meaning of creativity had shifted, or expanded, from an innate ability to something more like a skill.

Threading the Needle of the American Education Debates

Torrance's work was particularly salient at that moment in educational politics. As the preeminent champion of creativity in
American schools, Torrance hit the sweet spot between education hawks and liberal reformers, between progressive education's spirit of open-ended exploration and egalitarianism and
post-Sputnik Cold War needs. In this he shared a sensibility with
prominent policy intellectuals associated with what the historian
Arthur Schlesinger called at the time the "vital center" of American politics, who sought to balance individual freedom with social
goods and equality with excellence.[15] "Democracy is not . . . an
invitation to share a common mediocrity but . . . a system that allows each to express and live up to the special excellence that is in
him," John Gardner (the same one responsible for supporting the
IPAR creativity studies) wrote in a widely circulated 1958 Rockefeller Brothers Foundation report.[16] Defending the liberal arts and
some tenets of progressive education against hawkish advocates
of "rigid specialization," Gardner insisted that "a free society cannot commandeer talent," as the USSR was reportedly doing, but
must let individuals choose their own paths. "And yet," he wrote,
reflecting the managerial perspective, "at a time when we face
problems of desperate gravity and complexity an undiscovered
talent, a wasted skill, a misapplied ability is a threat to the capacity
of a free people to survive." The answer to this tension between
individualistic and social imperatives was to see American schools
not as egalitarian, but as pluralistic: minority education should be
improved and early tracking of students avoided, while at the same
time more attention should also be given to the naturally gifted for
the sake of national strategic interests. The common curriculum
was defended not only in the name of shared cultural heritage and
democratic citizenship but also as a strategy for workforce development in the face of rapid change. "We don't even know what
skills may be needed in the years ahead," Gardner wrote, in an argument that would echo down the decades. "That is why we must

train our young people in the fundamental fields of knowledge, and equip them to understand and cope with change."[17]

These liberal education reformers were attempting to reconcile what the historian of education David Labaree has called the three competing ideals in American education, each corresponding to a different end goal and a different model of the student subject. The goal of "democratic equality" sees students as citizens, with the role of schools being to make standard education widely available and thereby produce a well-informed populace. The goal of "social efficiency," by contrast, imagines students as future workers, with schools primarily preparing students "to carry out useful economic roles with competence." Both of these see education from the standpoint of the social good. The third ideal, "social mobility," imagines the student as a consumer of educational goods, and the school as providing them a competitive leg up in the labor market.[18] The liberal agenda for postwar school reform fused these into a pluralistic ideal wherein individualism and national greatness would reinforce one another: "A free society nurtures the individual not alone for the contribution he may make to the social effort," the Rockefeller Brothers report read, "but also and primarily for the sake of the contribution he may make to his own realization and development."[19]

Though he would often justify the importance of his research on national strategic grounds, Torrance also wrote with a warm and genuine concern for students' ability to cope emotionally and economically with modern life. Creative education was for him, above all, "a more humane kind of education."[20] His point, in effect, was that America didn't have to choose between imposing scientific specialization on its students and losing out to the Soviets; creativity could both foster individual expression and serve American strategic interests by cultivating not any particular knowledge or expertise but rather the general ability to think creatively:

> The Space Age is taking us places where old and comfortable ideas no longer apply. Much will be required of today's school

children. Threats to man's survival challenge us to consider what man may become, at his best, and to search for new ways of helping children realize this creative potential. . . . Today we proclaim that our schools exist for learning. We say that we should get tougher and make pupils learn more. (But) schools of the future will be designed not only for learning but for thinking. More and more insistently, today's schools and colleges are being asked to produce men and women who can think, who can make new scientific discoveries, who can find more adequate solutions to impelling world problems, who cannot be brainwashed, men and women who can adapt to change and maintain sanity in this age of acceleration.[21]

The overarching ability that enabled all of those others—thinking, discovering, inventing, problem-solving, imperviousness to brainwashing, and adaptability to change—was creativity. Torrance's assertion that schools existed not to inculcate knowledge but rather to teach students to "think" appealed to both an older progressive theory of education and a newly dawning anxiety about the unpredictability of the future. Torrance saw creativity itself as the force that would transcend the entrenched education policy battles. American schools would be saved "by neither critics nor defenders, but by prophets and frontier thinkers."[22] Torrance believed he was on the leading edge of a revolution in education, which would in turn revolutionize civilization as a whole: "Because of the continued development of man's thinking, his creative thinking," he wrote, "I suspect that the man of the 1960's will appear to be as naïve and brutish to future generations as the cave man seems to us."[23]

A Hero to Parents and Teachers

For his insistence on the teachability of creativity Torrance was criticized—unfairly, he insisted—from both sides of the education debate.[24] Progressive educators told him his divergent thinking exercises were nothing more than "operant conditioning," more like programming a machine than liberating a mind, and therefore a hollow simulacrum of true creativity. Conservatives, meanwhile, lumped his methods in with progressive education, criticizing them for being permissive and self-indulgent, and lacking specific content knowledge. But many parents, teachers, and counselors found Torrance's message incredibly refreshing. According to his biographer, Torrance received over two thousand letters after the *Look* article alone, including from over three hundred teachers requesting copies of the TTCT, leading to one hundred thousand new students taking the test.[25]

Teachers were excited to finally have a tool for catering to their more challenging but bright pupils. Marilyn Stassen, a high school teacher from Honolulu, was at the salon flipping through *Redbook* when she encountered an article on Torrance and "fairly leaped, from under the dryer." "Frequently," she wrote, "I have seen that high I.Q., punctuality, organization, discipline, 'good' homes did not always indicate an imaginative child. . . . I cringe to think of children in correction homes who feel they have NOTHING to offer. I.Q. average . . . manual dexterity average. . . . If we could tell them they have creative potential, maybe self-respect plus teacher help might change the lives of a few Juvenile delinquents." Stassen was also often frustrated by the guesswork involved in diagnosing and dealing with troublesome if imaginative children, and by the interference of parents who just wanted their children to be normal. Torrance's test, Stassen hoped, could help teachers make a more objective case. "Parents believe in tests," she wrote, "OHHHH! The possibilities!"[26]

For John R. Crowley, a high school teacher and parent of "at least one, perhaps several outstandingly creative children," reading about Torrance's work in *Redbook* and *Readers' Digest* was "a shot in the arm." Crowley, a believer in "the more proven ideas of progressive education," worried that schools like his in suburban New Jersey were "reverting" to "pre-World War I" practices: "schools for the financially and socially gifted," with "pressure for conformity and high grades." Like Stassen, Crowley was eager to prove "that the despised and the problem ones are frequently the most promising." "I have seen enough of life to recognize the kind of inner self-reliance, independence and odd-ballness it takes to survive as a creative personality," he wrote. "The average B/A student from the right side of the tracks just isn't it. He is going to be another anonymous paper-clip orderer in some large insurance company."

Many parents found hope in Torrance's message that their troubled youngsters might simply be creative. "I thank God for this article," wrote one Arkansas mother, "for I am sure it has helped many parents of children who have the qualities which you term as normal when all our lives we have been told our children are 'pestiferous,' 'too playful,' 'doesn't conform to the group,' etc." She attached a photo of her fifteen-year-old son, an adopted Native American boy, and wrote, "for the first time in my life I can relax concerning him since reading your article." Though she and her husband thought him a "lovely child," his teachers saw him as "stubborn" and a "know-it-all." Torrance's article had given them new "hope," that "if his teachers would only try to understand him and his problems they would not see him as a 'lazy-minded, playful, irresponsible day-dreamer' but as a child who, if understood, responds beautifully and works like a trojan for those who have a wave-length to him."

"I had the feeling that I was reading about my own son," wrote Margaret Mallory after reading the *Redbook* article, echoing the sentiments of many parents. Her sixteen-year-old junior was "a good-looking, friendly boy whose self-confidence has slipped." Hamstrung by an early physical handicap, he had "always been classed as a 'low-achiever,' a student who 'will not accept responsibility,' a student who 'is not interested in school.'" His arts and crafts teacher predicted a promising career in art or design, but his guidance counselor, "a man thoroughly sold on verbal and word skills," could see him "as a low-achiever only." Mallory and her husband were "puzzled about what to do next," and "very anxious to steer him in the right direction following his graduation from high school." She asked Torrance if there was anywhere in the Bay Area to find a test for creative ability, which she hoped might help clarify her son's prospects.

A Brooklyn mother told Torrance her son David, ten, "fits into your description of the creative child just as if you had written about him." David loved drawing, sculpting, and collecting animals, and tested average for intelligence. But he was also "sensitive" and socially troubled, "ridiculed, called names and the bane of the existence of his teachers," who dubbed him "'different from the other children'"—"'a non-conformist and a loner.'" The school recommended counseling, but his parents weren't so sure. "Will the therapy help or might it harm him and force him into convention?" they worried. "The price could be his individuality." "Please," his mother pleaded, "if there is anyone in New York that could perhaps give David your tests or advise us we would be most grateful. Above all we want our son to be happy. If he is happy in this world he has created for himself, then we are too."

Parents and teachers saw in Torrance's tests the hope that, in a school system increasingly colonized by tests that might decide their fate, and permeated by Cold War suspicions of "queerness" of any sort, there might be a place for their misfit children. As they looked anxiously toward a labor market increasingly dominated by college-educated, white-collar workers, many parents and teachers found in Torrance's message the reassurance that, whether their children suffered from a surfeit or a deficit of sociality, attention, or intelligence, the world might have a special plan for them, after all.

:::

Until his death in 2003 Torrance remained a passionate advocate for both unusually gifted students and the creative potential in all students. After arriving at the University of Georgia in 1966 he undertook a series of creative thinking programs with poor, rural, Black and White students. In the 1970s he founded the Future Problem Solving Program, which continues to this day, in which young people gather each year to compete in tasks of open-ended thinking around future scenarios. Between the 1970s and the 1990s he produced the Torrance Incubation Model for incorporating creativity into any subject area. Over this period he continued to publish in both *Gifted Child Quarterly* and the *Journal of Creative Behavior*, reflecting the persistence of his intersecting interest in the excellent and the "everychild."

The salience of Torrance's life's work ultimately lay in his ability to produce a new and satisfying answer to the question of what kind of person American schools should produce. His "creative child" embodied the potential for all three of Labaree's ideal forms: a liberal democratic subject, a skilled worker, and a competitive individual in a quickly changing white-collar labor market. One could see in the creative child whatever one wanted to see: a potential rocket scientist or a potential poet, a genius or simply a free and happy child. In Torrance's hands, creativity became both an update to the notion of giftedness and a new kind of skill that would enable every child to reach his or her full potential. In both cases, creativity was figured as a kind of productive thinking that was highly individualistic, not coerced or implanted but rather unleashed and unimpeded. Torrance thus deftly hitched the Cold War liberal critique of conformity to conservative fears of mediocrity and civilizational decline.

Thanks largely to Torrance's work, from the 1960s onward "creativity" became a key concept in this refiguring of American educational priorities. Applied broadly from arts education to "creative writing" programs to creative thinking techniques of the kind Torrance offered, creativity was a concept that uniquely embodied progressive education's spirit of individualized, open-ended exploration with the promise of national excellence.

Revolution on
Madison Avenue

6

The January 1959 issue of *Printers' Ink*, one of the two main organs of the American advertising industry, compiled a slew of daunting problems facing the industry. Despite being in the midst of an era of unprecedented billings—total annual advertising expenditures more than doubled between 1947 and 1957, and would almost double again over the next ten years—the recession of 1958 had shrunk advertising budgets and ad execs didn't know if or when they would recover. Apparently there was growing "skepticism" among manufacturers about whether advertising even worked, and it was decided that agencies needed to do a better job of explaining to their clients why they deserved money that could otherwise go into sales or R&D. One of the sources of skepticism, it was thought, was oversaturation—an ironic effect of Madison Avenue's success—which meant each individual ad needed to work especially hard to distinguish its clients' products from the crowd. "The average American is on the receiving end of up to 1,500 ad impressions daily," the piece read. "The ad message that shines through the mass must be exceptional."[1]

Adding to these nuts-and-bolts problems was the issue of advertising's "unfortunate" public image problem, about which executives had been "fretting" in the wake of Vance Packard's bombshell exposé *The Hidden Persuaders*. The ad industry had been the target of skeptics and muckrakers since its beginnings in the late nineteenth century. But in the 1950s Packard led a new flood of criticism that, dovetailing with Cold War political fears, cast Madison Avenue as a force of conformity, soulless consumerism, and quasi-totalitarian mind control. *Printers' Ink* considered this image problem a real existential threat, blaming it in part for an impending Federal Trade Commission "crack down" and, under a newly liberal Congress, Senate investigations into some of its shady practices.

The cure? Creativity. Creativity would be "the agency's key to '59," *Printers' Ink* declared, predicting it would "assume a new, much more important role."[2] Walter Guild, president of a San Francisco agency, explained how this "new emphasis on creativeness" would address the industry's multiple woes. It would, first, improve the quality of ads themselves. "Too much advertising is just plain dull!" he wrote, echoing the consensus among both advertising professionals and their critics. Clients "are increasingly aware and covetous of 'creative' advertising, and increasingly weary of the other kind." Creativity was, as the editors put it elsewhere in that issue, "the force that makes a product, a campaign, a company, a commercial or a thought stand above the crowd."[3]

Such "creative" advertising would, Guild explained, be accomplished only by liberating "creative" people—copywriters and artists—from the tyranny of the organization. As *PI* also noted, Madison Avenue was falling prey to the same bureaucratic bloat that infected the rest of America. A "merger splurge," as top agencies competed to match the growing size of clients (who, in an attempt to dodge antitrust laws, were undergoing a merger splurge of their own), caused agencies to balloon, with larger teams, more middle managers, more meetings.[4] Draper Daniels, vice president of creative departments at Leo Burnett (and a principal inspiration for the character Don Draper on the AMC show *Mad Men*), saw the situation much as William Whyte had described the plight of corporate capitalism in general, as the vanquishing of the genius entrepreneur by hordes of conservative managers. America was built "on ideas that wouldn't survive the first lower-echelon management meetings of today," Daniels complained. The public reputation of the typical adman reinforced this staid image. In a veritable cottage industry of exposés, memoirs, novels, and movies, advertising men were portrayed as the epitome of the bureaucratic organization man: spineless yes-men, traditional, grey-flannel-suited.[5] Within the industry a revolt was rising against the "researchers"—market researchers who with focus groups and polling tried to make even decisions about art and copy on scientific grounds. "The brilliant pioneers who built American business" were gone, Daniels wrote, and "in their place we have the cautious, caretaker management teams . . . with their batteries of research men and marketing experts superbly equipped to produce anything in the world but a new idea."[6] (Daniels clearly saw the link between bureaucratic bloat and all the creativity talk: "The bigger agencies get bigger and the interminable meetings become more interminable, and the less creative we get, the more we talk about the need for creativity."[7]) Going forward, Guild hoped, "pitches will contain fewer pie charts and more emphasis on our 'creative strength.'"

Crucially, the liberation of the creatives would improve not only the ads themselves, but the image of the entire industry. These newly prominent creatives would "put advertising on the professional level where it belongs," and "earn [the creative] the confidence and professional respect to which he is entitled as a worker in the profession that has helped build the highest living standards in history." Through its full-throated embrace of creativeness, Guild hoped, advertising could take its rightful place as an equal partner with industry in American prosperity. If clients would get out of the way and let the creative man do his job, he claimed, they would get ads that were "vital and productive," "less dull," and "really creative," "to the enormous benefit of themselves, the long-suffering public, and the noble profession of advertising."[8]

As advertisers attempted to produce more novelty against the forces of mass society they had in part created, "creativity" rang hopeful and pure. It would reenergize the industry and help transform its public image from the province of hucksters and corporate shills into one of authentic visionaries and iconoclasts, from the villains of a soul-deadening consumer society to the heroes of a consumers' utopia. The notion of creativity would render the creation of consumer desire a humane and high-minded pursuit. It would make capitalism a safe space for individuality and critique, while also transforming anti-consumerist critique into more consumption.

The agent of this transformation would be the "creative man": somewhere between an artist and a salesman, a liminal figure within if not totally comfortable with the business world, paradoxically committed to his own vision and his clients' needs simultaneously, a resident gadfly who would be the humane and rebellious face of capitalism and its ultimate font of value. It was during these years that the very term "creative man" went from merely a categorical designation to a personality type. Mixing homegrown stereotypes about creative personnel with the new psychological research—which, as we saw, was itself heavily inflected by existing stereotypes of "creative" people—the "creative man" in the advertising sense and the "creative man" in the psychological sense fused into a new heroic figure uniquely positioned to transcend the bureaucracy of the ad world and corporate America as a whole. The creative man himself would be Madison Avenue's unique selling proposition, its best foot forward, and a metonym for the industry as it vied to prove its value to industry and society.

The culmination of all of this creativity talk was an aesthetic and organizational upheaval remembered today as the "creative revolution." That moment in the history of advertising is still taught in business and marketing classes as a hopeful fable, a glorious moment in which creativity was unleashed against the forces of conformity. But what if we instead saw it as the moment in which the concept of creativity itself was solidified in the first place? Instead of seeing creativity as something that was already there, pent up and ready to burst out, perhaps it's more revelatory to see it as a new object in the advertising imagination, a container for the varied and often contradictory ambitions of one of postwar America's most emblematic institutions.

Catching Up

If we're looking for the moment the advertising industry embraced creativity as its guiding principle, an origin point may well be the two days in early April of 1958 in which the Art Directors Club of New York hosted five hundred advertising industry elites at New York City's Waldorf Astoria hotel to address the fact that everybody seemed to be talking about creativity but them. The meeting's organizer, Paul Smith, said he found it "interesting that the advertising business which is supposed to be so highly dependent on creativity and that employs so many high-priced creative personnel . . . should be so laggard in their investigation of this phenomenon."[9] Indeed, as Smith noted, advertising employed many people—such as visual artists and writers, photographers, graphic designers, audio producers, musicians, actors, and so forth—who were, since at least the 1920s, collectively referred to as "creative" personnel, as opposed to the people who brokered ad sales—historically the more fundamental aspect of the industry—who were sometimes referred to as "accounts" people. Volumes had been written about the art and craft of making good ads—how to write effective copy, how to lay out visuals, what kind of messages and images worked—but what Smith meant by creativity was something different, what *Printer's Ink* called in its writeup of the conference "creativeness in a man," not just the skill of making ads but an elemental faculty. Psychologists and management experts had in recent years produced a lot of knowledge about this faculty, from which, Smith felt, the advertising industry might learn something, and to which it might contribute in its turn.

The conference roster included some ad industry celebrities such as Saul Bass, who, after delivering the assault on brainstorming we saw in chapter 2, shared his thoughts on Creativity in Visual

Communications. But it also included guests from outside of advertising, such as Stanford's John E. Arnold, who spoke about Creative Engineering; the director of General Motors's AC Spark Plug creativity program (which drew heavily from Osborn) on Creativity in Industry; and the noted psychoanalyst Gregory Zilborg on the Creative Personality. Attendees also heard about Creativity in Science, Creativity in Music, Creativity in Marketing, and The Nature of the Creative Process, and they got a demonstration of creativity in action with a live performance by the jazz great Eddie Condon and his orchestra. The conversation was as wide-ranging as the roster. Toward the end of the conference's final day the record producer George Avakian asked, "has anyone found out what 'Creativity' means?" As usual, the true meaning of the term was not to be found in any one speaker's definition, but rather was implied in the very form of the conference, mixing art with science and technology.

Smith admitted the heavy emphasis on creativity in science and engineering might have struck his ad-industry audience as strange. But, he explained, creativity was something common across fields. There was really no difference, he said, between "so-called 'artistic' thinking and the practical, hard-headed, inquisitive, scientific method." This discovery had the potential to make Madison Avenue rethink itself, and for the rest of industry to rethink how they saw advertising people:

> In the past, hard-headed practical men of science and business were apt to under-rate creativity. They thought creative people were screwballs, wore berets, smocks, velveteen slacks and canvas sneakers, walked bareheaded in the rain, practiced free-love and starved in garrets. But of late, we have seen the emergence of a different point of view. Many people have come to recognize that whether it occurs in painting a picture, writing a poem or symphony, inventing a new jet propulsion system or a new marketing technique or a new wonder drug, the creative process is a manifestation of the same fundamental ability. . . . The arts and sciences are rediscovering the fact that they are siblings.[10]

As we've seen, this notion of a general creative faculty or process was attractive to those in scientific and technical professions because it gave them license to free their bohemian side without fear of being seen as self-indulgent or impractical. In advertising it served a similar function, legitimizing salaried artists and writers by making them seem less impractical and self-indulgent than their stereotypes might imply, assuring the "hard-headed" bosses and clients that they were no frivolous bohemians.

How to Keep a Creative Man Creative

Printers' Ink's coverage of the Waldorf Astoria conference, titled "How to Keep a Creative Man Creative," aptly summarizes the primary motivating force behind the sudden interest in creativity: management. It was not, by and large, the rank-and-file creative personnel who theorized about the creative process. In the magazine's new regular "Creativity" feature, for example, inaugurated in 1960, in which contributors were invited to share their "creative philosophies," copywriters and artists often opted to discuss how much text is too much or the finer points of visual hierarchy. As the old quip goes, when artists get together they don't talk about creativity, they talk about the price of paint. Whether because they wanted to protect their secrets or because they were genuinely uninterested in the question, it was not creatives who drove the conversation about creativity, but rather those who managed them. How, despite the multiplying layers of bureaucracy, would they "keep the creative man creative"? For, as Pierre Martineau, one of advertising's most prominent voices, put it, "Merely putting up a sign stating that here is the creative department . . . doesn't necessarily produce genuine creativity."[11] (Martineau may have been influenced in this belief by Alex Osborn, whom he apparently knew; he had attended the Creative Problem Solving Institute five years prior, serving on the brainstorming panel on juvenile delinquency.)[12]

Most of the advice about "proper understanding and handling" of creative personnel urged a laissez-faire approach: "The way you make a creative man creative is to let him be creative."[13] In a June 1958 article titled "The Creative Man: His Moods and Needs," a series of agency executives offered their advice: Hours should be flexible. "If someone wants to work at home, or take off during the day to sit in Central Park, that's all right, too."[14] "Creative men" shouldn't be saddled with administrative duties, and managers should be more flexible with them about rules than with other employees: "If you want conformity in the copywriter and artist, you get it in the copy and art, too." The new psychology was enlisted to explain why such methods were necessary. In "What Science Knows about Creative People," Paul Smith relayed the findings of J. P. Guilford and others, that creative people were "less authoritarian, less traditional, and less conventional in their attitude than their non-creative brothers." They were also "less prone not only to exercise authority, but also less inclined to accept it blindly," making a light managerial touch a necessity. Paradoxically, though they were supremely confident in their ideas and didn't tend to care about the opinions of others, they should be spared too much criticism or pressure while working. "Over motivation or anxiety kills creativity . . . so too, does a too highly evaluative atmosphere," whereas "a permissive atmosphere fosters creative ability."[15]

Often admen spoke of the "resurgence of interest in creativity" as a renaissance, a purification of advertising art and a return to the industry's golden age. That was the 1920s, when, likewise facing a reputation for trickery and the looming threat of government regulation, agencies turned ads into works of art, hiring well-known studio artists to lend the industry an air of refinement, respectability, even social responsibility. When budgets plummeted during the Depression, advertising returned to a brasher, matter-of-fact, "reason-why" style, and incorporated a host of other marketing ploys like tie-ins, coupons, giveaways, and direct mailings. Creativity partisans hoped the 1960s would bring "advertising, in its pristine sense, more to the fore," and not allow it to be "muted by casually lumping it with a number of marketing functions."[16]

Admen, like many postwar intellectuals and others engaged with creativity, had their own critique of science and rationality. In their case, they believed their industry was in the grip a scientific ethos. Indeed, following trends in the rest of industry and American society in general, advertising had, leading up to the middle of the century, carefully cultivated the notion that it was a proper profession and that it had "reached the status of a science," as one profile put it, "based on fixed principles" and "correct methods of procedure [that] have been proved and established."[17] *Madison Avenue, U.S.A.*, published in 1957 as a rebuttal of Packard, profiled the J. Walter Thompson agency, a bastion of the scientific approach, in which each ad went through a careful process of research, statistical analysis, and vetting, with artists and copywriters never given the final word. As historian Stephen Fox writes, the industry collectively celebrated the fact that campaigns were now developed based on "demographic studies and hard statistics instead of the intuitive hunches of a lone copywriter at his typewriter."[18]

Those who became associated with the creative revolution disagreed: "There are a lot of great technicians in advertising," said Bill Bernbach, an iconoclast copywriter and creative director known for giving his creative teams space to operate. "They know all the rules. . . . They are the scientists of advertising. But there's one little rub. Advertising is fundamentally persuasion and persuasion happens to be not a science, but an art."[19] Bernbach had no need for focus groups, relying instead on intuition: "We test everything on ourselves. If we like it, it's good. If we don't, it stinks."[20] Even more moderate voices often agreed, though, that research had overstepped its bounds. "Good advertising is the product of two types of minds, widely different," wrote advertising's senior statesman, Earnest Elmo Calkins, with echoes of Alex Osborn, "the orderly, systematic, business mind, and the free-wheeling, creative, inventive mind." Only the latter was the source of "the spark that gives an advertisement life and significance and results." "Preliminary statistical efforts—research, market surveys, tests, ratings—all help," he wrote, "but they stop short of the essential ingredient, *ideas*." And ideas could not be "dug up in field work or in the laboratory," but rather "spring up spontaneously—through instinct, intuition." In fact, Calkins believed, ideas eluded the accounting logics of science and commerce both: "Ideas cannot be measured. They cannot be bargained for."[21] The minds of creative men, though they may physically exist in a corporate office, were alleged to operate outside the bounds of commerce.

An Internal Other

The industry's ability to understand and incorporate the "creative man" became a symbol of the possibility of incorporating dissent and rebellion into the system without destroying it. Occasionally, in the early twentieth century, ad people would take to musing about the differences between account men and creative men, with the latter sometimes characterized as a bit unreliable and bohemian. But in the postwar era this imagined division hardened and the camps set upon one another in war. George Lois, a Pratt-trained artist known to occasionally physically assault those who dared disrespect his work, said of the account men: "They don't like the way we work, the way we talk, the way we dress. They don't know anything about advertising or how good advertising is created. They hold this business down. They help to create the bad advertising we are inundated with."[22] In 1960, in the iconic maneuver of the creative revolution, Lois became fed up with his management role and split from Doyle Dane Bernbach to form PKL, which enabled him to focus exclusively on creative work.

Partly to ward off such desertions, many firms began to rearrange their organizational charts to get the creative men out from under layers of bureaucracy. Many adopted the model already used at DDB where a copywriter-artist team would work closely together rather than separately down the chain from an executive, allowing their visions to come out whole rather than dented and distorted by a grapevine of often opposing and asinine opinions.[23] In 1958 the Leo Burnett agency promoted a number of creatives to top executive roles in order to "maintain fully the creative personality of the agency."[24] "Creative men are the men of the hour," Leo Burnett said, "it is high time they were given the respect they deserve. Agencies revolve around the men with the pencils."[25] By the early 1960s top creatives began to free themselves from the behemoths, splitting off to form "boutiques" or "hot shops" with leaner budgets and cocksure "creative" attitudes. This in turn prompted the big companies to woo them back, coupling big company pay with creative freedom, often by setting up in-house "think tanks" or "creative islands" for them.

It wasn't always easy to reconcile this freedom with the bottom line. There was much disagreement about how much free rein these creative types should get, and whether clients would like this new attitude. Many in fact feared the new deference to the creative man was at best ineffective, and at worst degrading to the profession. David Ogilvy, a senior adman who thought brainstorming was for "loafers," insisted that copywriters only "pretend that what they like best is to be left alone and have complete freedom to create, but what they really want is a great deal of pressure and interruption."[26] "They are not writing or painting in a garret," said another, "creative people need discipline to work toward a definite goal."

Opponents of the creative revolution often used Art as an effete and elite foil for their practical and muscular business. Art Tatham, chairman of a national agency, took out an ad in the *Wall Street Journal* to say there was no place in his firm for self-important aesthetes who could not handle criticism without feeling like "their delicate egos have been raped by the Huns of commerce. . . . All the great creative advertising people I know live and work in a creative climate that is appalling for its ruthless lack of self-indulgence." Truly creative men, he continued, "find fulfillment not in self-expression—in art for art's sake—but in the satisfaction of applying creative talents to make a mark not on posterity, but on next month's sales curve." Marion Harper, chairman and president of McCann Erickson, called "the cult of advertising creativity" "a waste of time," pointing out clients were not spending billions of dollars to "decorate" magazines and television, "so the people who prepare advertising should not go skipping around a Maypole of creativity."[27] Alfred Politz, a prominent advocate of scientific market research and "reason-why" advertising, thought admen who claimed corporate rules stifled their creativity were "seeking a license which the real creative geniuses in arts and sciences would consider embarrassing."[28] The true meaning of the word "creativeness," he wrote, was "the *advanced* form of imagination where it is *purposively* used by abiding to rigid rules and by meeting practical conditions."[29] Interestingly, it was not creativity itself such men opposed, but rather that the word was being used to justify a liberality they could not abide. Rather than reject the term, they attempted to reclaim it. "The only creativity that counts in our business," Tatham declared, "is that which is relevant to solving a sales and profit problem."[30]

Though there were extremists on both sides, the major tendency of most admen during the creative revolution was to push to the center, to thread the needle between images of the antisocial bohemian and the spineless yes-man. As Smith had said at the Waldorf Astoria, creativity was *not* just for "screwballs" but a "fundamental ability" shared by practical men as well. The creative revolution was just as much a process of claiming the bohemian sensibility as one of distancing itself from it, and "creativity" was the means for pressing the bohemian spirit into the service of selling stuff. It's no wonder, then, that the man still most closely associated with the creative revolution was Bill Bernbach, whose fierce independence nevertheless produced ads which, as we will see, were no indulgent artistic self-expressions but rather practices in functionalism and restraint, and which, above all, found ways of rising above the crowd and getting noticed.

There may not have been agreement about the proper care and feeding of creatives, but almost everyone agreed they were different. "You can't apply a basic description to all of them, nor should you apply a basic policy to all," one exec wrote. "The only overall conclusion you can make is that creative people shouldn't be treated the same way as other people." Or, as Draper Daniels confusedly put it, "we don't remember often enough how like creative people are unto other people—and how different."[31] It is indeed likely that from the experienced manager's point of view there was no one best way of managing an artist or copywriter, any more than there was one right way to manage an account man, a secretary, or a janitor. Still, even if they couldn't put their finger on how, managers were committed to the idea that "creative people" were somehow different from the rest.

The creative man was, at least in a symbolic sense, advertising's internal Other, the antidote to the industry's own feared over-rationalism. Defending the creative man's autonomy became a matter of importance well beyond the individual firm: the fate of American capitalism depended on it. A prominent 1960 ad for the Young & Rubicam agency touted its laissez-faire approach to creativity, depicting a man dangling by one arm, sloth-like, from the branch of a tree, with a contented smile. The copy ran:

> Say you're a man with an idea. You are in love with it. You are able to go way out on a limb for that idea without being afraid that anybody's going to saw it off or even snicker. When that is company policy it's good company policy. It frees people's minds to experiment. This kind of experimentation produces fresh new thinking . . . new ideas. And ideas are what people want. After all, it's not just the product itself that people buy. It's ideas about the product. People buy ideas.[32]

Out on a limb, the image punned, was the Y&R creative man's natural habitat. From his perch above the hustle and bustle of commerce he was happily at work creating the ideas that make business go. The ad seemed directed at potential employees looking for a permissive environment, but it was really making a larger claim about the significance of advertising in American capitalism: that the advertising industry, led by the unfettered creative man, was the ultimate source of profit.

Redeeming the Manufacture of Desire

The claim that people buy ideas rather than products, the conceit at the core of today's branding-design complex, was at the time a startling and somewhat unsettling assertion. It was, in a sense, an argument the ad industry had always made to explain its magical ability to differentiate essentially identical products, but this had traditionally been qualified by a larger belief that selling was, or at least should be, about the things themselves. The "reason why" paradigm that dominated for most of the industry's history had assumed rational consumers bought products because of their characteristics—that they cleaned twice as fast, that they smoked smoother, that they had patented technology—and that the role of the advertiser was simply to communicate these (or make them up if they had to). But the age of affluence, with its frank dependence on the manufacture of desire, seemed to demand a new theory of consumer behavior that went beyond use value.

Advertising, as the handmaiden of consumerism, had always struggled to defend itself against a certain Protestant suspicion of false needs, but the fact that the entire postwar economy seemed to depend on the manufacture of desire was profoundly alarming to critics. The economist John Kenneth Galbraith wrote, "the fact that wants can be synthesized by advertising, catalyzed by sales-manship, and shaped by the discreet manipulations of the per-suaders shows that they are not very urgent."[33] He argued that a society untethered to real needs lacked moral direction and tran-scendent purpose. The traditional justification of advertising, that it drove consumer spending and thus powered the economy, was compelling to many in the growth consensus, but to the charge of the tail wagging the dog the industry needed a better response. It needed to find a way for everyone to feel comfortable that all that was solid was melting into air.

One solution was to lean into the immateriality of it all: adver-tising did not simply get people to buy products, it also imbued those products with meaning. And it was actually this landscape of meaning that made consumer capitalism a force for good, even self-actualization.

Ironically, it would be a founding father of market research and a man largely responsible for advertising's bad reputation in the first place who would make the case for creative advertising as a means not only of economic prosperity, but of democratic freedom and self-actualization. Ernest Dichter fled Nazi Germany to become, as *Time* magazine wrote, "the first to apply to advertising really scientific psychology." At his Institute for Motivational Research, founded in 1946, Dichter applied pseudo-Freudian analysis to test consumers, helping manufacturers tap the "hidden desires and urges" lurking in the American consumer.[34] Vance Packard, bothered by the perversity of using deep psychoanalysis to sell pantyhose, turned Dichter into the titular hidden persuader that Americans found so troubling. A few years later Dichter would also be a target of Betty Friedan's *The Feminine Mystique*, which accused him of "deluding women about their real needs" in order to keep them at home and consuming. "Properly manipulated," Dichter candidly explained to Friedan, "American housewives can be given the sense of identity, purpose, creativity, the self-realization, even the sexual joy they lack—by the buying of things." It was Dichter, famously, who instructed manufacturers to remove the dehydrated egg from instant cake mix, because the simple act of adding a real egg would give housewives "a feeling of being creative" and assuage deep-seated fears of failing in the womanly arts. But Friedan saw this as nothing more than "the subversion of women's lives in America to the ends of business."[35]

The way Dichter saw it, convincing people to buy things was not trickery but a public service. As he argued, all the fretting about consumerism came from an outmoded "puritanical" strain in American culture. Thrift, moderation, and delayed gratification may have served prior generations, but in modern society they were not only obsolete but threatening. "Our economy would literally collapse overnight" without massive consumption, he wrote, so it was not the pointy-headed moralizers but rather "the individuals who defend the right to buy" who were the true "defenders of a positive outlook on life, the real salesmen of prosperity, and therefore of democracy."

Like a number of other Jewish émigrés including Herbert Marcuse and Theodor Adorno, Dichter believed that bourgeois self-restraint was to blame for the rise of totalitarianism and so much psychic and political dysfunction in the West. But Dichter also believed, as did some other émigrés, including Ludwig von Mises and Peter Drucker, that the rise of totalitarianism was a vindication of the market system.[36] In a potent if idiosyncratic combination of these postwar émigré intellectual currents, Dichter became a frank advocate of commodity fetishism.

Getting one's kicks through consumption was not, for Dichter, false or shallow, but rather a safe alternative to socially destructive behavior, and one that powered the very cycle of affluence. He often cited Abraham Maslow to argue that Western society was evolving beyond crass competitiveness to a more self-expressive and self-actualizing mode. If Dichter could help manufacturers and advertisers to "put the libido back in advertising," to understand that when men bought cars they were really buying the thrill of an illicit affair, all the better for car salesmen, millions of marriages, and the American economy.[37]

"Creativity," for Dichter, was what allowed marketers to pull off this feat. Although initially Dichter sold motivation research on the grounds that it was "scientific," by the late 1950s, threatened by the rise of highly sophisticated, computer-enabled quantitative market research, he began to argue that his approach was more "creative." Quantitative methods were "superficial," he said, while his were qualitative, interpretive, and even poetic, accessing "the deeper and more emotional factors" behind consumption patterns.[38] But it was also creative in that it necessarily led to unexpected territory. "Descriptive research" was for figuring out who consumes product, how much, and when, but when "you want to change or improve" consumer behavior, "you need the techniques of *creative* research." "Creative advertising," then, was the art of endowing a product with meaning. "The elementary fact," he wrote, "is that a cigarette is a cigarette is a cigarette and a soap is a soap. . . . Before a cigarette may become a Lucky Strike or a Pall Mall, and more a Lucky Strike or a Pall Mall than a cigarette, its perception by the consumer must be changed." Such changes in perception were the job not of the scientist but of the artist, working on the symbolic and emotional terrain of human consciousness rather than the logical "reason-why" level or the crass, almost behaviorist repetition that still dominated advertising. "Creativity," he wrote in 1959, should be a "Credo for the Sixties."

In a little-known postscript to his career, Dichter became so taken with the concept of creativity, and so desperate for work in the wake of the quantitative turn, that he reinvented himself as a creativity consultant: Ernest Dichter Creativity, Ltd. He began to offer three- and five-day "creativity seminars," gave talks to industry groups about "Creativity for Fun and Profit," and published a set of instructional cassette tapes titled *Everyday Creativity*.[39] Subscribers would learn "Dr. Dichter's 12 Steps to Creativity," cobbled together from various established creative thinking methods including Osborn's approach and Synectics (his papers include an itinerary and map for a week-long Synectics training in Cambridge). Dichter regularly repeated the don't-picture-an-artist trope: The glossy brochure for *Everyday Creativity* featured photos of a ballet dancer, a sculptor, and an oil painter, and on the inside two executives strutting confidently down a city street. "Artists call it creativity," the copy read, "Executives have another name for it . . . Success." It's not clear how well Dichter fared with this late career shift. He was left holding most of the tape sets, and he doesn't seem to have done more than a handful of executive creativity trainings. After a career spent divining consumer fads, perhaps he was simply too late to the creativity craze.

In any case, Dichter's point was that it was through "creativity," the source of symbolic meaning that copywriters shared with poets, that the ad industry spoke to consumers' authentic desires. In an age of affluence the "creative" professional, with his or her grasp of emotional and psychic needs, would be the source of both economic value and values in the deeper sense. The language of creativity could thus transform the manufacturing of desire from a sin against liberal democratic values into a high-minded and socially responsible pursuit.

The Creative Revolution and the Counterculture

The cover of *Newsweek*'s August 19, 1969 issue hailed "Advertising's Creative Explosion." With photos of bearded, betassled hipsters with their feet up on desks, gathered around tables to discuss accounts for TWA and Virginia Slims, it declared that "creativity has emerged from the writers' cubbyholes and the artists' bullpens." The "hardheaded dollars-and-cents men who long ruled the ad game . . . have had to move over for the imaginative, and frequently unconventional, men and women who are responsible for a new wave of ideas." The whole aesthetic and attitude of advertisements themselves reflected this youthful transformation, incorporating psychedelic imagery, hip jargon, and even a winking anti-consumerist attitude in order to appeal to the wealthiest, and most skeptical, generation the world had ever seen. Historians and marketing textbooks typically echo this narrative, associating the creative revolution with an outpouring of hip, exciting ads by a new cadre of maverick visionaries who took over the big agencies, bringing a countercultural sensibility to Madison Avenue. Like the *Newsweek* article, they highlight the irony that it was thanks to the incorporation of the very types known to be so hostile to business that the advertising industry was thriving again after an uncertain couple of decades in which its bottom line and its public image were threatened.[40]

According to the story told in every marketing class for the past sixty years, this Creative Revolution began in 1959 with a series of Volkswagen ads by DDB. Volkswagen, a German company still at the time associated with the Third Reich, needed to break into the American car market. The auto industry was the undisputed engine of the American economy at the time, dominated by the "Big Three" auto makers who pushed new models every year with ever more outlandish gizmos and space-age ornamentation such as rocket-like tailfins. The simple, utilitarian VW, then, might have seemed a challenge to market. But Bill Bernbach saw an opportunity.

Sensing the public weariness with the unceasing parade of fantastical car ads and the superficial consumer society they had come to represent, Bernbach tacked hard toward straightforward honesty. He traded the typical stylized drawings for simple black-and-white photographs against a neutral background, and the copy, printed in a utilitarian Helvetica font then rarely used outside of directional signage and instruction manuals, made self-deprecating stabs at the product. One ad, touting VW's unfashion-ableness to imply its steadiness, pictured a Beetle at center with the caption "The '51 '52 '53 '54 '55 '56 '57 '58 '59 '60 '61 Volkswagen." Another took aim at cars as status symbols: "If you want to show you've gotten somewhere, get a big beautiful chariot. But if you simply want to get somewhere, get a bug." There were two sly references here—the first to the frankly status-conscious slogan of the much-hyped, ill-fated 1958 Ford Edsel ("says you're going places"), and the second to the popular 1959 anti–auto industry screed *The Insolent Chariots*. With their winking humor, the DDB ads—or anti-ads—positioned VW as the "anti-automobile," the one company that shared the enlightened driver's disgust with empty consumerism.[41] Their new pitch was essentially, as Thomas Frank cleverly encapsulates it, "Alienated by the conformity and hypocrisy of mass society? Have we got a car for you!"

The DDB VW ads were instant classics, beloved in the industry not only because they successfully set their product off in a crowded field, but also because they seemed to hold a more fundamental lesson. They proved that an individual like Bernbach could channel his own antiestablishment sensibilities into effective advertising, and that it was possible to turn anti-consumerist sentiment into more consumerism.[42] It's no accident that by the time hippies started looking for ways to get from Point A to Point B they already knew which car was for them.[43] Maybe that trip would take them from Shaker Heights to the Haight, or perhaps they'd end up on Madison Avenue. For the creative revolution also demonstrated to young people with a humanistic bent that it was not necessary to "drop out" to find fulfilling work. One could exercise one's creativity from the comfort of a midtown suite. In advertising lore DDB's VW campaign became a symbol of the creative revolution because it captured the multiple ways in which "creativity" was brought to the fore—in the novelty of the ads, in the art-and-copy-forward approach, and in the nonconformist attitude that would remake Madison Avenue as the antidote to modern capitalism's ills.

Creativity was not a hippie value co-opted by Madison Avenue. Sure, Madison Avenue did its fair share of cooptation in the 1960s—using psychedelic imagery and feminist slogans to sell cars and cigarettes—but "creativity" was something more homegrown. In fact, it was the thing that made the incorporation of the counterculture feel authentic, as if the hippies and the ad industry were united in their pursuit of the new and different. Underpinning the new aesthetics and the new liberal management style of the creative revolution was a conceptual revolution: the solidification of the very concept of creativity within the profession, and its rapid rise to the status of a talisman to which every true advertising man would eventually bow down. Though it remained a fuzzy concept, creativity nonetheless provided a larger purpose, a rallying cry, to an industry in crisis. As in the rest of industry, the word had a special ring to it, sounding somehow both familiar and foreign—foreign enough to signal its disruptiveness to business as usual, yet familiar enough to be easily reconciled with industry's essential goal of permanent revolution.

: : :

By the mid-1970s the acme of the creative revolution passed. With recessions and a countercultural hangover, many of the hot shops closed, and overtly psychedelic imagery gave way to a partial return to pocketbook-conscious, "reason-why" advertising. But under the surface of ad aesthetics a key shift remained in place. The ad industry's identity as a force of cultural innovation and rebellion remains very much alive, evident in any number of anti–mass culture campaigns from Apple's "1984" and "Think Different" to Levi's Walt Whitman ads to the ill-fated Pepsi Super Bowl spot in which Kendall Jenner ditches a fashion shoot (for an ad, one presumes) for a protest featuring musicians, artists, and other creative types holding placards with anodyne 1960s slogans like "Love" and peace signs, plus the blandly corporate-sounding "Join the Conversation." The non-specificity of the issue being protested underscores the point that it's not the target of the rebellion that matters, but the rebellion itself, and the idea that the product in question can help one resist becoming part of the status quo. This kind of antiestablishment marketing, whether of chewing gum or yoga pants, powers what Frank calls "a cultural perpetual motion machine in which disgust with the falseness, shoddiness, and everyday oppressions of consumer society could be enlisted to drive the ever-accelerating wheels of consumption."[44]

The creative revolution also bequeathed to later generations a new professional identity—the "creative"—which would soon expand well beyond advertising to occupy what would (not coincidentally) come to be known as the "creative industries." With the rise of the aesthetic economy, branding, and the internet, the art and craft of forming impressions has become an ever more central part of our economy. As American businesses came to see themselves as producers not of goods (increasingly handled offshore) but of ideas and images, the advertising business and its offshoots became the template for American business writ large. It's now normal for businesses to model themselves after "creative agencies," or, borrowing from design and entertainment "studios," to signal that they are closer to art than commerce. The idea of putting the bohemians out front and highlighting the "creative" workplace environment is now de rigueur in the creative industries, or industries that would like to emulate their "creative vibe."[45]

As in the early days of advertising's cultural revolution, what exactly is "creative" about the "creative industries" or "creatives" themselves is multivalent. They are creative because they create new and valuable symbols, images, and messages. But they are also considered creative in a characterological sense. As we'll see, we speak of today's "creative" as both an economic role and a type, with particular consumption patterns, work habits, and personalities. Like the postwar creative revolutionaries, these creatives often see themselves as occupying a liminal space at the boundaries of capitalism, though in many ways they are at the center of it. They tend to hold a skeptical view of consumerism even as they pay their bills making Nike ads, and though they may be politically liberal or even leftist, they may hold their deepest ire, as any true artist would, for the "dull" and the hackneyed, about which they and their employers and clients are on the same page. In other words, the concept of creativity does moral work for those in the cultural industries—and, as we'll see, in the business of technology.

Creativity
Is Dead . . .

7

By the mid-1960s creativity research had already achieved many of its original goals: creative ability assessments were in use in major organizations from the Air Force and NASA to GE and Shockley Semiconductor. The lacuna that Guilford identified in 1950 had been robustly corrected: hundreds of articles had been published and were having a trickle-down effect, as creativity research was beginning to appear in psychology textbooks and undergraduate syllabi. In May and June of 1965, for example, *Machine Design* ran a three-part series on creativity tests, with several examples for readers to take, including divergent thinking tests used by Guilford and others, picture-completions from the Torrance Tests of Creative Thinking, and several of the personality inventories used by Barron and McKinnon at IPAR.[1] Through outreach in the popular press, creativity experts had informed the public about the importance of creativity for strategic, economic, cultural, and personal growth. By 1968, just a few years before he penned the very first entry on "creativity" for the *Encyclopedia Americana*,[2] Frank Barron crowed of the field's success in bringing attention to such a vital issue: "at no other time in all of human history has there been such general recognition that to be creative in one's own everyday activity is a positive good."[3] The palpable sense of forward momentum seemed to call for a communal stocktaking.[4] Between 1962 and 1964 Calvin Taylor, Frank Barron, E. Paul Torrance, Sidney Parnes, and other major figures in the field all published books synthesizing the progress of the field, eagerly citing one another and arguing that the diversity of methods was yielding results. Marveling at how far the field had come since 1950, Calvin Taylor boasted, "it can no longer be said fruitful research cannot be done on creativity."[5]

But not all psychologists agreed creativity research was, in fact, on such solid ground. Fourteen years after Guilford's speech, APA president Quinn McNemar took to the same podium and declared that "anyone who peeks over the fence into this field is apt to be astonished at the visible chaos."[6] Robert L. Ebel, president of the American Educational Research Association, which had supported Torrance's research, said creativity researchers were "chasing a will-o'-the-wisp."[7] A bemused Liam Hudson chalked creativity research up to "a bandwagon; one which all of us sufficiently hale and healthy have leapt athletically aboard," but essentially a dead end.[8]

These critics saw no evidence that "so-called tests of creativity," as McNemar put it, could really predict "actual creative performance."[9] A review of the field in August 1963 noted that "Guilford has yet to demonstrate that his creativity tests are related in any demonstrable manner to creative performance in the real world, but his work has become the basis for almost all current attempts to construct an applied test of creativity," including the flagship AC Spark Plug Test of Creative Ability in use throughout industry.[10] Hudson also noted this unfortunate habit of calling any open-ended test a "creativity" test, though he saw "scarcely a shred of factual support" for the assumption that one predicted the other. Robert Thorndike, a senior authority on mental testing, conceded Guilford's point that so-called general intelligence was an oversimplification, but warned that psychologists "would be well advised to use the term 'test of creativity' with even more circumspection than we are learning to use in speaking of 'test of intelligence.'"[11]

In fact, critics said, researchers had not actually proven that creativity was distinguishable from intelligence, or even distinguishable enough that standard intelligence tests should be abandoned when identifying top talent. They pointed out that even in the key studies creativity psychologists cited, IQ and creative accomplishment remained highly correlated. IQ tests, therefore, probably remained the best available predictors of success, especially in the applied sciences and to some extent even in the arts.[12] The Torrance Tests of Creative Thinking, in many ways the flagship creativity test of the era, came in for much of the criticism. Torrance himself would later admit disappointment that his twenty-five- and forty-year follow-ups revealed a low correlation between high scores as children and creative accomplishments as adults.[13] But Torrance also insisted, despite his belief in his tests' predictive power, that they could capture only a sliver of the total phenomenon of creativity. He reminded critics the tests were a necessary oversimplification for the sake of a large longitudinal study. (They were originally supposed to accompany two other studies, on biographical and personality factors.)[14]

But these were details often lost in researchers' excitement to use their new tools. Tests, once published, have a way of driving reification: between the administration of divergent thinking tests and the reporting of their results, the distinction between "creative thinking" and "creativity" became blurred, with the high scorers being classified as "creative." As the influential developmental psychologist Jerome Kagan noted in 1967, echoing the same criticism Guilford had made about the concept of "genius" years earlier, "creativity" had come to be defined by a score on a test rather than real-world ability. The cart was in front of the horse: "Where previous centuries saw fit to apply this label with some caution and in single units," he wrote, "our generation exuberantly assigns its adjective form every day to hundreds of young people. The intellectual priests of earlier generations assigned the label after the proof was in; our contemporaries wish to predict it, as if creativity resembled life expectancy, rather than number of children, to which it bears a closer conceptual tie."[15] For Kagan, creativity should refer to what someone has actually produced, not some supposedly latent ability. What psychologists had done was to turn "creativity" into a quantifiable mental trait and the "creative person" into an identifiable type. Perhaps as an inevitable consequence of making creativity into an object of empirical study, they had helped turn "creative" into something a person could simply "be."

Whether such a type existed in the absence of testing, however, was an increasingly important question. The technical root of the criticism was that the various so-called creativity metrics lacked significant "intercorrelation": the different attributes researchers were testing for—divergent thinking ability, ego strength, preference for asymmetry, etc.—did not in fact seem to cluster together in the same individuals. This led to doubt that all the things that researchers *called* creativity were, in any objective psychological sense, related. They had, in a sense, committed the same error intelligence testers had decades earlier: assuming that because the word "creativity" existed, there must be something called creativity residing somewhere *in there*, in the brain.[16] Yet it was not clear that any such thing—a distinct mental capacity or process responsible for novel products in any field—could be said to exist.

This basic critique of creativity research has been echoed by a number of psychologists. As recently as 2012, the *Journal of Creative Behavior* posed the fundamental question once again:

> Is there something analogous to the g of intelligence—call it c—
> that is predictive of creative performance across most domains?
> Can many of the creative-thinking skills that might help someone
> design a creative advertising campaign also be employed in helping that person write a creative sonnet, find a creative resolution
> to a scheduling conflict, develop a creative new approach to an
> engineering problem, choreograph a creative dance routine, and
> devise a creative scientific theory?[17]

The accumulated research suggested not necessarily. Apparently creativity (however defined) in one area depends on one set of traits and behaviors, and on another more or less distinct set in the next, and that "domain-general skills or traits contribute little to creative performance." The supposedly domain-general tests of creativity, such as Guilford's battery or the TTCT, moreover, "may have misled researchers to unsupportable interpretations." The validity of all the research conducted based on those tests—a significant portion of the creativity canon—needs to be reconsidered. As for the category of creativity itself:

> "creativity" is a convenient term for collecting many interesting artifacts, processes, and people into a single category, and the term "creative thinking skills" may be a useful way to connect a diverse set of unrelated cognitive processes that operate on different content and in different domains. These concepts are misleading, however, because although they connect things that may seem similar to observers, they lack any underlying cognitive psychological validity.[18]

In other words, although a jazz pianist, an engineer, and a child may all do things that strike us as "creative," there doesn't appear to be any psychological fact uniting them. From a psychological perspective, it seems, there may be no such thing as "creativity."

Already by the 1960s critics pointed out that "creativity" was often simply a catchall term for various qualities that researchers considered positive. Hudson, for example, wrote:

> This odd word is now part of psychological jargon, and covers everything from the answers to a particular kind of psychological test, to forming a good relationship with one's wife. "Creativity," in other words, applies to all those qualities of which psychologists approve. And like so many other virtues—justice, for example—it is as difficult to disapprove of as to say what it means.[19]

The definitional ambiguity was, as we have seen, long a point of frustration. The psychologist H. Herbert Fox, invited to a major creativity symposium in the late 1950s, became exasperated after hearing dozens of papers, none of which bothered to offer a precise definition of the word. "Words, more words and still more words. Vague, meandering, evasive, elusive, and incomprehensible," he wrote, "nothing is more indicative of the loose thinking and the chaotic state of the subject than the fact that one may read millions of words on any of the manifold aspects of creativity without ever once seeing it defined." Researchers used the term "with complete abandon" on the "tacit assumption" that readers knew what they meant by it, but "in the present inchoate state of the subject," Fox wrote, "there is no surety that others think of creativity as we do."[20] A reviewer of the proceedings of that symposium concluded, "one is almost persuaded that the term 'creativity' is a barrier to understanding and can be dropped as superfluous."[21]

Long Live Creativity

Creativity researchers often accused their critics of simply standing in the way of progress, stodgily hanging on to outdated notions of genius or intelligence. When on the defensive they sometimes compared themselves to the creative individual, always ahead of their time, pushing confidently and alone against society's natural resistance to change. But creativity researchers could not help but acknowledge their definitional difficulties. Already by the third Utah Conference in 1959, Calvin Taylor acknowledged that "no single definition [of creativity] has yet been prepared that suits all workers in the field," and that the plethora of incompatible criteria was an obstacle to further study.[22] The psychology professor Irving Taylor likewise acknowledged in 1959 that because creativity "means anything ranging from the child's first expressive 'tadpole' drawings of the human figure to Einstein's formulation of the relation between matter and energy, its communicative effectiveness is greatly reduced," and that "when a term embraces too many meanings, some of which may be contradictory, to avoid confusion the term itself must be examined."[23] His review of over a hundred definitions of creativity revealed five "distinct psycholinguistic clusters of usages." Yet, as a true believer in the viability of creativity research, he inferred not that there were five different phenomena going by the name of creativity, but rather that creativity was one thing with "five levels," ranging from the "expressive creativity" of a child to the "emergentive creativity" of the paradigm-shifting thinker. Similar schemes to account for the various "aspects" or "dimensions" of creativity abounded. One widely adopted scheme differentiated between "Big C" creativity, for great works of art and scientific breakthroughs, and "little c creativity" for everyday creations and problem-solving. Another posited the "Four P's of Creativity"—Person, Process, Product, and Place (meaning environment)—to account for the fact that studies of each of those would not necessarily overlap.[24]

In other words, even as doubts emerged that any general thing called creativity really existed, the true believers saw the problem as akin to the blind men and the elephant, as one described it—with individuals simply grasping small parts of one big thing. Calvin Taylor concluded that the multiplicity of definitions was to be expected since "creativity can be expressed variously in many different ways and media."[25] In Taylor's language we can see how thoroughly reified, hardened, the concept of creativity had become. Even though the research had made it abundantly clear that creativity was "complex" rather than "unitary," there had emerged a hardened sense that "it" was still there, waiting, as Taylor put it, to be "expressed."

Perhaps the best illustration of the faith that something called creativity existed, psychologically speaking, is the way creativity researchers were able to ignore other, likelier explanations for creative accomplishment. The most obvious of these were "external" or "environmental" factors such as education and class, which were generally considered outside the scope of psychology. One reputable study found that creative scientists often had professional fathers and were more likely to have supported their educations with scholarships or fellowships than with part-time work.

(Whether or not independent means were ruled out in the study is unclear.) The study also showed that creative scientists worked more hours and published more during graduate school than non-creative scientists. But rather than interpret this coincidence as linked—to theorize for example that those who had to pay their own way may have had less time to study and publish—the author ignored the various kinds of privilege likely at work and chalked up success to "motivation."[26]

In fact, motivation, dedication, and hard work (and the time and space to act on it) do seem to be the most common factors in creative accomplishment, whether in studies of successful scientists, architects, artists, or dead masters. The research was inconclusive on whether creative people had high IQs, showed promise early or late, were introverts or extroverts, were generalists or specialists, or were much better at divergent thinking than the general population. But one thing they all had in common was a single-minded devotion to their work. This should hardly have been surprising. The importance of persistence had long been established as both inherited wisdom and scientific fact. Catherine Cox's 1926 study had found that "high but not the highest intelligence, combined with the greatest degree of persistence, will achieve greater eminence than the highest degree of intelligence with somewhat less persistence."[27] But this was simply scientific evidence of the commonsense creed that, as Edison put it, success was "1 percent inspiration, 99 percent perspiration."

When the data from postwar creativity research confirmed this traditional wisdom, one might have expected Calvin Taylor, for example, to report back to his NSF funders that they should simply look for hard workers with reasonably high IQs and give them time and space. However, having committed themselves to something larger called creativity, Taylor and the others kept looking for it. Guilford even dismissed the idea that persistence was the single best predictor of creative success: "[Persistence] is a trait that may contribute to achievement and eminence in any field . . . [but] there is no indication that it has a unique relation to creativity." In retrospect, it is not clear there was any indication that the creative accomplishments Guilford was out to explain were a product of anything more than hard work, but such was the accumulated ontological mass of the concept of creativity. Such was its power to frame narratives and explain reality. The very concept of creativity, in other words, made scientists continue to look for it.

:::

We may never know how many psychologists, having foreseen or glimpsed the problems in creativity research, quietly avoided the field. It does seem that by the late 1960s the bubble was beginning to deflate. By 1965, a high-water mark in creativity publishing, funding for the Utah Conferences, the IPAR creativity studies, and Guilford's Aptitudes Project, among others, had expired. Torrance, possibly because of questions around his scholarship, left the University of Minnesota. By 1964, even Calvin Taylor admitted that "like creative effort itself, research on creativity must be able to live with imperfections, inevitable incompleteness, a poignant sense of unrealized intention, a need finally to recognize that in many ways it has fallen short."[28] By 1969, a somewhat chastened Frank Barron warned creativity researchers against "taking too seriously the singularity of its own vision."[29]

By the late 1960s, as their funders and departments began to move on, creativity psychologists found friendly terrain in the applied world of "creative problem solving." When the first journal dedicated to creativity research was established, in 1967, it was under the auspices of the Creative Education Foundation (CEF) in Buffalo, the organization Alex Osborn had established to spread his creative thinking gospel (see chapter 2). It seems likely to have been established at least in part to make space for creativity research that was no longer finding favor in existing academic journals.[30] From the 1960s until at least the 1980s Barron, Torrance, and Guilford were regular contributors and leaders of the organization.[31] Perhaps this was only natural. Despite some initial mutual misgivings between the empirical and the applied creativity camps, there was an ethic of mutual open-mindedness and common ground in their missions to promote creativity.

For all its troubles, creativity research reflected an earnest desire to recalibrate the tools with which psychologists sorted human resources around a new notion of excellence for the postwar world. Creativity signified something more democratic than genius, yet more heroic than intelligence; more whimsical than mere inventiveness or ingenuity, but more useful than mere imagination or artisticness. It was the common thread that connected—they imagined, anyway—military and cultural and spiritual progress, the Edisons of the past with the white-collar workers of the future. Navigating between humanistic ideals and the demands of the military-industrial complex, and looking for a way to "move between the commonplace and the sublime," these experts helped forge a new psychological category and the technologies that made it more real.[32]

The definitional expansiveness of creativity was both the fatal flaw and the enabling condition of creativity research. Though it made the consolidation of knowledge nearly impossible, it also facilitated the coming together of disparate methodologies, theoretical backgrounds, and tendencies within the psychological profession. These tendencies and the people who represented them were in a sense drawn to one another by the promise of mutual redemption. The humanistic ideas of Maslow, Rogers, and Barron helped the psychometricians articulate a more expansive social and moral ambit than simply staffing the military-industrial complex, while the humanists drew a sense of importance and urgency from the fact their wisdom was sought by those who held the survival of the free world in their hands. By embracing both the hyper-rational psychometric and the interpretive psychoanalytic approaches, the field of creativity research gained a powerful claim to significance, linking immediate strategic needs with broader questions about democracy, work, and the American character. The fact that creativity research brought military brass into the same room as those who wanted oddball schoolkids to thrive made all involved feel the importance of their pursuit. We can see in this synthesis a particularly Cold War desire to temper hardheaded rationalism with a humane touch. As Liam Hudson noted, one might have expected creativity researchers' preoccupation with physical scientists on behalf of the American "armaments industry" to "tell against the 'tender-minded' progressive traditions within psychology and to tell in favour of the 'tough-minded' scientific behaviorists and mental testers." But, he observed, "the overriding character of the 'creativity' literature is one of enlightened, progressive humanism."[33] True, in many cases these various voices were talking past each other, even sometimes against each other. But in their attempts to reconcile their differences we can see the striving of the psychological profession to match the ambitions of its age.

From Progress
to Creativity

8

If you went to school in America after 1968 there's a very good chance that once or twice your teacher pulled out the projector or A/V cart, dimmed the lights, and popped on a charming little twenty-five-minute film called "Why Man Creates." The Academy Award winner for best short film was written and directed by Saul Bass and originally aired on the first episode of CBS's *60 Minutes*. It now sits in the Library of Congress National Film Registry and is said to be the most viewed educational film of all time. The film begins with an animation—think *School House Rock* or *The Point*—recapitulating the history of Western progress in a hilariously accelerated four minutes. As the camera slowly pans up to accommodate the accumulating pile of discoveries, ideas, and inventions we watch the familiar stages of civilization unfold: a prehistoric hunt, painting on a cave, inventing the wheel, inventing new gods, building pyramids, chiseling an alphabet into stone, forging tools from iron and bronze. Greeks philosophize, Romans rise and fall. The Dark Ages give way to the Enlightenment, and up and up, ever faster, to Watt and his steam engine, Beethoven at his piano, Edison and his electric lamp. Freud says that Darwin says that man is an animal. As masses gather, men on soapboxes spout political slogans, a crescendo of cars, planes, and television sets pile up in a cacophonous blur until finally, suddenly, the camera stops. A single, tiny, lonely man stands atop it all, engulfed in a swirling radioactive cloud, coughing, howling something into the emptiness.

An odd start, perhaps, to a film extolling the virtues of creativity. But immediately following this arch overture, typical of a certain 1960s cynicism toward consumerism and technology run amok, the film abruptly shifts to a playful, optimistic tone. "Where do ideas come from?" a gentle-voiced narrator wistfully wonders, as we are led through a series of short "explorations, episodes, and comments on creativity." In an adorable stop-motion "parable" about defying social expectations, a Ping-Pong ball gets ejected from an assembly line for exceeding the standard bounce height, but eventually finds an admiring Ping-Pong-ball crowd who cheer as it bounces higher and higher, off into space. We learn that ideas come from "fooling around," but also (quoting Edison, Hemingway, and Einstein) from grit and hard work. We learn, as angry passersby sling insults at some off-camera piece of art, that society will resist new ideas. The film's protagonist, a vaguely hippie-ish white man, appears dressed as a movie cowboy and takes these criticisms as shots to the gut. At one point a cartoon snail wonders out loud, "have you ever thought that radical ideas threaten institutions then become institutions and in turn reject radical ideas which threaten institutions?" Finally, a tone of reverent wonder returns and the narrator poses the film's fundamental question, "Why does man create?" Over a montage of ancient art, a rocket launching, impressionist paintings, sheet music, and a bit of graffiti, he answers: "Among all the variety of human expression, a thread of connection, a common mark can be seen: that urge to look into oneself, and out at the world, and say 'this is what I am. I am unique. I am here. I am.'" The thesis seems to be that each advance, from the Pythagorean Theorem to Marxism to the atom bomb to the Boeing 747, came ultimately from one person's desire to express their individuality. This claim—more believable in the case of an oil painting than in the invention of TNT—is, as we've seen, the kernel of the postwar concept of creativity itself: the individual origin of every new thing under the sun. The myriad social factors—the institutions that decide what gets invented, that coordinate the labor of thousands—are ignored. All that is left is the lone creator, yearning to be seen.

The film never gets around to addressing why, if it all adds up to a heap of toxic rubbish, creativity is such a good thing to begin with. It turns out the "why" in the film's title does not refer to the question of ultimate purposes—*for what* does man create—but rather its inciting urges. The strange juxtaposition of techno-skepticism from the movie's opening with the glowing portrait of the creative process in the rest of the film can be summarized by a slogan: progress is dead; long live creativity.

The question is, why would Kaiser Aluminum, the Oakland corporation who hired Bass to produce the film, be interested in such a message? If Kaiser executives felt any misgivings about the sight of airplane fuselages in an apocalyptic pile, it certainly didn't stop them from releasing the film. In fact, the Oakland-based company, America's third-largest aluminum producer, which manufactured, among other things, military jet fuselages and TV tray dinners (a better encapsulation of the military-consumer nexus is hard to imagine), screened the film for thousands of their employees before the rest of the country got to see it. They concurrently distributed a spectacular special issue of *Kaiser Aluminum News*, called "You and Creativity," in which full-color psychedelic posters from San Francisco studios sat alongside quotations from Carl Rogers, Abraham Maslow, J. P. Guilford, Frank Barron, Alex Osborn, and Synectics, Inc., and creativity exercises, including one where readers could challenge themselves to list unusual uses for a brick. It was a sort of sampler platter of the various takes on creativity that had accumulated over the previous two decades, from the practical to the rhapsodic.

We have seen how corporate America both consumed and produced creativity knowledge, from scientific studies to applied creative engineering programs, as it attempted to foster innovation while also combating alienation and public skepticism. Through the notion of creativity the various critiques of mass society could be assimilated into the very heart of the system. (As we saw in his invective about brainstorming, Bass himself was ambivalent about his role in the march of modern civilization, acknowledging that advertising professionals might be simply "drug peddlers.") "The Creativity Film," as Bass privately called it, points to a specific way in which corporate America enlisted the idea of creativity to address a crisis of faith in technology during a time when the notion of progress, on which industry's moral claims had long rested, was seriously compromised.

But how, exactly? As Carl Rogers noted, creativity was essentially an amoral concept. "We get nowhere by trying to differentiate 'good' and 'bad' purposes in the creative process," he wrote, for "one man may be discovering a way of relieving pain, while another is devising a new and more subtle form of torture for political prisoners."[1] Even that boosterish issue of *Kaiser Aluminum News* admitted, "slums and wars and the weapons of war; poverty and crime, garbage and pollution are as much the created products of man as the painting on the easel, the machinery in the factory, the music in the air. . . . There is nothing in the creative act that guarantees that the creative product will be beneficial or useful."[2] Yet while the products of creativity might be heinous, creativity itself was considered innocent. It was, as Maslow said, "prevaluational, premoral, pre-ethical, precultural . . . prior to good and evil."[3]

For a firm like Kaiser, or any of the other companies in postwar America, to embrace creativity was to shift the focus, as the film quite literally does, from product to process. Indeed, the products in the film are always vague—literally off screen, or so silly and abstract that they don't point to anything in particular. Where actual products are pictured, a point is always made to include representative examples from art, science, technology, and the humane letters. In the slide from product to process, and in the equivalency of scribblings, high art, philosophy, and high tech, the act of creation becomes something both general and neutral. This supposed moral neutrality of the creative process made it an attractive subject for those who wanted to make technology more humane, or those who at least wanted to make it seem more humane. In some cases, as we'll see in this chapter, creativity was held up as an explicitly moralizing counterforce to technology, the assumption being that "creative" thinking was wiser and would lead to more socially responsible creations. But in other cases, creativity solved the moral dilemmas of science and technology by simply sidestepping them altogether, by shifting the focus from *products* to *process*, and from the social matrix to the individual creator. The concept of creativity recast technology not as the result of a mindless, inhuman system but as a series of innocent and passionate individuals who dared defy the crowd. This narrative gave scientific and technical workers and the companies that employed them a new transcendent value by which to understand, and communicate, the value of their work.

Technoscience Run Amok

The era after World War II was marked by a profound ambivalence about science, technology, and possibility of progress. The leftist theorist Lewis Mumford, who before the war had written breathlessly of the humane possibilities of "technics" in the hands of the collective, became a postwar pessimist of the "megamachine." As the Cold War gradually gave the lie to any swords-to-plowshares dream of the postwar order, Mumford was joined by others, such as the theologian Jacques Ellul, who took aim at the efficiency-obsessed, instrumentalist mindset that infiltrated every area of life, sucking all the humane and moral content out of society.[4]

Postwar observers were troubled by the Cold War's entangling of science and technology. As corporations snapped up a larger and larger share of PhDs, and universities set up research centers run like corporations, with personnel moving freely between academia, government, and industry, the lines between "research" and "development," "pure" and "applied" science were constantly being blurred.[5] One observer declared, "that we need a single word to mean both engineer and scientist, that the two form a single community, is obvious."[6] This was a dramatic departure from the traditional liberal model in which, according to the historian Steven Shapin, "the goal of scientific inquiry was Truth; the goal of business was Profit. The natural agent of pure scientific inquiry was the free-acting individual; the natural agent of applied research and development was the organized team."[7] William Whyte's concern that the over-management of scientists would shut down progress was accompanied by a concern that it would also stifle the moral agency of the individual scientist. The managers who championed the "social ethic," he wrote, "tend to assume the ends of the organization and morality coincide," while recent history, particularly the rise of the Third Reich, suggested otherwise.[8] Specialization, meanwhile, which the prior generation saw as the rational division of mental labor and the key to progress, was now blamed for narrowing the American mind. Industrial scientists and engineers, once seen as the enlightened leaders of a national technocracy, were in this view just so many organization men, blindly doing as they were told.

Particularly troubling from a moral point of view was how tied up science was with the military. President Dwight D. Eisenhower, in his famous speech warning of the rise of a "military-industrial complex," warned of the prospect that in universities, "historically the fountainhead of free ideas and scientific discovery . . . a government contract becomes virtually a substitute for intellectual curiosity." On the other hand was "the equal and opposite danger that public policy could itself become the captive of a scientific-technological elite."[9] The military-industrial complex, in other words, was a Faustian bargain for the white-collar professionals, giving them an undemocratic power over national life even as it sold their mental labor to the government and the capitalist class.

There was, in short, a crisis of faith not so much in technology but in technocracy. Even members of the counterculture and protest movements, with their messianic faith in the perfectibility of society, did not totally eschew the promise of technics. To the extent they had faith in a progressive technology, they (like an increasing number of technical workers) thought large-scale top-down organizations were unlikely to produce it, and instead forged a democratic, DIY ethic of technology.[10]

This all put scientists and engineers in an awkward position. They were either too powerful but not enlightened enough to serve as philosopher kings, or not powerful enough as moral agents to stand up to political pressure. Scientists and engineers were particularly sensitive to these criticisms not only because they potentially threatened public support for their livelihoods, but also because they challenged the ideals of self-negation and rationality that had justified technical work during the long Progressive Era going back to the beginning of the twentieth century. Rather than laying down their slide rules and joining a commune (or becoming humanities professors), however, most aspired to become saviors of the very technological order their ilk had created. Espousing what the historian Stephen Wisnioski calls the "ideology of technological change," they believed that technological change was inevitable and that, paradoxically perhaps, only technical experts could solve the problems caused by technology. But how? For some, creativity sounded like a good answer.

Creativity as Responsibility

One way for scientists and engineers to redeem their professions would be to take "responsibility" for the direction of technology. Prominent figures such as J. Robert Oppenheimer, the repentant father of the atomic bomb, spurred a national conversation about the importance of enlightened, democratic oversight of science and technology. While some focused on establishing regulatory institutions (e.g., the congressional Office of Technology Assessment), others focused on reforming technoscience from within.[11] This often meant inviting creativity into the mix. E. Finley Carter, director of the Stanford Research Center, acknowledged the "great deal of effort toward weapons of defense and destruction," and argued that as a countermeasure "we need to direct more creative thinking toward a better understanding of the conditions which have caused this situation."[12] Carter's center had been founded after World War II to apply Stanford University talent to for-hire projects for the military and industry. By 1959 it employed over a thousand scientists and engineers on projects ranging from social science to weapons systems. "Can we continue, with reckless abandon," Finley asked in that year, "begetting brain children which we leave to somebody else to bring up? Or does our responsibility continue? It is up to us to see that the devices we create are not left as orphans but to work with them to their maturity, so that we truly master them, so that they bring about a more abundant life."[13] Truly mastering technology also, Carter thought, would entail encouraging creativity, which involved "inward motivation" and a "sense of broader significance that the scientist derives from the work."[14] He did not spell out how intrinsically-motivated creative scientists would end up taking this greater responsibility, but he implied that their morality would serve as a rudder.

For MIT and Stanford professor John E. Arnold, who pioneered the Creative Engineering programs at General Motors, creativity could sensitize the technical mind to "social" problems. For Arnold, creative thinking meant liberation from the traditional engineering mindset.[15] The "creative engineer of the future," Arnold wrote, was "a blend . . . of the scientist and the artist": "He forms new combinations and tries to invent, as the artist does," but also "tries to do this in a very organized and deliberate fashion, as the scientist does." As the founder of the Stanford Design Institute within the Mechanical Engineering department, with a joint appointment in Mechanical Engineering and Business Management, Arnold assigned courses in literature, composition, and the fine arts to make engineers more effective at designing for people's emotional needs as well as better at communicating their ideas to others—both necessary skills in the modern consumer economy.[16] The creative engineer—which Arnold also called the "comprehensive engineer"—would be a social thinker, "world-oriented," eager to solve big problems like hunger and economic inequality. "One of the aims of Creative Engineering is to bring about a union between the physical sciences, social sciences, and the arts," he wrote. "In this way and perhaps only in this way can we be assured that our innovations better satisfy some need of man."

Arnold's purpose was surely to alleviate suffering, but it was just as much to save the engineering profession from itself. Rather than leave the design of society to the politicians, engineers should actually colonize even more areas of life. Wherever there were "creative problems"—Arnold's term for problems without a right or wrong answer—the "creative engineer" would be there. As we saw with Osborn and brainstorming, there were often anti-statist and apolitical assumptions in the notion that creative thinkers would solve "people problems." Arnold said the creative engineer would be aware of social injustices but would also understand "that these inequalities can not be corrected by a political redistribution," but must ultimately find technical solutions: "Somehow he must make every pound of material more useful, every kilowatt of energy go further, every human life . . . more effective, more efficient." Despite Arnold's overtures to the arts, his campaign to make engineering more "creative" was at heart a thoroughly rationalistic and technocratic ethos. Through the person of the engineer, creativity would somehow succeed where regulation and policy would not.

Art and Science as Acts of Creation

Finley and Arnold's faith that creativity could make technology more moral channeled a belief, inherited from the eighteenth and nineteenth centuries, that the artist had a kind of priestly role. To be creative in this sense was to approach technologies with wisdom. But the artist was a key figure for another reason: as a model of autonomy. This view of the creative artist—single-minded, in it for their own intrinsic motivation to create—was a powerful image in navigating the moral ambiguities of postwar technoscientific work. The concept of creativity named what scientists and engineers shared with artists, and artists with them.

Take for example the September 1958 issue of *Scientific American* dedicated to "Innovation in Science," which featured a detail of a Renaissance painting of baby Jesus, mother Mary, and an archangel. *Scientific American* was a key shaper of public perception of technoscience during the Cold War, pitching itself at a broad swath of engineers, scientists, and research executives but also at "the scientific layman: the growing community of US citizens who have a responsible interest in the advance and application of science."[17] Its pages boasted the newest rocket science, radar, and semiconductors—the fruits of Pentagon dollars. Most months, the cover would feature high-definition photos or mod, stylized images of gadgets, labs, or outer space.

Why, in an issue devoted specifically to innovation, with national security on everyone's minds and a world of amazing gadgets to show off, would the editors have chosen a five-hundred-year-old religious image? The British polymath Jacob Bronowski, who penned the lead article, explained that the choice of Leonardo da Vinci's *Madonna of the Rocks* (1483–1486) was to index its creator. Leonardo, Bronowski explained, was the embodiment of the natural unity between science and art; he noted the anatomical details of the bodies and the plants in the scene, which Leonardo had perfected by close scientific observation. Bronowski was known as something of a Renaissance man himself. A physicist and mathematician who also wrote on the poetry of William Blake, his influential report on the effects of the bombing of Hiroshima and Nagasaki, followed up by his book *Science and Human Values* (1956), earned him a reputation as a man of science who wasn't afraid to ask big philosophical questions.[18] (It was apparently Bronowski, by the way, who had so shaken Saul Bass by calling advertisers "drug peddlers.")[19]

Bronowski argued here that on a psychological level the distinction between science and art was artificial. In particular, science was not nearly as "rational" as its stereotypes implied. To begin with, there was something aesthetic about scientific understanding: Copernicus' theory of planetary motion came to him not by pure reason but rather by an "esthetic sense of unity," and the controversy over whether light was a wave or a particle was ultimately "a conflict between analogies, between poetic metaphors." A scientific theory was not a simple transcription of objective reality, but a creation, "an imaginative choice which outstrips the facts." Echoing John Dewey's notions that scientific understanding relied on the intuitive perception of "esthetic" unity, and that all knowledge was pursued by some underlying purpose, Bronowski argued that both science and art were driven by a will to "control our surroundings." Why should we see *Othello* as "genuinely a creation," but not Columbus's discovery of the West Indies or Bell's invention of the telephone? Just because the latter do not show "the presence of a single mind" as obviously as does a work of art, they are, according to Bronowski, essentially made of the same stuff.

In temperament, too, Bronowski said, artists and scientists were similar; the stereotype of the sober scientist and the tempestuous artist was a myth. The Irish scientist William Rowan Hamilton's drinking himself to death was "as much part of his prodigal work as is any drunken young poet."[20] (This assertion was backed up in this issue by Frank Barron, from the Institute for Personality Assessment and Research, who wrote, "certain uniformities do seem to characterize highly original scientists and artists.")[21] Tellingly, Bronowski provided few examples of the converse— rational and well-behaved artists—for his purpose here was not to convince artists they were like scientists, but to convince scientists and engineers that they were artists at heart. The article, bookended by images of cave paintings at Montignac and contemporary sculpture by Henry Moore, invited readers to place themselves in a long tradition of individual imaginations that drove the march of Western progress.

Most important for Bronowski was that true scientists, like true artists, were individualistic. Where mid-century critics celebrated science—and, to a great extent, art as well—as a collective project taken on by self-negating investigators, Bronowski cast it as a lonely and an individualistic pursuit. Science and art, he said, flourished together[22] in individualistic milieus like ancient Greece and the Renaissance, not in the "anonymous" Middle Ages or "the craftsmanlike countries of the East." This sort of claim was practically an article of faith in Cold War America. Dripping with racist and anti-Catholic assumptions, it made it easy to characterize the Soviet Union, which was both Orientalized and collectivist, as a relic in the making.

Yet this all clearly flew in the face of the reality of postwar science and technology. Not only was the Soviet Union, an expressly collectivist society, running circles around the US in technological progress; most American scientists and engineers would have had trouble seeing themselves as heroic lone geniuses in their highly collaborative, managed labs.

More relevant, perhaps, was Bronowski's implicit argument on behalf of applied science—that is, for invention over discovery. The Western individualism that allowed for new ideas to flourish, Bronowski said, went hand in hand with an "active" as opposed to a monastic or "contemplative" orientation. Against the idea that science was, or should be, essentially about objective discovery, Bronowski emphasized the scientist's inventive role. What were theories if not creations, tools, things to think with? The dichotomy between "pure" and "applied" science, he seemed to say, was as illusory as that between art and technology. All of it came down to the human drive to master our world.

Readers may have found in Bronowski's particular configuration of art, science, and technology a way to reconcile their conflicted professional identities. According to the traditional liberal view of science, independence of mind and disinterested truth-seeking went hand in hand. The mark of a true scientist was that he or she worked for themselves, or at least was protected by academic freedom, and did not invent but rather discovered. Neither presupposition fit the Cold War context very well. But if deep down everything was an invention anyway, as Bronowski suggested, there was not necessarily anything wrong with being a scientist enlisted in the invention and manufacturing of goods. Moreover, by construing independent-mindedness as a psychological rather than an institutional state, Bronowski's argument made it possible to imagine a true scientist working on an assignment rather than a project of his or her choosing. The notion that there was no such thing as passive discovery may have helped Cold War scientists feel less tension between their identities as objective truth-seekers and agents of frankly practical aims.[23] And as salaried members of a system beyond their comprehension or control, they may have also taken comfort in the idea that at least in their own heads they could be every bit as individualist as an artist. Rather than a contradiction in terms, the "creative scientist" was a new ideal.

But once again, the particular vagueness of the concept of creativity allowed it to represent the opposite side of this debate between utilitarianism and non-utilitarianism as well. Case in point: the term "creative science," though sometimes used as a synonym for "applied science," in that it created as opposed to simply discovered, also sometimes meant the opposite: a zone of pure ideas. Shortly before the *Scientific American* innovation issue came out, the magazine's editor, Dennis Flanagan, told the Art Directors Club of New York conference on creativity that the atomic bomb was not a truly creative act. This was not because it was destructive, but because it was merely a gadget. "A truly creative act in science is the discovery of a new principle, and the invention of an atomic bomb is the application of principles already known. A creative act in science is Copernicus putting the sun in the center of the solar system."[24] Our institutions, Flanagan argued, must respect this truth and protect creative scientists from the practical concerns of technology—"we must jealously maintain the distinction between science and technology."[25]

"Our society cheerfully provides funds for practical things," Flanagan continued, "but it is still suspicious of longhairs"—referring to connoisseurs of high art out of step with bourgeois respectability—and "puts cruel economic pressure on young people with scientific talent to become practical men." Flanagan believed what set these "longhairs" apart was a pure and unstoppable curiosity. Echoing Maslow, who said "a musician must make music, an artist must paint, a poet must write," Flanagan said of the creative person, "nothing on earth can stop them from wanting to know, just as nothing on earth can stop a gifted painter from wanting to paint."[26] In addition, longhairs also thought more like artists than like the practical man. Echoing Bronowski, Flanagan described the process of fundamental scientific discovery not as "the patient, mechanical collection of facts," but rather as "intuitive," "below the level of consciousness," "the way of the poet, the painter, the composer."[27] For Flanagan, true creativity was about the search for meaning itself. For the editor of a magazine that generally celebrated the marriage of science and technology, this speech is striking, though of its moment. And of course it did not make Flanagan anti-technology in the slightest. The creative person's non-utilitarianism was not, in his formulation, an ideological or political position but rather a psychological one that ultimately, through the labors of other less creative functionaries down the line, would result in material progress for the rest of us.

No matter where one stood in the technoscientific ecosystem, creativity, embodied in the artist, provided a perfect ideal. The true engineer could look to the true artist as a fellow inventor, united in the making of new things. Meanwhile the true scientist could look to the true artist as a fellow thinker, united in a dedication to ideas for their own sake. Whether one saw creativity as a trait of the pure scientist or the applied scientist, the disinterested discoverer or the solver of everyday problems, everyone could agree creativity was something technical people needed more of.

Creativity as a Corporate Value

> The ability of the creative person to communicate his ideas into practical application is universal in all fields of endeavor . . . Science as well as in the Arts. The same basic phenomenon conceives an idea and carries it through to a benefiting conclusion whether the individual is composing a symphony, writing a sonnet, developing a miracle drug, formulating a mathematical model or designing a nuclear reactor.

So ran an advertisement for the Westinghouse Bettis Atomic Energy Division, a government-owned, corporate-run research and development laboratory near Pittsburgh founded in 1949 to develop the US Navy's nuclear program. We've seen how this refrain was used by psychologists to establish the scope of their subject. But what resonance could it have with readers of *Scientific American?* The advertisements in the September special issue are just as revealing as the articles, because they show us how corporations used the concept of creativity to appeal both to the public and to the great mass of American engineers, many of them potential employees. They reveal a strategy of aligning themselves with the arts and the individual creator to portray a counter-image to that of cold, rational, and bureaucratic behemoths.

An ad for Boeing Scientific Research Laboratory featured an abstract painting of overlapping, jagged quadrangles streaking across concentric amoeboid rings. This was a painting of the constellation Cygnus created by a team of "artist-scientists" who explained, "knowledge of the Universe is not a matter of man's sight, but of his imagination's vision. Our eyes show us Cygnus. But creations of our genius, such as the radio-telescope, reveal unexplored, unexplained sources of energy that man may someday master." Echoing Bronowski, the ad copy equated telescopes and paintings, arguing that both were expressions of an impulse to master the universe. An Alcoa Chemicals ad featured a brightly colored, cubist rendering of four missiles jabbing up into the sky. (The artist, S. Neil Fujita, would provide similar abstract images for the covers of the Dave Brubeck Quintet's *Take Five* and Charles Mingus's *Mingus Ah Um*, both released the following year.) The ad boasted that engineers at an unnamed company "mix imagination with Alcoa Aluminas," a proprietary chemical product, to come up with a more heat-resistant nose cone.

One way to interpret this is as an attempt to make terrible violence look pretty. But considering how proudly missiles were on display throughout the magazine, readers of *Scientific American* were likely not gun-shy. Rather, the idea was to transform the missiles from technology into art. As art they could be seen as the product not of technical problem-solving by a corporate army but of "imagination." The viewer's eye turns from the product, a thing with a very real and potentially devastating effect on the world, to the process. Just as Bronowski and the Boeing ad had compared scientific theories and satellites to poems and paintings, so the

mix imagination with Alcoa Aluminas and see ceramics do what ceramics never did before! A case in point: Missile designers needed a nose cone material transparent to electronic impulses and able to withstand a holocaust of friction heat. Looking to high alumina ceramics—products of imagination plus Alcoa® Aluminas—they found the answer. Another case in point: Metalworkers wanted improved tool performance for finer, less costly machining. Ceramic engineers blended imagination with Alcoa Aluminas . . . developed sapphire-hard alumina ceramic cutting tools now setting new records of metalworking quality and tool durability. The cases in point are almost endless. When *you* are faced with a tough materials problem, see what ceramics can do when you mix imagination and engineering with Alcoa Aluminas. Contact our nearest sales office or outline your problems in a letter to ALUMINUM COMPANY OF AMERICA, CHEMICALS DIVISION, 706-J Alcoa Building, Pittsburgh 19, Pennsylvania.

For finer products . . . let Alcoa add new directions to your creative thinking!

Figure 8.1 "Let Alcoa add new directions to your creative thinking!" Mixing art with technology during the Cold War. Alcoa 1958.

Alcoa ad rendered ICBMs as stylized expressions of the human imagination.

This whimsical sensibility of the "mix it with imagination" ads was part of a larger Alcoa campaign around mixing art and engineering. In 1957, Alcoa hired the designer John Neuhart of the

Charles and Ray Eames studio to design a "Do-nothing Machine" using Alcoa's materials and photovoltaic cells. Art, embodied by Neuhart himself and by the colorful and openly non-utilitarian gizmo he designed, here signified the human imagination in its purest form. This was a nonutilitarian twist on the Bronowski thesis: innovation comes not out of a drive for mastery, but out of play and whimsy. It also implied that pure technology, like pure science, had no determined underlying purpose. Whatever those photovoltaic cells had originally been invented for—maybe it was powering satellites, maybe it was powering cars—the eventual applications were as boundless as the human imagination. That a manufacturer known for creating utterly purposeful products backed by hard-core materials science would pay a designer for a machine that did nothing, or a painter to soften its nose cones in brush strokes, suggests some of the ambivalence corporations were feeling about technological progress.[28]

Taken together, these ads and promotional gizmos can be read as attempts to show that these companies were guided not by a smug notion of technological progress nor the impersonal forces of geopolitics but rather by the individual minds of their creative employees. These public image campaigns seem to have been targeted not only to a general public but specifically to employees and would-be employees themselves. As they beckoned new engineers to sprawling corporate campuses in suburban New Jersey, Boston, and the Sunbelt, these companies projected an image of autonomy, free play, and respect that went under the heading of creativity. The Westinghouse Atomic ad that compared a nuclear reactor to a sonnet also claimed the company was "one of the foremost champions of the creative individual in Science." "We take pride in recognizing [creativity] in the individual," developing it through "training and exercise, and by making available the environmental factors that encourage it." Many firms emphasized a creative environment. "The Climate's Right at Link-Palo Alto," boasted an ad for Link Aviation, clarifying that they meant both the temperate weather and the proper "mental" climate for creative work. Referencing the recently announced "missile gap" between the United States and the USSR, an ad for General Electric's Missile and Ordnance Systems Department boasted it "Narrows the Gap . . . between an engineer's inborn potential and creative output." Emphasizing that "many—perhaps a majority—of engineers and scientists are acutely aware that the full force of their creative powers are seldom, if ever, brought to bear upon a problem," GE promised that the common roadblocks to the "full realization of creativity," such as "inflexible directives," "assignments lacking in scientific challenge," and "indifference to an individual's ideas," were not to be found there.[29]

The sheer number of ads begging for talent attests to the meteoric rise of the engineering profession in the Cold War. The fact that they appealed to would-be employees not by highlighting pay, benefits, or esprit de corps, but by emphasizing the opportunity to be creative (in its multiple senses), attests to the challenge of legitimacy the profession was beginning to face along the way. Due to overlapping concerns about white-collar alienation, militarism, and the moral limits of a technocratic society, traditional appeals to professionalism and expertise were now being joined by more personal, expressive values. And innovation itself was beginning to be recast not as the mechanized social process envisioned by the original champions of organized science, but rather as an accumulation of ideas, each one emanating from a single, unfettered, whole—in a word, creative—mind.

: : :

We have seen how the concept of creativity served as a psychological fix for the structural contradictions of postwar America. It reconciled a newfound individualism—which itself contained progressive, liberal, and reactionary ingredients—with the seemingly incontrovertible facts of mass society. We saw it blossom in the soil of Cold War America, where a particular mix of strategic, economic, and ideological pressures came together. We have seen how, for its most ardent champions, the notion of creativity had it all: it represented excellence against mass mediocrity but also

the democratic potential of an open society; it represented dynamism and innovation without being anarchic; and it stood for a
much-needed shot of humanism into a world of engineers, while
fundamentally endorsing innovation, consumerism, and economic growth. And we've seen how it fused productivity with
self-actualization, enabling the return of an older bourgeois producer ethic, albeit in a softer, more psychological, and somewhat
feminized form, in a consumerist era.

What remains to be done is to explain how this all relates to the
very different world that arose after the 1960s.

Long Live Creativity

9

So far we've seen how the concept of creativity was a creature of postwar America, with its Cold War and consumerism and its particular hang-ups about conformity and alienation. But the career of creativity was only just getting started. The decades since the 1970s are really when creativity worked its way into our collective vocabulary and common sense to the point that the culture of America as well as many parts of Europe, Australia, and Asia can be characterized by what the scholar Andreas Reckwitz calls a "creativity dispositif," a general orientation toward creativity built into our language, our institutions, our identities.[1]

This has been accomplished by innumerable utterances and initiatives, mission statements and lesson plans, miniseries and graduation speeches. In pure numerical terms, according to Google Books, in the year 2000 we used the term "creativity" twice as frequently as in 1970. In many ways this is a sign of general diffusion of the term into our everyday speech, including in casual instances in which we might previously have reached for other terms like "imagination" or "ingenuity." To that extent we're seeing some lessening specificity; as many a critic has pointed out, the term is becoming a buzzword far beyond the bounds of official creativity discourse. But at the same time, the word's meaning has been scaffolded along the way by the production and institutionalization of creativity knowledge and expertise. This has largely been due to the continuation of the two strands we've been following so far: academic psychology and "applied creativity." According to the editors of the *Encyclopedia of Creativity* (one flagship of new creativity knowledge), between 1999 and 2011 there were more books and articles published on creativity than in the previous forty years combined.[2] In this final chapter we will briefly drop in on those fields from the 1970s through the 2000s before looking at a cluster of phenomena in the late 1990s and early 2000s—the rise of "creative industries," "the creative class," "creative cities," and so on—that represents both a product of and a major new development in the reification of creativity. These examples will help us see how the concept of creativity thrived in, and in some senses even enabled, the significant upheavals that divided our own era from the immediate postwar decades.

The Post-Postwar

Sometime around 1973 the postwar order, the crucible in which the concept of creativity first solidified, began to fall apart. Economically, it was the first time in a generation that domestic growth slowed and real wages began to stagnate. Soon came oil shocks, pollution, stagflation. Suddenly all the worrying about what we would do with ourselves in an "affluent society" seemed almost quaint, yielding to deep doubts about the possibility of never-ending growth upon which the whole postwar order had been based. With the Democratic Party riven by internal contradictions and Keynesian planners momentarily without answers, a new cadre of cheerleaders for the free market came into power, enacting a raft of measures meant to shrink the state. The postwar assumption that rules and regulations were necessary to prosperity gave way to a new Wild West of deregulation, devolution, and casualization of labor.

These so-called neoliberal reforms intensified the trend toward postindustrialism that had started in the 1950s. Transnational corporations, while ballooning in absolute size through mergers and acquisitions, also began to dissolve in many ways. To escape unions and shrink labor costs they not only moved their factories abroad, but in many cases sold them off completely, contracting out orders to increasingly complex and faceless global networks of interchangeable bidders, and retaining in-house only the production of intellectual property, design, and marketing. It's a phenomenon perhaps best summed up by the eight words stamped onto every Apple product: "Designed by Apple in California. Assembled in China."

The postindustrial narrative is, it must be said, a selective picture and something of a self-fulfilling prophecy. The US was still the largest manufacturer in the world well into the twenty-first century, and money was still being made in manufacturing; it just wasn't getting spread around the country as much. The brightest spots seemed to be in the functions that were slower to be exported and that could still thrive amidst, or even on, growing inequality—the so-called FIRE industries (finance, insurance, and real estate), and engineering, design, marketing, entertainment, and media. These remaining sources of high-quality American jobs were, consequently, the sectors that got the most attention from economists, policy makers, and those hoping to find an optimistic tale to tell about America's future. Hence, although the largest job growth was in the low-wage service sector of retail, hospitality, and the like, this "new economy" became understood to be an "information," or "knowledge," or, as we'll see, "creative economy," as if dirty industry had simply been replaced by something cleaner and smarter.

Where the old order, the Fordist order, thought of itself as rooted in the hard stuff of manufacturing and the grit of labor, the new order, or so it tells itself, doesn't make goods but rather experiences, lifestyles, identities, images. Companies are now routinely referred to as simply "brands"; Even restaurants, apparently, are now merely "concepts." Indeed, many of us have found ourselves in some way in the business of creating content, messaging, ideas, designs, identities. Even our leisure time somehow seems bound up in producing or consuming free content for the platforms of the attention economy. All that was solid has melted into air. The whole vibe is one of flux, a state of "liquid" modernity, as Zygmunt Bauman put it: capital, like fluid, seeks the lowest ground, and, with nothing left to stop it, we all try to go with the flow.[3]

This new economic order was attended by a change in values. Where once society prized dependability, loyalty, expertise, and teamwork, this new order preaches entrepreneurship, flexibility, going against the grain.[4] Now everyone, from hospitals to whiskeys, claims to be "innovative" and "disruptive." The job security promised under Fordism has gone out the window. No more gold watch after forty years at a company; now we work for four companies by the time we're thirty. More and more work is done on a project basis involving contractors and subcontractors and consultants and freelancers and temps. Precarity is the norm. We work gigs (the artsy phrase is not a coincidence), and even though a lot of work seems as rote and pointless as ever, we try hard to follow the instructions Steve Jobs bestowed upon the Stanford graduating class of 2005: "do what you love."[5]

In one popular version of this narrative, this new ethos was an internet-era product of hippies who grew up to be entrepreneurs. Indeed, the 1970s onward has been a boom time for personal liberation, self-help, human potential, the free play of identity and lifestyle. And though many of these efforts have at least an implicitly revolutionary program, they have also, as observers have been saying since the end of the 1960s at least, dovetailed nicely with a hypercharged consumer capitalism that caters to our yearnings for self-actualization. As we have seen, though, the seeds of this "new" culture of capitalism were already sprouting in the 1950s. The prophets of the postindustrial society, including those who championed creativity, had already begun to make the arrival of that society seem like a commonsense outcome. And though they might not have predicted or supported the erosion of social contract liberalism, they would likely have smiled upon the new norms that they helped promote. The disdain for bureaucracy and the complacent, 9-to-5 culture of industrial work; the valorization of rootlessness, adaptability, and uncompromising individualism; the conviction that passion can and should drive one's work; and the unwavering faith in the power of crazy new ideas to solve every sort of problem—all of these values, born out of the failings of the Fordist corporate order, have become the animating ideals of the new economy. In this sense the cult of creativity can be seen as a kind of ideological bridge between the postwar era and our own—despite all the fractures of the post-Sixties era, creativity is one thing that remained intact.

Continuity and Change in the Institutions of Creativity

When we left our story of creativity research in the mid-1960s the field was in an awkward moment, having established an impressive corpus of research and institutional might, but also conceptually confused about its very subject and facing a backlash from the wider profession. After a lull in academic creativity studies in the 1970s, a new generation of researchers picked up the banner of creativity.

Some of this new research reflected larger trends in the social sciences. On one hand was the rediscovery of the "social" that attended the New Left's entry into academia. Many researchers felt the first generation of creativity research was overly concerned with the "creative individual," and turned to looking at how social and cultural contexts affected creative behavior.[6] Nevertheless, this socially oriented research still concerned itself primarily with how context affects the creativity of the individual and has often reinforced autonomist notions of creativity, such as the finding by Theresa Amabile that creativity depends on "intrinsic motivation" rather than external rewards.[7]

A second and somewhat opposite trend has been the rise of neuroscience. The allure of being able to crack the mysteries of everything from love to drug addiction by looking inside the brain has captured the imagination of our era, and it's no surprise that people should turn their magnetic gaze to creativity, in much the same spirit in which Guilford applied his empirical methods. One widely reported 2008 study had a jazz pianist lie down in a fMRI machine with a keyboard suspended in front of him, to see what regions of his brain lit up when playing a solo.[8] Many studies in both social psychology and neuroscience have continued to utilize divergent thinking tests such as the Guilford battery and the Torrance Tests of Creative Thinking, despite long-standing questions about their predictive validity.

Through it all, the "great person" tradition has also continued apace in, for example, Howard Gardner's book *Creating Minds: An Anatomy of Creativity Seen Through the Lives of Freud, Einstein, Picasso, Stravinsky, Eliot, Graham, and Gandhi*. Dean Keith Simonton, a leading authority on creativity and the author of such books such as *Genius, Creativity, and Leadership* and *Greatness*, has devoted his career to understanding "eminence, giftedness, and talent in science, philosophy, literature, music, art, cinema, politics, and war." Perhaps the most widely cited turn-of-the-millennium creativity writer, Mihalyi Csikszentmihalyi, who spent his early career under the tutelage of Jacob Getzels (whose landmark 1962 study *Creativity and Intelligence* argued that creativity deserved to be seen as its own distinct kind of ability), later criticized his mentor for overly generously equating creativity with "divergent thinking," and sought to put the study of creativity back on solid ground by starting with an unambiguously creative test population. He studied dozens of eminent individuals including the sociologist David Riesman, the naturalist Steven Jay Gould, and the pianist Oscar Peterson. (He also included John Gardner, the psychologist, statesman, and funder of creativity research; and Motorola CEO Robert Galvin, a longtime champion of creativity who reportedly distributed copies of Alex Osborn's *Your Creative Power* to every employee of his company.)[9]

But as always the point of these works is not to understand genius or eminence for its own sake; rather, it is to extract lessons for the rest of us. Amabile explained that scholars "strive to understand the experiences of Picasso, da Vinci, Einstein" to see "what, if anything, we ourselves have in common with these amazing individuals." Understanding creative people could, Csikszentmihalyi wrote in his 1997 study *Creativity*, "make our own lives directly more interesting and productive."[10] The creative life could be a "model," "a way of being that is more satisfying than most lives typically are." The purpose of his book was to tell readers "how to make your life more like that of the creative exemplars" therein.[11]

Despite the waning of the Cold War and the Fordist order, creativity researchers have continued to be motivated by a fear that the institutions of modern society are hampering progress, and a faith that only through creative thinking can civilization be saved. Amabile and Hennessey write, "it is only with creativity that we can hope to address the myriad problems facing our schools and medical facilities, our cities and towns, our economy, our nation, and the world. Creativity is one of the key factors that drive civilization forward."[12] Csikszentmihalyi, calling creativity the "cultural equivalent" of biological evolution, said we must understand creativity because "solutions to poverty or overpopulation will not appear magically by themselves."[13] As in the beginning, research on creativity is motivated by a distinct worry that there's not enough of it.

Contemporary creativity researchers still deal with the criteria problem that plagued their postwar forebears. It is still not clear that findings from an fMRI study of jazz pianists is commensurate with the biographies of eminent scientists. Still, the urge to unify the field is strong. Amabile and Hennessey worry that the outpouring of new creativity research is leading to "fragmentation" in the field and recommend an "all-encompassing" theory to bring together research ranging from "the innermost neurological level to the outermost cultural level."[14] They represent such a hypothetical theory by a series of concentric circles with neurological research at the center, then cognitive, personality, group, and finally society factors radiating out from there.[15] Despite the social turn, the creative person—or really, the creative brain—is still at the center of this concept.

As before, the growth of the field of academic creativity studies went hand in hand with the growth of the field of "applied creativity." As brainstorming became so ubiquitous that we forgot it even had a history, the numbers of creativity methods, classes, and consultants has expanded every year, introducing ever more people to the gospel that they, too, can be creative. It's also spread around the world. In 2019 I went to work in the Industrial Design Engineering Department at the Delft University of Technology, the Netherlands' largest science and technology school. On my first day I walked by a studio where the word "synectics" was up on a screen. Baffled at my excitement, students explained that they were in a course on design methods and were learning about techniques for stimulating creativity. Not long after, I was invited to join a team of instructors developing a new minor in creativity. Having studied creativity in various university programs around the world, they considered Alex Osborn, Sidney Parnes, and Joy Paul Guilford the undisputed founders of the field, and included them in the new curriculum. Shortly thereafter, I attended an event of the European Association for Creativity and Innovation, where Bea Parnes, the widow and longtime standard-bearer of Sidney Parnes's Buffalo legacy, was an honored (virtual) guest.

Buffalo remains a hub for the field—the Creative Problem Solving Institute is still held every year there and the International Center for Creativity Studies at Buffalo State College, which Parnes established in 1967, now grants both a Master of Science and an undergraduate minor in creativity—but it has since been joined by a number of other centers for the study and practice of creativity, including the Torrance Center for Creativity and Talent Development at the University of Georgia. Though many alumni from such programs go on to careers in management, marketing, and the arts, many become consultants and facilitators themselves. New variants have been proliferating all the while, the latest it seems being Design Thinking, which bears amazing parallels with brainstorming. Both are characterized by a series of replicable steps and their signature material accoutrements—if brainstorming's was the idea list, Design Thinking's is the Post-it note, which multiplies across every surface of a DT session. Both were institutionalized in quasi-academic centers—DT has the Hasso Plattner Institute of Design, better known as the d.school, at Stanford. Like Osborn, DT's main exponent, David Kelley, believes DT can be used to solve any kind of problem. Kelley, a practitioner of "human-centered design," believes design should focus on "systemic" change and that true creativity involves "empathy" that produces more humane solutions. Accordingly, like Osborn, Kelley believes DT should be practiced in every field and incorporated into the curriculum in every department. Like brainstorming, Design Thinking has faced some push-back both among designers (who see it as a rosy oversimplification of what designers actually do) and in the liberal arts (where some consider it overly utilitarian and geared toward commercial problems rather than the tricky political and philosophical issues it implies it can solve).

Indeed, as always, the quest for creativity, be it in academia or in applied creativity, is most often implicitly or explicitly oriented around industry. Much of the recent creativity research has come out of the field of organization studies, and many of the top researchers are located within business schools. Many academic centers that support creativity research tend to be collaborations with design, engineering, or business schools rather than with the arts, humanities, policy, or social justice.[16] Applied creativity folks, a warm and lively bunch, have an ambivalence about the fact that business accounts pay most of their bills. They often see themselves as on the fringe of, or even outside of, staid business culture. Within those spaces they are often the ones urging for a more "human-centered" or "responsible" approach to problem solving. At the same time, they have an almost pure faith that solving problems in any context is a good thing, as long as it involves creativity.

The Permanent Myths

One of the most curious things about contemporary creativity literature is that even after seventy years creativity experts are apparently *still* waging war against the Romantic misconceptions about creativity that Guilford and Barron and Maslow said they were trying to clear up when the field emerged.

"We've romanticized the notion of the lone poet starving in a garret or scribbling away by a pond far from civilization," writes the former *BussinessWeek* editor and Parsons Professor of Innovation and Design Bruce Nussbaum, but "a growing body of research reveals that we all have the capacity to be creative."[17] The popular training video *Everyday Creativity* promises to reveal "a surprising truth about creativity: that it's not a magical, mysterious occurrence, but a ready tool." The psychologist Robert Sternberg, editor of the *Encyclopedia of Creativity*, writes that "people often speak of creativity as though it were a prized possession of only a few. . . . Although the contributions of people like Van Gogh, Milton, or Beethoven are of great interest . . . we believe that creativity, like intelligence, is something that everyone possesses in some amount."[18] Tom and David Kelley, founders of IDEO and the Stanford d.school, write, "When you hear the word 'creativity' . . . [i]f you are like many people, your mind immediately leaps to artistic endeavors like sculpture, drawing, music, or dance. You may equate 'creative' with 'artistic.' . . . Or you may feel that being creative is a fixed trait, like having brown eyes—either you're born with creative genes, or you're not." This the authors dub "the creativity myth."

But do we readers really think creativity is only for artists and geniuses? Do we think it's mysterious, irrational, frivolous, or any of the other things we are told we believe it to be? Did we ever? As the research in this book suggests, at least among those who wrote about creativity, not really. The outdated notions creativity writers are battling, it seems, are not really about creativity but about other things. Has society often emphasized the role of geniuses in driving progress? Yes. But did anyone ever say only geniuses were capable of coming up with new ideas? Of course not. Do we often see artistic talent as distinct from mechanical ingenuity? Sure. But was it ever said that inventors were not creative? Not as far as I can tell.

So, are creativity writers really frustrated by these persistent myths, as they attest? Or is it that the presence of such myths, even as straw men, is essential to any claims about creativity? To the extent we *do* believe these things about creativity—and according to creativity experts they do regularly meet people who insist they are "not creative"—could it have something to do with the fact that everybody who has ever written about creativity always brings up artists and geniuses, ushering them onstage only briefly just to shunt them off the next moment, disowning the very idea that the show was ever about them in the first place? In Kelley's book, the illustration facing the passage about the "creativity myth," in our periphery as we are reading it, is an unmistakably artsy, abstract watercolor composition. Throughout the book one finds illustrations—in the same vibrant, slightly cartoonish style—of a painter at his easel and an itinerant guitarist strolling, even though the book never addresses how to paint or write a song.[19]

The very genre of creativity literature, whether academic or how-to, is practically defined by this constant push-pull between art and not-art (and, increasingly in the post-1960s era, between High Art and commercial art) and between genius and not-genius. It's almost as if the very idea of creativity cannot be discussed, or ceases to be interesting, without this intervention. It's as if the intervention itself—an intervention against the "Great Man" theory of history (that nonetheless regularly praises great men), and against the supposed elitism and obscurantism of the Romantics (that nonetheless tries to re-enchant our everyday existence)—is what the concept of creativity allows people to do.

It's a savvy rhetorical maneuver. The "everybody thinks x but it's really y" formula, whether or not everybody really thinks x, is the starting point for nearly every work of popular nonfiction, and a good chunk of academic writing too. But it also says something about the deeper logic of the genre. Just as postwar researchers endeavored to define creativity as distinct from genius even as they kept studying members of the pantheon, and just as humanistic psychologists insisted creativity was not just about art even as they took the artist as the archetype of the creative person, so does contemporary creativity literature depend on the very notions it denies in order to define the new space it occupies.

In fact, as we've seen, the term itself never really meant just acts of genius or artistic self-expression. Rather, it always named a trait more universal than genius, and one that pertained as much to invention as to art. It's not that we've discovered hidden truths about something long misunderstood, but rather that we invented a concept that could embody the truth we wanted to see.

Creative Everything

Creative industries. The creative class. Creative cities. Creative spaces. These have become part of the twenty-first-century lexicon. At first blush they seem self-explanatory: the creative industries, for example, are made up of creative occupations like design, film, publishing, and fashion. And insofar as these sectors have grown over the last few decades, it makes a certain amount of sense that we would develop new terms to encompass them. But these terms are not merely descriptive; they are also aspirational. In all cases the term "creative" doesn't just point to a categorical distinction (e.g., the arts rather than science or engineering); it also, as Keith Negus and Michael J. Pickering write, "provides a means of according value, and establishing a cultural hierarchy."[20]

The term "creative industries" first came into widespread use in the UK and Australia in the 1990s. The British New Labour government made it the center of its agenda, with a corresponding push for creativity in schools. The term was a subtle shift from a prior term, "cultural industries," which included the traditional arts and commercial entertainment. The new term allowed the category to be expanded to include parts of "information industries," "intellectual property industries," and "knowledge industries," which were much more lucrative. The benefits went both ways: the tech and information sector imparted to the arts an economic importance attached to the concept of innovation, while the arts brought the ITE an aura of cool and of contributing to the larger cultural life of the nation.[21] The educational reforms instituted to support this creativity push likewise appealed to both vocational and progressive impulses.

Much of the growth in this sector came from advertising and related fields, which expanded to include media production, writing, design, and strategy, and which one can find under one roof in today's "creative agencies." These businesses inherited the advertising industry's conventions, narratives, and language, including the creative revolution framework in which they are the fun, rebellious visionaries who bring value to their clients whether they like it or not. As Sean Nixon writes, those within the advertising field cultivate "a distinct habitus . . . in which speaking the language and pursuing the signs of creativity [is] central to the successful shaping of an identity at work."[22] The creative industries literature also drew on postwar knowledge about the flexible creative personality to make the hip freelancer or independent studio artist, rather than the unionized musician or actor who had been at the heart of the cultural industries, the star of this new economy.

A similar act of re-categorization was at work in the 2002 hit book *Rise of the Creative Class*. In it, Richard Florida argued that the new dominant group in society are those who "create new ideas, new technology and/or new creative content."[23] This included scientists, engineers, teachers, and even bankers, but at its center was a "super creative core" of artists, writers, designers, filmmakers, architects, and the sort. In a dramatic reversal of the status quo, Florida wrote, "Capitalism has . . . expanded its reach to capture the talents of heretofore excluded groups of eccentrics and nonconformists . . . taking people who would once have been viewed as bizarre mavericks operating at the bohemian fringe and setting them at the very heart of the process of innovation and economic growth. . . . The creative individual is . . . the new mainstream."[24] Smaller than the low-wage service sector but with greater cultural influence, the creative class was remaking norms. Florida noted how certain markers of bohemian lifestyle had been generalized to all kinds of corporate work—working from cafes, casual dress, keeping odd hours. He called this work-hard-play-hard combination of "Protestant" and "bohemian" values the "creative ethos," the spirit of our time.

The rise of the creative class explained why people were moving back into urban centers, after a generation of disinvestment and white flight. Cities, Florida said, are good for creativity. Whereas classic economic theory said workers flow to wherever they're paid the most, Florida said creative people were motivated by more than money, and sought the fuel for their creativity—authentic community, sensual experience, diversity, and cheap studio space—in the very cities their parents had fled. Florida called the factors to urban success the "3 T's": Technology, Talent, and, Tolerance, measured by hospitality to gays and lesbians, which Florida hypothesized was a proxy for open-minded attitudes toward all kinds of unconventional thinking. The composite of the 3 T's yielded Florida's "Creativity Index," with which he ranked American cities.

Luckily, just as every person had creative potential within them, every city had a chance to become a new creative hub, if only it embraced a creative "lifestyle mentality." Pittsburgh and Detroit were "trapped in the organizational age," with a conservative, "Protestant," "patriarchal, white . . . 9 to 5" attitude toward work. Austin, on the other hand, welcomed weirdos.[25] Florida recommended that cities forgo tax breaks for corporate offices, malls, and stadiums, and instead focus on walkable streets, bike paths, historic preservation, and the kinds of "authentic" cultural amenities favored by the creative class.

Florida traveled the world advising governments and business leaders on how to profit from creativity. In 2003 he hosted a conference in Memphis (at #49, dead last on the Creativity Index of cities with over one million inhabitants). At its conclusion, the participants, dubbed "the Creative 100," from cities across North America signed on to the three-page "Memphis Manifesto" of the gospel of creativity. The preamble began: "Creativity is fundamental to being human and is a critical resource to individual, community and economic life. Creative communities are vibrant, humanizing places, nurturing personal growth, sparking cultural and technological breakthroughs, producing jobs and wealth, and accepting a variety of life styles and culture. . . . The Creative 100 believe in the vision and the opportunities of a future driven by the power of ideas."

Soon "creative cities" began popping up all over the world— often following a consultation from Richard Florida's Creative

Class Group—from Providence, Rhode Island to Singapore. The creative cities phenomenon is a loose collection of practices and policies including everything from local "design districts" to urban rebranding, and ranging from subsidies for a few artists' studios to massive "innovation hubs." Creative cities partake of a mix of cultural policy, urban design, and regional economic planning ideas, some dating to the 1960s. This includes grassroots community arts practices and tactical urbanism, "creative clusters" theory, the "Bilbao effect"—where museums and cultural amenities would spur tourism—and the "SoHo effect," by which artists attract more affluent residents to down-market neighborhoods, spurring real estate investment. Parallel to all of this, a new generation of urban planners promoted walkable, vibrant, mixed-use urban spaces. The creative cities phenomenon—thanks in no small part to the work of Richard Florida—brought these currents together in an economic model tied together by the concept of creativity: creative amenities would attract creative workers, who would then drive economic creativity.[26]

The creative cities paradigm brought together unusual coalitions. Leaders of de-industrialized cities saw in it an untapped source of economic growth that seemed to mesh with their emphasis on diversity and community development. Small-is-beautiful urban planners liked having economic grounding for their beliefs, while real estate developers saw new possibilities in abandoned warehouses that could be converted into live-work lofts. Culturally liberal business leaders liked having a bottom-line case for supporting the arts, and many artists and cultural institutions, from legacy art museums to scrappy community theater groups, found a new and powerful language to advocate for support. In fact, it encouraged a whole new paradigm of arts practice, "creative placemaking," enshrined in an NEA initiative reportedly influenced by Florida's work, which put artists to work beautifying and revitalizing downtrodden urban spaces.

The whole creative economy paradigm, including creative industries, creative class, and creative cities movements, is the postwar mass culture critique coming of age. It prefers creative entrepreneurs to large corporations, adaptive reuse to shiny new office complexes, the blending of live-work-play to the Fordist segregation of functions. It also partakes of the postmodern breakdown between high and low culture, seeing a blues bar as just as valuable, both culturally and economically, as a fine art museum. It feels no compunction to segregate, and indeed cultivates connections between, art and commerce, art and technology.

Of course reality is more complicated. The coalition-building and sectoral conglomerations the champions of creativity encouraged were not so easily achieved. There were divisions within the creative class: as Doug Henwood put it, "someone writing electronic music in a former industrial space in Bushwick, Brooklyn, or an investment banker crafting derivatives in midtown Manhattan, or somebody writing an app in DUMBO Brooklyn . . . lead very different lives and earn very different kinds of income." While there were indeed rapidly expanding opportunities in design, fashion, and other "super-creative core" jobs, the real growth, and money, went to other, less sexy kinds of brain workers in the FIRE industries (finance, insurance, real estate, and engineering). Real estate speculation priced out the artists who made those cities cool.[27]

The very idea of a creative sector, as the scholar Nicholas Garnham puts it, "helps to mobilise a very disparate and often potentially antagonistic coalition of interests."[28] Within the super-creative core, many fine artists felt uneasy being lumped in with advertising and app developers, and being used as "decoys" for a new economic regime they often hated. In 2009 a group of artists and musicians in Hamburg, Germany occupied a building slated to be replaced by luxury real estate, issuing a manifesto called "Not in Our Name," which read, "a spectre has been haunting Europe" since Richard Florida arrived.[29] (Florida had argued that artists didn't really care about politics and were therefore happy to work for corporations as long as they got to be creative; this backlash exposed the fact there was still some oppositional sentiment in bohemia.)

Scholars and social justice activists also took aim at the creativity script for being "the funky side of neoliberal urban development," and a thin "veneer" for gentrification. Despite its progressive vibe, the "creativity script" played into disillusionment about the social safety net. The notion that creative people aren't motivated by money, are always happy to be working, and prefer odd gigs to a stable career normalized the precarity and overwork of the post-Fordist world. The successful creative life calls to people like a siren song but fails to materialize for so many, who chalk their failure up to deeper personal deficiencies. The creative economy, critics point out, demands a "creative underclass" of aspiring creatives who romanticize their own exploitation as the timeless struggle of the starving artist. The creative economy narrative was sold on the idea that everyone possessed creativity, so it would be more meritocratic, more open to diverse voices, but it can be particularly rough for aspiring creatives of color and working-class backgrounds, who seek creative work as a means of self-determination but lack the social and financial capital that benefit many of their white peers.[30] According to the blog "Creative Class Struggle," which popped up shortly after Florida took a position at the University of Toronto, the "glossy myth of the 'creative class,' serves only to increase the vulnerability of the vulnerable and further empower the powerful."[31]

To many people, however, at least momentarily, all of these contradictions seemed unapparent. The vision of a creative society was, and continues to be, amazingly popular, and one can clearly see why: it seems to reconcile innovation and growth with more holistic humane values. And the glue that holds these things together is none other than the concept of creativity itself. It allows people to lump engineers and avant-garde filmmakers into the same "class"; to paint an essentially finance-, tech- and IP-driven economy as having a bohemian core; to acknowledge that cities are competing for a limited pool of "talent" while also believing that we can simply "creatify" everyone's jobs. The notion of creativity allowed people to interpret career and lifestyle preferences as expressions of innate personality traits rather than as exercises in class distinction; to imagine a direct link between personal and economic growth. It allows us to see late capitalism as a natural consequence of human beings striving to express themselves as opposed to the result of a decades-long series of political choices.

What's most remarkable is not so much the flurry of sleight-of-hand tricks the creativity discourse performs, but how easily they are pulled off. Such a feat is possible only insofar as the concept of creativity is already so firmly baked in, contradictions and all, to our collective consciousness. Richard Florida told me that, in fact, his obsession with creativity probably had something to do with the creativity psychology that was being popularized when he was a child in the 1960s, and that the "creative person," the hero of his narrative, was in some way a "subconscious" attempt to "unify the artist or the musician in me with the scholar in me, trying to say . . . they can go together in one human being."[32]

The early twenty-first-century cult of creativity is the logical conclusion of fifty years of creativity discourse structuring our worldview so thoroughly that we hardly noticed the slippages it was capable of producing. We don't even realize how effortlessly it hides the contradictions we don't want to see.

The Cultural Contradictions of Creativity

Yet these are also the tensions that, once played out, lead to that sense that creativity is being coopted, bastardized, eviscerated of all meaning. In a recent book called simply *Against Creativity*, Oli Mould says that "the language of creativity has been subsumed by capitalism," and that today's notion is but an "economized and capitalism-friendly version of creativity." He proposes an alternative "revolutionary creativity," one dedicated to "creating new phenomena to which capitalism is unaware [and] that resist co-optation, appropriation and stabilization by capitalism."[33] But if true creativity is only that which actively resists capitalism, then what are we supposed to call everything that doesn't? Is a writer of pop songs or a developer of a food delivery app not being authentically creative?[34] Mould seems to believe the same myths creativity tells about itself—that creativity is fundamental, naturally pre-commercial and pre-political, that it is a Romantic value originally seen to resist capitalism and industrial logics.

By now we know otherwise. As this book has shown, the concept of creativity never actually existed outside of capitalism, and in retrospect that shouldn't really surprise us; if we know one thing about capitalism, it's that it loves novelty. In fact, the notion that capitalism stifles new ideas is a product of an earlier time, a fairly specific era of capitalism as seen by liberal critics with a particularly Cold War concern with the fate of the individual. No, creativity is not really being trivialized or sullied; actually it's being used to do exactly what it was created to do.

That's not to say creativity is inherently capitalistic. The very universality that made creativity appealing to business also makes it appealing to those on the left, who are also interested, for their own reasons, in locating the power of the individual within oppressive systems, blurring the boundaries of art, and shifting the focus from process to product.[35] Kirin Narayan's 2016 book *Everyday Creativity*, about Himalayan women's singing, for example, notes that creativity "can be a way to reclaim space amid repressive, disciplining institutions." Post-1970s African American historiography has often emphasized the ways in which Black people have creatively adapted and improvised to carve out pockets of freedom in the midst of oppression. Cultural scholars of the post-structuralist persuasion, emphasizing contingency and flux, often deploy Gilles Deleuze's theory of "the creative act" to talk about the ways in which cultural producers actively reconfigure oppressive ideas of race, gender, and class. Many radical art practices since the 1960s have emphasized "process over product" to resist capitalist commodification. Cynthia Cohen, the director of Brandeis University's "Creativity, the Arts, and Social Transformation" program, which has an explicit social justice agenda, told me she needed a word "that signified more than the arts . . . because cultural practices (i.e. collective expressive forms) don't necessarily fall within the category of art." (Yet, Cohen continued, an added bonus was that "creativity" was also "ambiguous" enough to cover traditional arts as well as design and entrepreneurship, thus making her program legible to the more business-focused areas of the school.)[36]

Creativity, in other words, embodies much of the shared sensibility of our time, and in that way can be seen as a bridge between the postwar era and our own. Creativity is in one sense a quintessentially modern value: it extols humanity's ability to make its own world. But in another sense it's quintessentially postmodern. It is not particularly invested in an idea of truth and lacks the telos of Progress. For all their postindustrial utopianism, champions of creativity do not envision a final stage when everything has been solved, but rather see the world in a constant state of churn— problems and solutions in perpetual co-creation. This jibes well in an intellectual climate disabused of master narratives and attuned to flux and contingency.

So many of those who dedicate their careers to creativity have, like many of us, been motivated by a sometimes unconscious desire to reconcile the various contradictions of our era: between utility and transcendence, a yearning for greatness and a belief in the dignity of the everyday, between the work available and the work we want to do. If anything, those contradictions have only intensified in the post-postwar era. For all the fault in his rosy take on the world, Richard Florida proved an apt conduit for the aspirations of his generation when he called the "Creative Ethos" the spirit of our time.

Conclusion

What Is to Be Done?

At this point it's probably reasonable to expect that, having now fully taken the concept of creativity down to its studs and shown that it's at best unstable and at worst a vector of false consciousness for a bad system, I might suggest we do away with the concept altogether. A few have suggested such a thing.[1] But I'm not so prescriptive.

The concept of creativity is a tool, and it can do many things. By pointing out the roots of the cult of creativity in Cold War capitalism I do not mean to argue that it's tainted or compromised, or that it will doom any progressive agenda that embraces it. I'm simply saying we shouldn't imagine there is some kind of pure spirit of creativity to reclaim. From a historical perspective such a thing simply doesn't exist, and that shouldn't surprise us, because "the ability to create" is obviously as important to capitalism as to any other kind of system. As the example of Abraham Maslow shows, we can try to theorize creativity in a way that resists utilitarianism and commodification, but that won't stop it from being taught in business schools. If the concept of creativity never really actually existed outside of capitalism in the first place, it makes less sense to try to reclaim it than to simply let go of the idea that creativity is the fundamental source of revolutionary power. But that doesn't mean we need to reject it.

In fact, I'm still sort of attached to it. That feeling of making something, of having an idea and then making it happen, of seeing something take shape in your hands, the one I occasionally had writing this book—it's beautiful and mysterious and life-affirming and I'm not sure what to call it other than creativity. Even during this project I occasionally found myself, when stuck in some rut or being too academic, in the market for some general advice about how to unleash my own creativity.

I also think many of the problems to which creativity addresses itself need to be taken seriously. This book is in some ways a record of people beginning to name something they felt was missing from the industrial work of the mid-twentieth century, and we need to listen to that. As much as I loathe the cult of work that prevents us from getting our four-hour workday (or even four-hour work week), I am sympathetic to the socialist William Morris's idea that people do inherently enjoy a job well done. As we sort through the questions around what to do with work in the future, it seems like one priority should be allowing people access to work that gives them a sense of agency and constructiveness. The fight for a minimum wage and even a universal basic income must also be accompanied by a focus on the quality of work itself, and if that for some people involves building stuff, or solving problems, or making their own decisions, or any of the other vague criteria that go under the heading "creative," then creative it should be.

The cult of creativity also came as a response to encroaching rationality that in many ways has only grown stronger. In a world in which every last thing is being quantified, in which science, technology, engineering, and math get beefed up at every level of education while art and humanities programs are cut, any attempts to push back and restore such art education opportunities should be celebrated. Creativity advocates are in many cases the only ones telling engineers they should visit an art museum or suggesting the value of other-than-scientific ways of thinking.

Nevertheless, a few critiques of the cult of creativity seem to suggest themselves. First, as regards the arts, while I have no interest in patrolling the boundaries between high art and everyday culture, and even between science and art—not least because much of our lived reality challenges many of those boundaries—I worry about some of the effects of clumping them in the particular way the concept of creativity does. As I've suggested, the idea of creativity, accompanied with images of art and youthful self-expression, is often used to valorize other more questionable or uninteresting forms of progress, like gentrification or oil extraction. I also worry that these speech acts constrain the very possibilities of art. When we accept the equivalency of art and creativity we assume art is essentially *about* novelty. When we posit creativity as the source of art we cut off our minds from other motivations, such as recognition or communication or the passing down of traditional wisdom, and accept instead the values of a regime of intellectual property that demands constant differentiation. Equally for science, when we valorize creativity over discovery, we sideline other motivations, like curiosity or understanding, that could belong to a less aggressive ethic. Of course people who champion creativity would also, I'm certain, champion curiosity and communication and care. But what would it mean to foreground those other ideas? To advertise art museums as places that "foster communication" rather than "creativity"? How would that reorganize our conceptual universes? Would we then populate our how-to books and psychological studies with diplomats and marriage counselors rather than inventors and entrepreneurs? That would of course come with its own blind spots and problems, but the thought experiment helps us see the implicit values embedded in our supposedly uncontroversial language.

Second, I take issue with the cult of creativity's obsession with the importance of new ideas. The champions of creativity have long said that creativity is necessary to solve the world's thorny problems. I'm not so sure. When I look around it seems to me most of the biggest problems actually have a plethora of solutions already lined up, and the necessary technology chugging along at approximately the rate we choose to prioritize it. What's lacking is the political will. It ultimately serves the status quo to convince us that we suffer not from one big problem with one big solution, but from lots of little problems each one representing an opportunity for an entrepreneurial intervention. Evgeny Morozov has shown how Silicon Valley "disruptors" believe their job is to transcend all institutions and established norms to provide individual solutions for each problem. The discourse of creativity often partakes of this anti-institutional ethos, but it makes it even broader than technological solutionism. When we combine an idolization of innovators with the constant messaging that to save the world one must come up with a bold new idea, we encourage our idealistic youth to see themselves as "social entrepreneurs" rather than members of ongoing collective projects of change. Yes, institutional calcification is a real phenomenon, and leaders who come from outside and aren't afraid to shake things up can be incredibly generative (as long as "shaking things up" isn't just a euphemism for privatizing, downsizing, etc.). But when the whole business of "changing the world" reflexively demeans career experts and specialists and activists who have been working thoughtfully and carefully through tricky issues, we often also ignore their systemic analyses as well as systemic—i.e., political—means for dealing with them, and are more likely to propose piecemeal interventions that can be called radical only because nobody has tried them before.[2]

As we saw, the concept of creativity was forged as a psychological solution to structural problems, in an age that preferred to see problems in psychological terms. In many ways we are still in such an era—see how quickly we turn to medical and neurological explanations for widespread problems like loneliness and depression that have profound social roots. The idea that what stands between us and a better world is our own "creative thinking" both puts too much pressure on us as individuals and lets us off the hook as political actors.

Last, I think the cult of creativity has a way of valorizing people who do "creative work"—defined, as we've seen, fairly narrowly—at the expense of those who do other types of work. The notion that creativity is what makes us human is both toothlessly vague and far too limiting, especially if it makes us think of other very human impulses—to care, to maintain, to collect, to reuse, to copy, to fight, or even to follow—as less relevant.

As it happens, the events of the last several years have forced a reckoning with some of the tenets of the cult of creativity. The COVID-19 pandemic revealed newfound willingness to disentangle the equivalency of inner growth and productivity. The titles of books that have come out over the last few years—*Do What You Love: And Other Lies About Success and Happiness*; *Work Won't Love You Back*; *The Trouble with Passion*; and *No More Work*—betray a collective questioning of the exploitative pressures to find deep creative fulfillment in our jobs. Many people, deprived of so many loved ones and so much purely social connection, have begun to rediscover a sense of self defined not by what we produce, but by who we are as social beings. Meanwhile, the pandemic almost immediately reconfigured our ideas of who was "essential," and it was almost uniformly occupations not considered creative—poultry plant workers, grocery store stockers, nurses, delivery drivers—that sustain our society. We began to see the infrastructure of care and maintenance and physical goods—not ideas—that keeps us all alive.

Above all, the escalating environmental catastrophe, from climate change to microplastics in everything, has made it abundantly clear that the cults of innovation, growth, and disruption are literally killing us. The rejection of neoliberalism by both the left and the right across much of the world and the rejuvenation of organized labor in both the service and white-collar sectors also reveal a renewed appetite for collective projects and a rejection, at least in some parts, of the individualism that for several decades seemed to be the chief cultural legacy of the post–World War II era.

Perhaps another ideal is possible, even necessary. The artist and writer Jenny Odell, for example, sees the constant impulse to both create and consume in our screen-based, socially mediated environment as part of the capitalist plot to harvest our attention.

Aggressively uncreative practices such as aimless wandering or birdwatching (or, as she perceptively calls it, "bird listening") offer "an antidote to the rhetoric of growth" that surrounds us every day. There is ultimately a feminist and environmental case to be made for doing nothing: if we can shift our notion of constructive social behavior from the creation of novel products to "maintenance and care," she writes, perhaps we can build the collective will to rebalance an unsustainable and unjust system.[3]

The "Maintainers," a group of Science and Technology Studies scholars, agrees. For too long their own field has fetishized "innovation." But "what happens *after* innovation," Lee Vinsel and Andrew Russell write, is more important. "Maintenance and repair, the building of infrastructures, the mundane labour that goes into sustaining functioning and efficient infrastructures, simply has more impact on people's daily lives than the vast majority of technological innovations." Like Odell, the Maintainers see the importance of maintaining the maintainers, whether they be the 70 percent of rank-and-file engineers tasked with keeping up existing systems, or the many more nurses, tradespeople, janitors, cooks, garbage removers, and others who keep our world from falling apart rather than introducing new things.

Serious economists have also begun to fundamentally question the growth consensus, proposing so-called de-growth and donut economy models that are not only less wasteful but also demand that societies talk about *what* should be produced in the first place. As we've seen, the discourse of creativity, like that of innovation, has little to say about these moral questions. "Innovation-speak worships at the altar of change, but it rarely asks who benefits, to what end?" Vinsel and Russell write. "[A] focus on maintenance provides opportunities to ask questions about what we really want out of technologies. What do we really care about? What kind of society do we want to live in?"[4]

None of this is to say new ideas are not important, or that new technology doesn't have a part to play in saving the world. It's simply to suggest that those things will probably happen whether or not we encourage "creative thinking" or understand "how creativity works." We need not return to a blind faith in technocracy or reestablish a strict hierarchy of culture. But a little shift back to an appreciation of the power of collective goals, to an ethic of care and maintenance, a love of art not necessarily for art's sake but for more than just a stimulus of new ideas, a respect for thoughtful research and knowledge, and above all the space to question the goodness of the new might just be the big idea we need right now.

ACKNOWLEDGMENTS

Working on this project over the last decade I have accumulated so many debts. Creativity is one of those topics lots of people want to discuss, and I am grateful to everyone I've talked to at conferences and on planes, at parties and seminars, that have helped me think through it. There are too many of you to name.

This project began under the sage advisership of Sandy Zipp, Steve Lubar, Robert Self, and Jamie Cohen-Cole. It would not have been possible without my Brown University community: Anne Gray Fischer, Patrick Chung, and Alicia Maggard, who gave thoughtful and encouraging feedback on early versions of this work; and my cohort, Horace Ballard, Chris Elias, Majida Kargbo, Crystal Ngo, and Micah Salkind, as well as Sara Matthiesen, Ben Holtzman, John Rosenberg, Elizabeth Searcy, Sarah Brown, Oddný Helgadóttir, Cornel Ban, Robyn Schroeder, and Elena Gonzalez, who made the whole experience worthwhile. I am also grateful to Kira Lussier, Bretton Fosbrook, Matthew Hoffarth, Victoria Cain, Ethan Hutt, Matthew Wisnioski, Fred Turner, and Alana Staiti for their valuable input and academic companionship.

Shelly Ronen and Lee Vinsel deserve particular thanks for their abiding enthusiasm. The blazing minds of Liz Searcy, who edited many, many early drafts, and Daniel Platt, who was there at the beginning and the bitter end, have greatly improved the book you hold.

My research was made possible with support from the Brown University Library's Center for Digital Scholarship, the Hathi Trust Research Center, the Hagley Museum and Library, and the Smithsonian Institution's Lemelson Center for the Study of Invention and Innovation under the enthusiastic guidance of Eric Hintz. I would also like to thank the knowledgeable staffs of the Archives Center at the National Museum of American History, SUNY Buffalo State, The University at Buffalo, the Hargrett Rare Book and Manuscript Library at the University of Georgia, the Library of Congress in Washington, DC, and the Rockefeller Library at Brown. The field of creativity is full of enthusiastic, big-hearted, and knowledgeable people, including Theresa Amabile, Bob Johnston, Leo Boudreau, Richard Harriman, Cavas Gobhai, Dorie Shallcross, and John Osborn, all of whom were generous with their time and expertise and indispensable in helping me find my way through the history of their world. Thanks also to Karin Hibma, Bruce Burdick, and Andy Kramer for their archives and recollections.

This book would not exist without Peggy Phelan and Michael Kahan plus my co-fellows and participants in the Stanford Creative Cities Initiative and the Stanford Humanities Center. The encouragement and input from the members of the Stanford History working group was indispensable. My valued colleagues at the Delft University of Technology, including Paul Hekkert, Pieter Desmet, Adjaan van der Helm, Roy Bendor, Geertje van Achterberg, Vincent Cellucci, Milene Gonçalves, Willemijn Brouwer, Katrina Heijne, and so many more, have given me a new understanding of the real professional resonance of creativity. I am forever indebted to Bregje van Eekelen, who has been a caring mentor, provocative interlocutor, and enthusiastic cheerleader for the past three very strange years.

I want to thank my editor, Tim Mennel, for believing in this project and in me. He, Susannah Engstrom, Caterina MacLean, and Adrienne Meyers at the University of Chicago Press and Evan Young guided this project with a steady and very patient hand. Thanks also to the wonderful Howard Brick and an anonymous reader for their invaluable feedback. Diane Cady, Catherine Osborne, Anne Horowitz, Kali Handelman, and Tana Wojczuk helped me through the laborious process of figuring out how to say what I wanted to say.

In life there are people who let you know you can do it. There were many times in this project I started to think I could not, but the kind and supportive voices of Avi Decter, Melissa Martens, Lauri Halderman, Martin Schwabacher, Dorothy Fishman, and Ahren Cohen echoed out over the distance of geography and time and told me to keep going. I would never have had the confidence to take on such a project were it not for my parents, Andrew Franklin and Audrey Fishman Franklin. Brooke Lamperd played most of the roles listed above. She has borne so much of this project and will never know how grateful I am for all the love, wisdom, and sacrifice she has delivered.

NOTES

Introduction

1. Daniel H. Pink, *A Whole New Mind: Why Right-Brainers Will Rule the Future* (New York: Riverhead Books, 2006); David Brooks, *Bobos in Paradise: The New Upper Class and How They Got There* (New York: Simon & Schuster, 2000); Richard Florida, *The Rise of the Creative Class: And How It's Transforming Work, Leisure, Community and Everyday Life* (New York: Basic Books, 2002); Ken Robinson, *Out of Our Minds: Learning to Be Creative* (New York: Capstone, John Wiley, 2001); Kimberly Seltzer and Tom Bentley, *The Creative Age* (London: Demos, 1999).

2. Austin Carr, "The Most Important Leadership Quality for CEOs? Creativity," *Fast Company*, May 18, 2010.

3. "This Is the One Skill that Will Future-Proof You for the Jobs Market," *World Economic Forum*, October 22, 2020, https://www.weforum.org/agenda/2020/10/andria-zafirakou-teacher-jobs-skills-creativity/.

4. Norman Jackson et al., eds., *Developing Creativity in Higher Education: An Imaginative Curriculum* (London and New York: Routledge, 2006), xviii.

5. Scott Barry Kaufman and Carolyn Gregoire, *Wired to Create: Unraveling the Mysteries of the Creative Mind*, reprint edition (New York: TarcherPerigee, 2016); Jonah Lehrer, *Imagine: How Creativity Works* (Boston: Houghton Mifflin Harcourt, 2012).

6. Christopher Peterson and Martin E. P. Seligman, *Character Strengths and Virtues: A Handbook and Classification* (New York: Oxford University Press, 2004), 4.

7. This quote favored by creativity experts is often attributed to Albert Einstein, but as with many Einstein quotes, it was probably not Einstein who said it, and it appears to have originally been said about "imagination," not "creativity."

"Creativity Is Intelligence Having Fun," *Quote Investigator*, accessed November 10, 2021, https://quoteinvestigator.com/2017/03/02/fun/.

8. Mihalyi Csikszentmihalyi, *Creativity: Flow and the Psychology of Discovery and Invention* (New York: Harper Perennial, 1997), 1–2.

9. Beth A. Hennessey and Teresa M. Amabile, "Creativity," *Annual Review of Psychology* 61, no. 1 (January 2010): 570.

10. When the UK's New Labour government enshrined creativity in major education and economic development policy documents in the 1990s, a group of scholars discovered seven different notions or "discourses" of the term, encompassing behaviors ranging from High Art to the street culture of urban teens to imaginative play in schoolchildren, and denoting everything from a personality trait to a social phenomenon. See Shakuntala Banaji, Andrew Burn, and David Buckingham, *The Rhetorics of Creativity: A Review of the Literature*, revised edition (London: Creativity, Culture and Education, 2010); for other useful discussions of the meanings of creativity, see Mark Readman, "What's in a Word? The Discursive Construction of 'Creativity'" (PhD diss., Bournemouth University, 2010); Rob Pope, *Creativity: Theory, History, Practice* (New York: Routledge, 2005); Keith Negus and Michael Pickering, *Creativity, Communication and Cultural Value* (London and Thousand Oaks, CA: Sage Publications, 2004).

11. Though the word "creativity" is fairly new, the word "creative" has been in common use for centuries, leading many scholars to assume therefore that the concept of creativity existed in some primordial form. But "creative" did not yet mean what it does today. If you had told someone in 1900 that they were "creative" they would likely have responded, "creative of what?" And that's because the term most nearly meant generative, as in "God's creative power"—closer to constructive than to imaginative or clever. At some point during the early twentieth century, "creative" did take on a secondary sense as a near synonym for "artistic," since over the course of the nineteenth century art had increasingly come to be seen as a source of new ideas rather than simply a way to imitate nature. But even as we start to see references to "the creative artist" or the poet's "creative imagination," creative meant generative. An 1890 economics textbook included in a list of "creative industries" farming, construction, manufacturing, transportation, retail, and anything else that generated new value—basically everyone except landlords and financiers. As late as the 1940s Joseph Schumpeter used the term "creative destruction," and in the 1950s Martin Luther King Jr. wrote of "creative protest"; both of these cases lack any sense of artistic imagination. In the few cases in which creativity or "creativeness" does appear in the historical corpus, the words tend to refer not to an individual capacity but rather to a generative tendency—e.g., "God's creativeness" or "the creativity of the Renaissance." Today, by contrast, when we say someone had a "creative idea," we're not saying the idea itself creates, but that it is a product of a faculty or process we now have a name for: "creativity." R. W., Burchfield, ed., *A Supplement to the Oxford English Dictionary*. Vol. 1. (Oxford: Clarendon Press, 1972).

12. *The Random House Dictionary of the English Language*, ed. Jess M. Stein (New York: Random House, 1966).

13. Paul Oskar Kristeller, "'Creativity' and 'Tradition,'" *Journal of the History of Ideas* 44, no. 1 (1983): 105.

14. Jean-Baptiste Michel et al., "Quantitative Analysis of Culture Using Millions of Digitized Books," *Science* 331, no. 6014 (January 14, 2011): 176–82. A virtually identical pattern emerges from a variety of other corpora, including the Corpus of Historical American English at Brigham Young University, ProQuest Historical Newspapers. For a more detailed account of my research on the historical use of the terms "creative," "creativeness," and "creativity," see Samuel W. Franklin, "The Cult of Creativity in Postwar America" (PhD diss., Brown University, 2018).

15. For good examples of this, see Vlad Petre Glaveanu, ed., "Revisiting the Foundations of Creativity Studies," in *The Creativity Reader* (Oxford and New York: Oxford University Press, 2019), 5–12; Robert Weiner, *Creativity & Beyond: Cultures, Values, and Change* (Albany: State University of New York Press, 2000); John Hope Mason, *The Value of Creativity: The Origins and Emergence of a Modern Belief* (Aldershot, Hampshire, England, and Burlington, VT: Ashgate, 2003); Pope, *Creativity: Theory, History, Practice*; Mark A. Runco and Robert S. Albert, "Creativity Research," in *The Cambridge Handbook of Creativity*, Cambridge Handbooks in Psychology (Cambridge: Cambridge University Press, 2010); James Engell, *The Creative Imagination: Enlightenment to Romanticism* (Cambridge, MA: Harvard University Press, 1981)..

16. Dorothy Parker, *The Portable Dorothy Parker*, ed. Marion Meade, deluxe edition (New York: Penguin Classics, 2006), 567. To be sure, artists were regularly asked for their thoughts on creativity, or the creative process, but they often only seemed half interested in grand theories. James Baldwin, solicited to write an essay on "The Creative Process" for a book called *Creative America*, essentially changed the subject and wrote about the role of the artist in society; the phrases "creativity" or "the creative process" hardly appear in it.

17. In many ways postwar American art reflected the same concerns shared by the psychologists and businesspeople in this book. Many postwar artists and critics, for their own ideological reasons as well as those of their Cold War liberal funders (including in some cases the CIA), experienced their own individualistic, apolitical turn in the 1950s—cf. Frances Stoner Saunders, *The Cultural Cold War: The CIA and the World of Arts and Letters* (New York: New Press, 2000); Mark McGurl, *The Program Era: Postwar Fiction and the Rise of Creative Writing* (Cambridge, MA: Harvard University Press, 2009); Eric Bennet, *Workshops of Empire: Stegner, Engle, and American Creative Writing During the Cold War* (Iowa City: University of Iowa Press, 2015). But even Harold Rosenberg's memorable phrase to describe the art of that era, "the tradition of the new," like Ezra Pound's earlier injunction to "make it new," perhaps overemphasize the importance of innovation as an end in itself to modern artists. Moreover, no sooner had the hyper-individualistic postwar moment crested than many artists in the 1960s began to again reject the cult of originality and embrace distinctly anti-authorial projects, seeing themselves by turns as art workers, reproducers, or facilitators rather than godlike creators—Michael North, *Novelty: A History of the New* (Chicago: University of Chicago Press, 2013).

18. A handful of scholars have written about the concept of creativity in the postwar era, and I build on their work in what follows. Jamie Cohen-Cole, "The Creative American: Cold War Salons, Social Science, and the Cure for Modern Society," *Isis* 100 (2009): 219–62; Jamie Cohen-Cole, *The Open Mind: Cold War Politics and the Sciences of Human Nature* (Chicago and London: University of Chicago Press, 2014); Michael Bycroft, "Psychology, Psychologists, and the Creativity Movement: The Lives of Method Inside and Outside the Cold War," in *Cold War Social Science: Knowledge Production, Liberal Democracy, and Human Nature*, ed. Mark Solovey and Hamilton Cravens (New York: Palgrave Macmillan, 2014), 197–214; Amy Fumiko Ogata, *Designing the Creative Child: Playthings and Places in Midcentury America* (Minneapolis: University of Minnesota Press, 2013); Bregje F. van Eekelen, "Accounting for Ideas: Bringing a Knowledge Economy into the Picture," *Economy and Society* 44, no. 3 (2015): 445–79; Sarah Brouillette, *Literature and the Creative Economy* (Palo Alto, CA: Stanford University Press, 2014); Andres Reckwitz, *The Invention of Creativity* (Malden, MA: Polity Press, 2017); Camilla Nelson, "The Invention of Creativity: The Emergence of a Discourse," *Cultural Studies Review* 16, no. 2 (September 2010): 49–74. A valuable chronicle of creativity research from within the field is Runco and Albert, "Creativity Research."

19. Those who think the criterion of "useful" rules out art because art is useless by definition offer the variant "new and appropriate," or, as Theresa Amabile puts it, "appropriate, useful, correct, or valuable." In every case the intent is the same: creativity, though originating as an internal phenomenon, has to be "expressed," and involves producing something that is not merely random or bizarre or lucky, but that somehow "works" for a community outside the creator.

20. Rollo May, *The Courage to Create* (New York: W. W. Norton and Co., 1975), 40.

21. Carl R. Rogers, "Toward a Theory of Creativity," *ETC: A Review of General Semantics* 11, no. 4 (1954): 249–60.

22. William J. J. Gordon, *Synectics: The Development of Creative Capacity* (New York: Harper & Row, 1961).

23. Isaac Asimov, "Published for the First Time: A 1959 Essay by Isaac Asimov on Creativity," *MIT Technology Review*, October 20, 2014, http://www.technologyreview.com/view/531911/isaac-asimov-asks-how-do-people-get-new-ideas/.

24. Hugh Lytton, *Creativity and Education* (New York: Schocken Books, 1972), 2.

25. *Fortune* 43, no. 2 (February 1951).

26. Robert M. Collins, *More: The Politics of Economic Growth in Postwar America* (New York: Oxford University Press USA, 2002). On consumerism see Lizabeth Cohen, *A Consumers' Republic: The Politics of Mass Consumption in Postwar America* (New York: Vintage Books, 2003); Charles McGovern, *Sold American: Consumption and Citizenship, 1890–1945* (Chapel Hill: University of North Carolina Press, 2006); Gary S Cross, *An All-Consuming Century: Why Commercialism Won in Modern America* (New York: Columbia University Press, 2000).

27. Warren Weaver, "The Encouragement of Science," *Scientific American,*

September 1958, 172–73; Daniel Bell, *The Coming of Post-Industrial Society: A Venture in Social Forecasting* (New York: Basic Books, 1973), 17. On the white-collar class see C. Wright Mills, *White Collar: The American Middle Classes* (New York: Oxford University Press, 1951). In this book I try to use "white-collar," "middle-class," and "professional" as precisely as possible in the context, but they are ultimately overlapping and imprecise concepts. For discussions of the tradition of theorizing this "middle," "new," or "professional managerial class" from Karl Marx onward, and the problems therein, see Jean-Christophe Agnew, "A Touch of Class," *Democracy* 3 (1983): quote on 61; Lawrence Peter King, *Theories of the New Class: Intellectuals and Power* (Minneapolis: University of Minnesota Press, 2004); Robert D. Johnston, *The Radical Middle Class* (Princeton, NJ: Princeton University Press, 2003), esp. chapter 1; Barbara Ehrenreich and John Ehrenreich, "The Professional-Managerial Class," *Radical America* 11, no. 2 (April 1977): 7–31.

28. Theodore Roszak, *The Making of a Counter Culture: Reflections on the Technocratic Society and Its Youthful Opposition* (Garden City, NY: Anchor Books, 1969), 13. Key critiques of mass society include James Burnham, *The Managerial Revolution* (Westport, CT: Greenwood Press, 1972); Mills, *White Collar*; David Riesman, Nathan Glazer, and Reuel Denney, *The Lonely Crowd: A Study of the Changing American Character* (Garden City, NY: Doubleday, 1953); William Whyte, *The Organization Man* (New York: Simon and Schuster, 1956); Paul Goodman, *Growing Up Absurd: Problems of Youth in the Organized System* (New York: Random House, 1960); David Riesman, *Abundance for What?* (New Brunswick, NJ: Transaction Publishers, 1993); Herbert Marcuse, *One-Dimensional Man* (Boston: Beacon Press, 1964); Jacques Ellul, *The Technological Society* (New York: Knopf, 1964). The notion of progress was famously destabilized in the wake of the First World War, as evidenced by the first attempts to historicize the concept soon after the war. See J. B. Bury, *The Idea of Progress: An Inquiry into Its Origin and Growth* (London: Macmillan, 1920); but it remained a keyword in public and political discourse in the interwar period. See Christopher Lasch, *The True and Only Heaven: Progress and Its Critics* (New York: W. W. Norton, 1991).

29. O. Hobart Mowrer, quoted in William J. Clancey, "Introduction," in John E. Arnold, *Creative Engineering*, ed. William J. Clancey (n.p.: William J. Clancey, 2016), 43.

30. William H. Whyte, "Groupthink," *Fortune*, March 1952.

31. James Livingston, *Pragmatism, Feminism, and Democracy: Rethinking the Politics of American History* (New York: Routledge, 2001).

32. John J. Corson, "Innovation Challenges Conformity," *Harvard Business Review* 40, no. 3 (June 1962): 67. On the ideals of order and organization see Max Weber, *The Protestant Ethic and the Spirit of Capitalism* (New York: Routledge, 2001); Thorstein Veblen, *The Engineers and the Price System* (New Brunswick, NJ: Transaction Publishers, 1990); Adolf A. Berle and Gardiner C Means, *The Modern Corporation and Private Property* (New Brunswick, NJ: Transaction Publishers, 2009); Walter Lippmann, *Drift and Mastery: An Attempt to Diagnose the Current Unrest* (Madison: University of Wisconsin Press, 2015). On the progressive sensibility see Robert H. Wiebe, *The Search for Order, 1877–1920* (Westport, CT:

Greenwood Press, 1980); Andrew Delano Abbott, *The System of Professions: An Essay on the Division of Expert Labor* (Chicago: University of Chicago Press, 1988). On the rise of the professions and professionalism see David F. Noble, *America by Design: Science, Technology, and the Rise of Corporate Capitalism* (New York: Knopf, 1977).

33. Rockefeller Brothers Fund, *Prospect for America: The Rockefeller Panel Reports* (Garden City, NY: Doubleday, 1961) .

34. Jerome Bruner, "The Conditions of Creativity," in *Contemporary Approaches to Creative Thinking: A Symposium Held at the University of Colorado*, ed. H. E. Gruber, G. Terrell, and M. Wertheimer (New York: Atherton Press, 1962), 2–3.

35. My understanding of the history of middle-class selfhood in America comes from Wilfred M. McClay, *The Masterless: Self and Society in Modern America* (Chapel Hill: University of North Carolina Press, 1993).

36. Betty Friedan, *The Feminine Mystique* (New York: W. W. Norton & Company, 2010), 472; see also Daniel Horowitz, *Betty Friedan and the Making of the Feminine Mystique: The American Left, the Cold War, and Modern Feminism* (Amherst: University of Massachusetts Press, 2000).

37. Daniel Immerwahr, "Polanyi in the United States: Peter Drucker, Karl Polanyi, and the Midcentury Critique of Economic Society," *Journal of the History of Ideas* 70, no. 3 (2009): 446; Nelson Lichtenstein, *American Capitalism: Social Thought and Political Economy in the Twentieth Century* (Philadelphia: University of Pennsylvania Press, 2006); Howard Brick, *Transcending Capitalism: Visions of a New Society in Modern American Thought* (Ithaca, NY: Cornell University Press, 2006).

Chapter 1

1. Kenneth Rexroth, "Vivisection of a Poet," *Nation* 185, no. 20 (December 14, 1957): 450–53.

2. J. P. Guilford, "Creativity," *The American Psychologist* 5, no. 9 (1950): 444, 451; Sidney J. Parnes and Eugene A. Brunelle, "The Literature of Creativity (Part I)," *Journal of Creative Behavior* 1, no. 1 (1967): 52.

3. Calvin W. Taylor, *Creativity: Progress and Potential* (New York: McGraw-Hill, 1964), 3.

4. J. P. Guilford, "Creativity: Yesterday, Today, and Tomorrow," *Journal of Creative Behavior* 1, no. 1 (1967): 6.

5. Guilford, "Creativity," 444.

6. Taylor, *Creativity*, 6.

7. Jamie Cohen-Cole, *The Open Mind: Cold War Politics and the Sciences of Human Nature* (Chicago: University of Chicago Press, 2014), 5–6; Ellen Herman, *The Romance of American Psychology: Political Culture in the Age of Experts* (Berkeley: University of California Press, 1995).

8. Calvin W. Taylor and Frank Barron, eds., *Scientific Creativity: Its Recognition and Development* (New York: John Wiley, 1963), xiii.

9. Liam Hudson, *Contrary Imaginations: A Psychological Study of the Young Student* (New York: Schocken Books, 1966), 220.

10. Calvin W. Taylor, ed., *Widening Horizons in Creativity: The Proceedings of the Fifth Utah Creativity Research Conference* (New York: Wiley, 1964), preface.

11. John Carson, *The Measure of Merit: Talents, Intelligence, and Inequality in the French and American Republics, 1750–1940* (Princeton, NJ: Princeton University Press, 2007).

12. Guilford, "Creativity," 445.

13. Irving A. Taylor, "The Nature of the Creative Process," in *Creativity: An Examination of the Creative Process*, ed. Paul Smith (New York: Communication Arts Books, 1959), 21.

14. Quoted in Darrin M. McMahon, *Divine Fury: A History of Genius*, 1st edition (New York: Basic Books, 2013), 174.

15. Galton restricted his studies to the English for practical reasons, but he was also interested in the Italians and the Jews, "both of whom appear to be rich in families of high intellectual breeds." He was less interested in studying the French, "where the Revolution and the guillotine made sad havoc among the progeny of her abler races." Francis Galton, *Hereditary Genius: An Inquiry into Its Laws and Consequences* (London: Macmillan and Co., 1869), quoted in Pierluigi Serraino, *The Creative Architect: Inside the Great Midcentury Personality Study* (New York: Monacelli Press, 2016), 100–101.

16. Guilford, "Creativity," 447.

17. Carson, *The Measure of Merit*, 260–63.

18. See David A. Varel, *The Lost Black Scholar: Resurrecting Allison Davis in American Social Thought* (Chicago: University of Chicago Press, 2018).

19. Calvin W. Taylor, ed., *Climate for Creativity: Report of the Seventh National Research Conference on Creativity* (New York: Pergamon Press, 1972), viii.

20. Taylor and Barron, *Scientific Creativity: Its Recognition and Development*, 6.

21. Guilford, "Creativity: Yesterday, Today, and Tomorrow," 3.

22. Guilford, "Creativity," 445.

23. Guilford, 446.

24. L. L. Thurstone, "Creative Talent," in *Testing Problems in Perspective*, ed. Anne Anastasi (Washington, DC: American Council on Education, 1966), 414.

25. Guilford, "Creativity," 446.

26. Howard E. Gruber, Glenn Terrell, and Michael Wertheimer, eds., *Contemporary Approaches to Creative Thinking: A Symposium Held at the University of Colorado* (New York: Atherton Press, 1962), x.

27. Guilford was even more conservative than Galton, estimating one person in two million had ever accomplished anything truly creative. Guilford, "Creativity," 445.

28. Quoted in Herman, 46.

29. Serraino, *The Creative Architect*, 10.

30. Serraino, 100–101.

31. Serraino, 61.

32. Anne Roe, *A Psychological Study of Eminent Biologists* (Washington, DC: American Psychological Association, 1952); Anne Roe, *The Making of a Scientist* (New York: Dodd, Mead, 1953); Anne Roe, *A Psychological Study of Eminent Psychologists and Anthropologists, and a Comparison with Biological and Physical Scientists* (Washington, DC: American Psychological Association, 1953).

33. Taylor, *Creativity*, 13.

34. Serraino, *The Creative Architect*, 55.

35. Cohen-Cole, *The Open Mind*, 45.

36. For the historical construction of taste and class in America, see Lawrence Levine, *Highbrow/Lowbrow: The Emergence of Cultural Hierarchy in America* (Cambridge, MA: Harvard University Press, 1990); Michael Kammen, *American Culture, American Tastes: Social Change and the Twentieth Century* (New York: Knopf, 1999).

37. Frank Barron, *Creativity and Psychological Health* (Princeton, NJ: D. Van Nostrand Company, Inc., 1963), 2–3.

38. Cohen-Cole, *The Open Mind*.

39. X, "WOMAN's QUALITIES; Not Dependable for Creative, Judicial, and Executive Labors," *New York Times*, April 7, 1909; on "pink collar" or "white blouse" labor see Nikil Saval, *Cubed: A Secret History of the Workplace* (New York: Doubleday, 2014), chapter 3.

40. "Women in Business," *Fortune*, July 1935.

41. Nancy MacLean, *The American Women's Movement, 1945–2000: A Brief History with Documents*, illustrated edition, The Bedford Series in History and Culture (Boston: Bedford/St. Martin's, 2009), 72.

42. McMahon, *Divine Fury*, 114.

43. McMahon, 22, 71.

44. Taylor, *Creativity*, 384.

45. Cohen-Cole, *The Open Mind*, 44.

46. John Riddick, "Boys Predominate in Creativity Beginning at Age of Puberty," *Tucson Daily Citizen*, May 26, 1962, 2.

47. Nathan Kogan, "Creativity and Sex Differences," *Journal of Creative Behavior* 8, no. 1 (1974): 1.

48. Kogan, 11.

49. Jerome Kagan, *Creativity and Learning* (Boston: Houghton Mifflin, 1967), ix.

50. Kogan, "Creativity and Sex Differences," 12.

51. Betty Friedan, *The Feminine Mystique* (New York: W. W. Norton & Company, 2010), 472.

52. Phyllis Schlafly, "What's Wrong with 'Equal Rights' for Women?" in *Debating the American Conservative Movement: 1945 to the Present*, ed. Donald T. Critchlow and Nancy MacLean, Debating 20th Century America (Lanham, MD: Rowman & Littlefield, 2009), 200.

53. Israel Shenker, "Spock Still Cares about Babies, Wishes More Women Did," *New York Times*, January 28, 1970, sec. Archives, https://www.nytimes.com/1970/01/28/archives/spock-still-cares-about-babies-wishes-more-women-did.html.

54. Paul Goodman, *Growing Up Absurd: Problems of Youth in the Organized System* (New York: Random House, 1960), 13.

55. Shulamith Firestone, *The Dialectic of Sex* (New York: Bantam Books, 1970), 91.

56. Friedan, *The Feminine Mystique*, 541.

57. Friedan, 479.

58. Friedan, 458.

59. Friedan, 436–37.

60. Hubert E. Brogden and Thomas B. Sprecher, "Criteria of Creativity," in *Creativity: Progress and Potential*, ed. Calvin W. Taylor (New York: McGraw-Hill Book Company, 1964), 162, 158.

61. Morris I. Stein, "Creativity and Culture," *The Journal of Psychology* 36 (1953): 311.

62. Harold H. Anderson, "Comments on Viktor Lowenfeld's 'What Is Creative Teaching?'" in *Creativity: Proceedings of the Second Minnesota Conference on Gifted Children, October 12–14, 1959*, ed. E. Paul Torrance (Minneapolis: University of Minnesota Center for Continuation Study of the General Extension Division, 1959).

63. Taylor, *Creativity*, 6.

64. Anne Roe, "Psychological Approaches to Creativity in Science," in *Essays on Creativity in the Sciences*, ed. Myron A. Coler (New York: New York University Press, 1963), 153–82.

65. Brogden and Sprecher, "Criteria of Creativity," 176.

66. Abraham H. Maslow, "The Creative Attitude," in *The Farther Reaches of Human Nature*, An Esalen Book (New York: Viking Press, 1971), 58.

67. Brogden and Sprecher, "Criteria of Creativity," 156.

68. Brewster Ghiselin, "Ultimate Criteria for Two Levels of Creativity," in *Scientific Creativity: Its Recognition and Development*, ed. Calvin W. Taylor and Frank Barron (New York: John Wiley, 1963), 30–31.

69. Taher A. Razik, "Psychometric Measurement of Creativity," in Ross Lawler Mooney, *Explorations in Creativity* (New York: Harper & Row 1967), 302.

70. Chapter 2. For ties between industry and creativity research, see also Michael Bycroft, "Psychology, Psychologists, and the Creativity Movement: The Lives of Method Inside and Outside the Cold War," in *Cold War Social Science: Knowledge Production, Liberal Democracy, and Human Nature*, ed. Mark Solovey and Hamilton Cravens (New York: Palgrave Macmillan, 2012).

71. J. H. McPherson, "How to Use Creative People Effectively," paper presented at the American Management Association, Chicago, March 1958, cited in Calvin W. Taylor and Frank Barron, *Scientific Creativity: Its Recognition and Development* (New York: John Wiley, 1963). See chapter 2 for more examples of this school of thought.

72. Gary A. Steiner, ed., *The Creative Organization* (Chicago: University of Chicago Press, 1965), Introduction.

73. Steiner, 10.

74. Steiner, 14.

75. Steiner, 21.

76. Ayn Rand, *The Fountainhead* (New York: Signet, 1943).

77. Steiner, *The Creative Organization*, 11–12.

78. Steiner, 13.

79. Eugene Von Fange, *Professional Creativity* (Hoboken, NJ: Prentice Hall, 1964), 2.

80. Von Fange, 218.

Chapter 2

1. "BBDO Worldwide (Batten, Barton, Durstine & Osborn)," *AdAge Encyclopedia*, September 15, 2003, http://adage.com/article/adage-encyclopedia/bbdo-worldwide-batten-barton-durstine-osborn/98341/.

2. Alex F. Osborn, *How to Think Up* (New York: McGraw-Hill, 1942), 29.

3. Phillip E. Norton, "Thinking Unlimited: More Companies Adopt Unorthodox Techniques for Generating Ideas," *Wall Street Journal*, September 13, 1962.

4. Alex F. Osborn, *Your Creative Power: How to Use Imagination* (New York: C. Scribner's Sons, 1948); title brainstorm list from Box 1, Alexander F. Osborn Papers, 1948–1966, University Archives, State University of New York at Buffalo.

5. Alex F. Osborn, *Wake Up Your Mind: 101 Ways to Develop Creativeness* (New York: Scribner, 1952), front matter.

6. Alex F. Osborn, *The Gold Mine Between Your Ears* (New York: Ticonderoga Publishers, 1955), 4.

7. Alex F. Osborn, *Applied Imagination: Principles and Procedures of Creative Problem-Solving* (New York: Scribner, 1953), 36.

8. Osborn, *How to Think Up*, v, 3, 5.

9. Osborn, 5.

10. Harold A. Littledale, "Imagination Yea—Shyness Nay," *New York Times*, November 7, 1948, 131.

11. Osborn, *How to Think Up*.

12. Bregje F. Van Eekelen, "Uncle Sam Needs Your Ideas: A Brief History of Embodied Knowledge in American World War II Posters," *Public Culture* 30, no. 1 (January 1, 2018): 113–42, https://doi.org/10.1215/08992363-4189191.

13. See Catherine L. Fisk, *Working Knowledge: Employee Innovation and the Rise of Corporate Intellectual Property, 1800–1930* (Chapel Hill: University of North Carolina Press, 2009); Harry Braverman, *Labor and Monopoly Capital: The Degradation of Work in the Twentieth Century* (New York: Monthly Review Press, 1975); David F. Noble, *America by Design: Science, Technology, and the Rise of Corporate Capitalism* (New York: Knopf, 1977); David F. Noble, *Forces of Production: A Social History of Industrial Automation* (New York: Knopf, 1984).

14. Osborn, *How to Think Up*, 32.

15. "Brainstorming: More Concerns Set Up Free-Wheeling 'Think Panels' to Mine Ideas—Ethyl Gets 71 Ideas in 45 Minutes: Reynolds Metals Develops Marketing Plans," *Wall Street Journal*, New York, December 5, 1955, 1.

16. "Federal 'Brains' Brace for Storm: Apostle of Madison Avenue Technique to Try to Stir Up Sluggish Thinkers," *New York Times*, May 20, 1956; Jhan and June Robbins, "129 Ways to Get a Husband," *McCall's*, January 1958.

17. Alex F. Osborn, "Developments in the Creative Education Movement," Creative Education Foundation, 1962, 3, Box 13, Alexander F. Osborn Papers, 1948–1966, University Archives, State University of New York at Buffalo; C. M.

Mullen, "G. & C. Merriam Company to Sidney J. Parnes," October 9, 1962 (unprocessed), Alex Osborn Creative Studies Collection, Archives & Special Collections Department, E. H. Butler Library, SUNY Buffalo State.

18. Dr. Daniel Pursuit to Alex Osborn, quoted in Alex F. Osborn, "Is Education Becoming More Creative?" Creative Education Foundation, 1961, Box 16, Alexander F. Osborn Papers, 1948–1966, University Archives, State University of New York at Buffalo.

19. Various letters, Box 11, Alexander F. Osborn Papers, 1948–1966, University Archives, State University of New York at Buffalo.

20. "The Third Year: Current Developments in the Movement for the Encouragement of a More Creative Trend in Education," Creative Education Foundation, 1958, Box 13, Alexander F. Osborn Papers, 1948–1966, University Archives, State University of New York at Buffalo.

21. Rosalie Deer Heart and Doris J. Shallcross, *Celebrating the Soul of CPSI* (Buffalo, NY: Creative Education Foundation, 2004), 10.

22. Heart and Shallcross, 10.

23. John E. Arnold, *Creative Engineering*, ed. William J. Clancey (n.p.: William Clancey, 2016), 20.

24. Whiting, *Creative Thinking*, 2.

25. Kyle VanHemert, "Creative Complex: Brainstorming in American Business in the 1950s" (unpublished paper, May 22, 2017), 15. For the story of brainstorming at DuPont I am indebted to Kyle VanHemert, who generously allowed me to use material from an unpublished research paper.

26. Memorandum, "Pilot Brainstorming Session," July 13, 1956, Box 27, Folder 6, E. I. Du Pont de Nemours & Co. Advertising Department, Hagley Museum and Library, Wilmington, Delaware.

27. Memo from James H. McCormick to V. L. Simpson, March 5, 1956 [likely date from context March 5, 1957], Box 28, Folder 7, E. I. Du Pont de Nemours & Co. Advertising Department, Hagley Museum and Library, Wilmington, Delaware.

28. VanHemert, 5.

29. M. R. Hecht, "Brainstorming—Bunk or Benefit," *Canadian Chemical Process*, September 11, 1956; "Brainstorming: Cure or Curse?" *Business Week*, December 29, 1956; Harry Stockman, "The Limits of Brainstorming," *Proceedings of the Institute of Radio Engineers*, October 1957; B. B. Goldner, "Why Doesn't Brainstorming Always Seem to Work?" *Sales Management*, October 5, 1956.

30. Donald W. Taylor, Paul C. Berry, and Clifford H. Block, "Does Group Participation When Using Brainstorming Facilitate or Inhibit Creative Thinking?" *Administrative Science Quarterly* 3, no. 1 (June 1, 1958): 42.

31. Heart and Shallcross, *Celebrating the Soul of CPSI*, 10. In 1958, probably due to criticism of brainstorming in the press, enrollment dropped to two hundred again, but by 1963 it was back up to a steady five hundred, which it held for the next three decades.

32. Taylor, Berry, and Block, "Does Group Participation When Using Brainstorming," 23–47; "'Brainstorming' for Ideas Criticized," *New York Herald Tribune*,

January 20, 1958; Sidney J. Parnes, *A Source Book for Creative Thinking* (New York: Scribner, 1962).

33. W. A. Peterson, "Groups Don't Create: Individuals Do," *Printers' Ink*, October 26, 1956; Mildred Benton, *Creativity in Research and Invention in the Physical Sciences* (Washington, DC: US Naval Research Laboratory, 1961).

34. William Whyte, *The Organization Man* (New York: Simon and Schuster, 1956), 51.

35. Quoted in Stephen R. Fox, *The Mirror Makers: A History of American Advertising and Its Creators* (New York: Morrow, 1984), 181.

36. Paul Smith, ed., *Creativity: An Examination of the Creative Process* (New York: Communication Arts Books, 1959), 180.

37. Saul Bass, "Creativity in Visual Communication," in *Creativity: An Examination of the Creative Process*, ed. Paul Smith (New York: Communication Arts Books, 1959), 123.

38. Bass, 126.

39. Bass, 126–27.

40. Smith, *Creativity: An Examination of the Creative Process*, 198.

41. Osborn, *Your Creative Power*, 7.

42. "Report of Proceedings of the Second Annual Creative Problem Solving Institute," Creative Education Foundation, 1956, 6, Box 16, Alexander F. Osborn Papers, 1948-1966, University Archives, State University of New York at Buffalo.

43. Alex F. Osborn, *Applied Imagination*, 3rd revised edition (New York: Charles Scribner's Sons, 1963), 12.

44. Osborn, 10. These were apparently more than idle musings. It seems Osborn did put some effort toward communicating his plans to government, as he reported in 1960: "We have been progressing in most areas of public affairs. We have fallen flat, however, in our efforts to persuade Washington to apply creative procedures to our foreign problems." Osborn, "Developments in Creative Education," 18.

45. Osborn, *Applied Imagination*, 28.

46. Alex F. Osborn, "High Lights of the First Five Months in My Endeavor to Encourage Education to Include Indoctrination in Creativity," 1954, Box 11, Alexander F. Osborn Papers, 1948-1966, University Archives, State University of New York at Buffalo.

47. Osborn, "Developments in the Creative Education Movement."

48. Osborn, "Is Education Becoming More Creative?"

49. For this characterization of the liberal arts philosophy compared to those of classical and vocational schooling, see David F. Labaree, "Public Goods, Private Goods: The American Struggle over Educational Goals," *American Educational Research Journal* 34, no. 1 (1997): 39–81.

50. Osborn, "Is Education Becoming More Creative?"

51. Aaron Lecklider, *Inventing the Egghead: The Battle over Brainpower in American Culture* (Philadelphia: University of Pennsylvania Press, 2013); Richard Hofstadter, *Anti-Intellectualism in American Life* (New York: Knopf, 1963).

52. James Gilbert, *A Cycle of Outrage: America's Reaction to the Juvenile Delinquent in the 1950s* (New York: Oxford University Press, 1988).

53. Bregje van Eekelen has previously described brainstorming as carnivalesque (van Eekelen, "The Social Life of Ideas").

54. Richard P. Youtz, "Psychological Foundations of Applied Imagination," in *A Sourcebook for Creative Thinking*, ed. Sidney J. Parnes and Harold F. Harding (New York: Charles Scribner's Sons, 1962), 193–215.

55. Arnold Meadow and Sidney J. Parnes, "Evaluation of Training in Creative Problem-Solving," *Journal of Applied Psychology* 43, no. 3 (1959): 189–94; Arnold Meadow and Sidney J. Parnes, "Influence of Brainstorming Instructions and Problem Sequence on a Creative Problem-Solving Test," *Journal of Applied Psychology* 43 (1959): 413–16; Sidney J. Parnes and Arnold Meadow, "Effects of 'Brain-Storming' Instructions on Creative Problem-Solving by Trained and Untrained Subjects," *Journal of Educational Psychology* 50, no. 4 (1959): 171–76; Sidney J. Parnes and Arnold Meadow, "Evaluation of Persistence of Effects Produced by a Creative Problem-Solving Course," *Psychological Reports* 7 (1960): 357–61; Sidney J. Parnes, "Effects of Extended Effort in Creative Problem-Solving," *Journal of Educational Psychology* 52, no. 3 (1961): 117–22.

56. Alex F. Osborn, "Developments in Creative Education, as Reported to the Sixth Annual Creative Problem-Solving Institute at the University of Buffalo," 1960, Box 13, Alexander F. Osborn Papers, 1948–1966, University Archives, State University of New York at Buffalo.

57. Osborn, 25.

58. Untitled document, c. 1963, Box 11, Alexander F. Osborn Papers, 1948–1966, University Archives, State University of New York at Buffalo.

59. J. P. Guilford, "Creativity: Yesterday, Today, and Tomorrow," *Journal of Creative Behavior* 1, no. 1 (1967): 12–13.

60. Osborn, *Applied Imagination*, 3rd revised edition.

Chapter 3

1. Carl R. Rogers, "Toward a Theory of Creativity," in *Creativity and Its Cultivation*, ed. Harold H. Anderson (New York: Harper & Brothers, 1959), 72.

2. Rogers, "Toward a Theory of Creativity," 69–70.

3. For a recent account of humanistic psychology in postwar business and culture see Jessica Grogan, *Encountering America: Sixties Psychology, Counterculture and the Movement that Shaped the Modern Self* (New York: Harper Perennial, 2012).

4. Harold H. Anderson, ed., *Creativity and Its Cultivation* (New York: Harper & Brothers, 1959); Carl R. Rogers, "Toward a Theory of Creativity," *ETC: A Review of General Semantics* 11, no. 4 (1954): 249–60; Rollo May, *The Courage to Create* (New York: W. W. Norton and Company, Inc., 1975); Abraham H. Maslow, "Emotional Blocks to Creativity," in *A Source Book for Creative Thinking*, ed. Sidney J. Parnes and Harold F. Harding (New York: Charles Scribner's Sons, 1962), 93; Abraham H. Maslow, "Creativity in Self-Actualizing People," in *Creativity and Its Cultivation*, ed. Harold H. Anderson (New York: Harper & Brothers, 1959), 83; Abraham H. Maslow, *The Maslow Business Reader*, ed. Deborah C. Stephens, 1st edition (New York: John Wiley & Sons, 2000), 21.

5. Abraham H. Maslow, "Emotional Blocks to Creativity," in *The Farther Reaches of Human Nature*, An Esalen Book (New York: Viking Press, 1971), 78.

6. "Creativity" was not listed in Maslow's original "Hierarchy of Needs," in 1943, though it would appear in later versions.

7. Abraham H. Maslow, "A Holistic Approach to Creativity," in *The Farther Reaches of Human Nature*, An Esalen Book (New York: Viking Press, 1971), 69.

8. Abraham H. Maslow, "The Creative Attitude," in *The Farther Reaches of Human Nature*, An Esalen Book (New York: Viking Press, 1971), 66.

9. Maslow, "A Holistic Approach to Creativity," 71–73.

10. Quoted in Ian A. M. Nicholson, "'Giving Up Maleness': Abraham Maslow, Masculinity, and the Boundaries of Psychology," *History of Psychology* 4, no. 1 (2001): 82, https://doi.org/10.1037//1093–4510.4.1.79.

11. Quoted in Nicholson, 80.

12. Maslow, "Emotional Blocks to Creativity" (1971), 83.

13. Maslow, 80–81, 86, 90.

14. Darrin M. McMahon, *Divine Fury: A History of Genius*, 1st edition (New York: Basic Books, 2013), 165, 169.

15. Fred Turner, *From Counterculture to Cyberculture: Stewart Brand, the Whole Earth Network, and the Rise of Digital Utopianism* (Chicago: University of Chicago Press, 2006); Grogan, *Encountering America*.

16. Quoted in Alfonso Montuori, "Frank Barron: A Creator on Creating," *Journal of Humanistic Psychology* 43 (April 1, 2003): 8, https://doi.org/10.1177/0022167802250582.

17. Frank Barron, *Creativity and Psychological Health* (Princeton, NJ: D. Van Nostrand Company, Inc., 1963), 1–2.

18. Donald W. MacKinnon, "The Highly Effective Individual," in *Explorations in Creativity*, ed. Ross Lawler Mooney, 1st edition (New York: Harper & Row, 1967), 65.

19. Frank Barron, "The Psychology of Imagination," *Scientific American* 199, no. 3 (1958): 150–56.

20. Barron, 164.

21. Barron, *Creativity and Psychological Health*, 5.

22. Maslow, "The Creative Attitude," 55.

23. Maslow, "Emotional Blocks to Creativity" (1971), 62.

24. Maslow, "The Creative Attitude," 59–65.

25. Frank Barron, "The Psychology of Imagination," 163.

26. Timothy Leary, "The Effects of Test Score Feedback on Creative Performance and of Drugs on Creative Experience," in *Widening Horizons in Creativity: The Proceedings of the Fifth Utah Creativity Research Conference*, ed. Calvin W. Taylor (New York: Wiley, 1964), 87–111.

27. Maslow, "Emotional Blocks to Creativity" (1962), 80.

28. Maslow, *The Maslow Business Reader*, 185.

29. Maslow, "A Holistic Approach to Creativity," 70.

30. quoted in Sarah Brouillette, *Literature and the Creative Economy* (Stanford, CA: Stanford University Press, 2014), 69, originally in "See No Evil, Hear No Evil:

When Liberalism Fails," in *Future Visions: The Unpublished Papers of Abraham Maslow*, ed. Edward L. Hoffman (Thousand Oaks, CA: Sage Publications, 1996).

31. Abraham H. Maslow, "The Need for Creative People," in *The Farther Reaches of Human Nature*, An Esalen Book (New York: Viking Press, 1971), 94–95.

32. Brewster Ghiselin, *The Creative Process: A Symposium* (New York: New American Library, 1955), 3.

33. May, *The Courage to Create*, 12.

34. Maslow, "The Need for Creative People," 94.

35. Maslow, "The Creative Attitude," 57.

36. Frank Barron, "The Disposition Toward Originality," in *Scientific Creativity: Its Recognition and Development*, ed. Frank Barron and Calvin W. Taylor (New York: John Wiley & Sons, 1963), 151.

37. Jamie Cohen-Cole, "The Creative American: Cold War Salons, Social Science, and the Cure for Modern Society," *Isis* 100 (2009): 226–30.

38. Barron, "The Disposition Toward Originality," 150.

39. For the historical construction of taste and class in America, see Lawrence Levine, *Highbrow/Lowbrow: The Emergence of Cultural Hierarchy in America* (Cambridge, MA: Harvard University Press, 1990); Michael Kammen, *American Culture, American Tastes: Social Change and the Twentieth Century* (New York: Knopf, 1999).

40. Barron, "The Disposition Toward Originality," 150.

41. Barron, 151.

42. Barron, "The Psychology of Imagination," 163.

43. Frank Barron, "The Needs for Order and for Disorder as Motives in Creative Activity," in *Scientific Creativity: Its Recognition and Development*, ed. Calvin W. Taylor and Frank Barron (New York: John Wiley & Sons, 1963), 158, emphasis in original; Barron, "The Disposition Toward Originality," 151.

44. Maslow, "The Creative Attitude," 58–59.

45. Michael F. Andrews, ed., *Creativity and Psychological Health* (Syracuse, NY: Syracuse University Press, 1961).

46. Maslow, "Creativity in Self-Actualizing People," 94; Arthur Koestler, *The Act of Creation* (New York: Macmillan, 1964).

47. Victor Lowenfeld, "What Is Creative Teaching?" in *Creativity*, Second Minnesota Conference on Gifted Children (Minneapolis: University of Minnesota Press, 1959), 43.

48. Maslow, "The Creative Attitude," 55.

49. Maslow, "Creativity in Self-Actualizing People."

50. Maslow, "The Creative Attitude," 59.

51. Maslow, "Emotional Blocks to Creativity" (1971), 83.

52. Donald W. MacKinnon, "The Nature and Nurture of Creative Talent," *American Psychologist* 17, no. 7 (1962): 484–95.

53. Nathan Kogan, "Creativity and Sex Differences," *Journal of Creative Behavior* 8, no. 1 (1974): 4–6.

54. Quoted in Nicholson, "'Giving Up Maleness,'" 80.

55. Nicholson, "'Giving Up Maleness.'"

56. Abraham H. Maslow, *Maslow on Management*, ed. Deborah C. Stephens and Gary Heil (New York: John Wiley, 1998).

57. Nadine Weidman, "Between the Counterculture and the Corporation: Abraham Maslow and Humanistic Psychology in the 1960s," in *Groovy Science: Knowledge, Innovation, and American Counterculture*, ed. David Kaiser and Patrick McCray (Chicago: University of Chicago Press, 2016), 109; for the corporate aspects of Maslow's ideas on creativity, also see Brouillette, *Literature and the Creative Economy*.

58. Maslow, *Maslow on Management*, 243.

Chapter 4

1. George M. Prince, *The Practice of Creativity: A Manual for Dynamic Group Problem Solving* (New York: Harper & Row, 1970), 3.

2. Dean Gitter, quoted in "Synectics' Art of Analogy Makes Creativity a Science," *Executive's Bulletin*, October 1965.

3. "Synectics' Art of Analogy Makes Creativity a Science," *Executive's Bulletin*, October 1965.

4. Prince, *The Practice of Creativity*.

5. Tom Alexander, "Invention by the Madness Method," *Fortune*, August 1965, 190.

6. "Synectics: A New Method for Developing Creative Potential," n.d., Box 29, Folder 8, United Shoe Machinery Corporation Records, Archives Center, National Museum of American History, Washington, DC.

7. DeWitt O. Tolly, "The Creativity Review," 1963, Box 11, Alexander F. Osborn Papers, 1948–1966, University Archives, State University of New York at Buffalo.

8. Gordon, quoted in Eugene Raudsepp, "Intuition in Engineering: Learn to Play," *Machine Design*, April 15, 1965.

9. William J. J. Gordon, "How to Get Your Imagination Off the Ground," *Think*, March 1963; Gordon, quoted in Raudsepp, "Intuition in Engineering."

10. On the legacies and transformations of scientific management in the postwar era see Stephen P. Waring, *Taylorism Transformed: Scientific Management Theory since 1945* (Chapel Hill: University of North Carolina Press, 1991); for a good overview of Taylor, the Gilbreths, and scientific management see Nikil Saval, *Cubed: A Secret History of the Workplace* (New York: Doubleday, 2014).

11. Carter to Abel, June 22, 1962, Box 29, Folder 8, United Shoe Machinery Corporation Records, Archives Center, National Museum of American History, Washington, DC.

12. "Reaction to Discussion on Synectics," Jackson to Goodchild, June 22, 1962, Box 29, Folder 8, United Shoe Machinery Corporation Records, Archives Center, National Museum of American History, Washington, DC.

13. Goodchild to Prince, March 8, 1963, Box 29, Folder 8, United Shoe Machinery Corporation Records, Archives Center, National Museum of American History, Washington, DC.

14. Tape transcript as reproduced in Tom Alexander, "Invention by the Madness Method," *Fortune*, August 1965.

15. Alexander, 165.

16. William J. J. Gordon, *Synectics: The Development of Creative Capacity* (New York: Harper & Row, 1961), 8.

17. *20/20*, date unknown.

18. Prince to Overly, June 21, 1962, Box 29, Folder 8, United Shoe Machinery Corporation Records, Archives Center, National Museum of American History, Washington, DC.

19. "Synectics' Art of Analogy Makes Creativity a Science," *Executive's Bulletin*, October 1965.

20. Chris Argyris, *Personality and Organization: The Conflict between System and the Individual* (New York: Harper & Row, 1957); Douglas McGregor, *The Human Side of Enterprise* (New York: McGraw-Hill, 1960).

21. McGregor, *The Human Side of Enterprise*.

22. McGregor, 22.

23. Gordon, *Synectics: The Development of Creative Capacity*, 10.

24. Box 29, Folder 8, United Shoe Machinery Corporation Records, Archives Center, National Museum of American History, Washington, DC.

25. Prince to Overly June 21, 1962, Box 29, Folder 8, United Shoe Machinery Corporation Records, Archives Center, National Museum of American History, Washington, DC.

26. "Synectics' Art of Analogy Makes Creativity a Science,"" *Executive's Bulletin*, October 30, 1965.

27. John E. Arnold, *Creative Engineering*, ed. William J. Clancey (n.p.: William J. Clancey, 2016), 115.

28. Peter Vanderwicken, "USM's Hard Life as an Ex-Monopoly," *Fortune*, October 1972, 124.

29. Pamphlet, "An Intensive Course on Creative Problem Solving," 1963, Box 29, Folder 8, United Shoe Machinery Corporation Records, Archives Center, National Museum of American History, Washington, DC.

30. Tolly, "The Creativity Review."

Chapter 5

1. Diane Ravitch, *The Troubled Crusade: American Education, 1945–1980* (New York: Basic Books, 1985), 231.

2. Quoted in Chandler Brossard, "The Creative Child," *Look*, November 7, 1961, 113.

3. Teresa Amabile, *Creativity in Context: Update to "The Social Psychology of Creativity"* (Boulder, CO: Westview Press, 1996), 24.

4. For more on creativity and childhood in postwar America see Amy Ogata, *Designing the Creative Child* (Minneapolis: University of Minnesota Press, 2013).

5. Kristie L. Speirs Neumeister and Bonnie Cramond, "E. Paul Torrance (1915–2003)," *American Psychologist* 59, no. 3 (April 2004): 179; unidentified persons affiliated with the Creative Education Foundation, Interview with E. P. Torrance, videotape, c. 1989, Box 34, E. Paul Torrance Papers, MS 2344, Hargrett Rare Book and Manuscript Library, University of Georgia Libraries. It is unclear how much Torrance's adoption of the word "creativity" owed to what we might call

234 NOTES TO CHAPTER 5

the Guilford effect. It seems clear the very fact that the president of the national professional association named creativity as worthy of investigation prompted more than a few researchers whose work might otherwise have remained in the categories of "imagination," "effectiveness," "ingenuity," or "intelligence" to take up the new label. Torrance repeatedly claimed that his interest in creativity began in the 1930s, a narrative that later biographers would repeat. He claimed to have been heavily influenced by a 1943 book, *Square Pegs in Round Holes*, and *Ideophoria*, a 1945 career psychology book, both of which dealt in part with "creative imagination." But Torrance's first use of the word in any systematic way came in the late 1950s.

6. Robert Genter, "Understanding the Pow Experience: Stress Research and the Implementation of the 1955 US Armed Forces Code of Conduct," *Journal of the History of the Behavioral Sciences* 51, no. 2 (2015): 158, https://doi.org/10.1002/jhbs.21696.

7. Brossard, "The Creative Child," 113.

8. E. Paul Torrance, ed., *Creativity: Proceedings of the Second Minnesota Conference on Gifted Children, October 12–14, 1959* (Minneapolis: University of Minnesota Center for Continuation Study of the General Extension Division, 1959), 25.

9. Harold H. Anderson, ed., *Creativity and Its Cultivation* (New York: Harper & Brothers, 1959), 181–82.

10. E. P. Torrance, *Norms-Technical Manual: Torrance Tests of Creative Thinking* (Lexington, MA: Ginn and Company, 1974), 8.

11. Unidentified persons affiliated with the Creative Education Foundation, interview with E. P. Torrance.

12. The tests were originally called the Minnesota Tests of Creativity Thinking but were renamed in 1966, when Torrance left Minnesota for the University of Georgia. Because they have been known as the Torrance Tests of Creative Thinking ever since, I have chosen to use the more familiar name for simplicity.

13. Philip E Vernon, *Creativity: Selected Readings* (Harmondsworth, UK: Penguin, 1970), 339.

14. Calvin W. Taylor, *Creativity: Progress and Potential* (New York: McGraw-Hill, 1964), 178.

15. Arthur M. Schlesinger, *The Vital Center: The Politics of Freedom* (Boston: Houghton Mifflin Company, 1962).

16. Rockefeller Brothers Fund, *The Pursuit of Excellence: Education and the Future of America* (Garden City, NY: Doubleday & Company, Inc., 1958), 205.

17. John W. Gardner, *Excellence: Can We Be Equal and Excellent Too?* (New York: Harper & Brothers, 1961), 35.

18. David F. Labaree, "Public Goods, Private Goods: The American Struggle over Educational Goals," *American Educational Research Journal* 34, no. 1 (1997): 42.

19. Rockefeller Brothers Fund, *The Pursuit of Excellence*, v.

20. E. Paul Torrance, "Towards a More Humane Kind of Education," paper presented at the Annual Statewide Meeting of the Florida Association for Childhood Education, Tampa, Florida, October 5, 1963.

21. E. Paul Torrance, ed., *Education and the Creative Potential* (Minneapolis: University of Minnesota Press, 1963), 3–4.

22. Torrance, 3.

23. Torrance, 4.

24. E. Paul Torrance, "Is Creativity Research in Education Dead?" paper presented at the conference Creativity: A Quarter Century Later, Center for Creative Leadership, Greensboro, North Carolina, 1973.

25. M. K. Raina, *The Creativity Passion: E. Paul Torrance's Voyages of Discovering Creativity* (Westport, CT: Greenwood Publishing Group, 2000), 12.

26. "Various Parent Letters," n.d., MS3723—Torrance Personal Papers, Carton 4, University of Georgia Special Collections.

Chapter 6

1. *Printers' Ink*, January 2, 1959, 17–19.

2. *Printers' Ink*, January 2, 1959, cover, 17–19.

3. "How to Keep a Creative Man Creative," *Printers' Ink*, April 11, 1958, 51.

4. *Printers' Ink*, January 2, 1959, 18–19.

5. Thomas Frank, *The Conquest of Cool: Business Culture, Counterculture, and the Rise of Hip Consumerism* (Chicago: University of Chicago Press, 1998), 35–36.

6. Draper Daniels, "Don't Talk Creativity—Practice It," *Printers' Ink*, May 26, 1961, 52.

7. Daniels, 52.

8. "Printers' Ink Predicts for 1959: More Creativity, Agency-Client Rapport, New Products and Marketing Pressures," *Printers' Ink*, January 2, 1959, 31–32.

9. Paul Smith, ed., *Creativity: An Examination of the Creative Process* (New York: Communication Arts Books, 1959), 16.

10. Smith, 17–18.

11. Pierre D. Martineau, "The World Can Be Added to Me," *Printers' Ink*, April 2, 1961, 46.

12. "Report of Proceedings of the Second Annual Creative Problem Solving Institute," Creative Education Foundation, 1956, Box 16, Alexander F. Osborn Papers, 1948–1966, University Archives, State University of New York at Buffalo.

13. "How to Keep a Creative Man Creative," 51.

14. "The Creative Man: His Moods and Needs," *Printers' Ink*, June 13, 1958.

15. Paul Smith, "What Science Knows about Creative People," *Printers' Ink*, April 14, 1961.

16. *Printers' Ink*, January 2, 1959, 17.

17. Quoted in Frank, *The Conquest of Cool*, 40.

18. Stephen R. Fox, *The Mirror Makers: A History of American Advertising and Its Creators* (New York: Morrow, 1984), 182.

19. Quoted in Frank, *The Conquest of Cool*, 56.

20. Carl Ally, a PKL defector, in 1966, quoted in Frank, 99.

21. Earnest Elmo Calkins, "My Creative Philosophy," *Printers' Ink*, March 18, 1960, 54.

22. Quoted in Frank, *The Conquest of Cool*, 96.

23. Frank, 57.

24. *Printers' Ink*, January 2, 1959, 7.

25. Quoted in Fox, *The Mirror Makers*, 222.

26. "The Creative Man: His Moods and Needs," 31.

27. Robert Alden, "Advertising: 'Cult of Creativity' Is Scored by Harper," *New York Times*, October 28, 1960.

28. Alfred Politz, "The Dilemma of Creative Advertising," *Journal of Marketing*, October 1960, 1–6.

29. Politz. The most famous advocate of the "reason-why" approach in the 1950s was Rosser Reeves, who, like Politz, believed advertising was no art but "a science, like engineering." "The most dangerous word of all in advertising," he thought, was "originality" (quoted in Fox, *The Mirror Makers*, 193).

30. "Display Ad 38," *Wall Street Journal*, May 6, 1963.

31. "The Creative Man: His Moods and Needs," 32.

32. *Printers' Ink*, February 5, 1960, inside cover.

33. John Kenneth Galbraith, *The Affluent Society* (Boston: Houghton Mifflin, 1958), 129.

34. Daniel Horowitz, *The Anxieties of Affluence: Critiques of American Consumer Culture, 1939–1979* (Amherst: University of Massachusetts Press, 2004), 52–53.

35. Betty Friedan, *The Feminine Mystique* (New York: W. W. Norton & Company, 2010), 300–301.

36. Drucker apparently once said he remembered playing soccer with Dichter when they were boys.

37. Ernest Dichter, "Motivations," Newsletter, July-August 1957, Box 127, Ernest Dichter Papers, Hagley Museum & Library, Wilmington, Delaware.

38. Ernest Dichter, "Creativity: A Credo for the Sixties," unpublished manuscript, March 25, 1960, Box 173, Ernest Dichter Papers, Hagley Museum & Library, Wilmington, Delaware.

39. Box 175, Folder 8, Ernest Dichter Papers, Hagley Museum & Library, Wilmington, Delaware.

40. "Advertising's Creative Explosion," *Newsweek*, August 18, 1969. (The cover read "Advertising's Creative Revolution.")

41. Frank, *The Conquest of Cool*, 53–73.

42. Frank, 60.

43. Frank, 67.

44. Frank, 31.

45. Frank, 8.

Chapter 7

1. *Machine Design*, May 27 and June 10, 1965.

2. "Putting Creativity to Work," in *The Nature of Creativity: Contemporary Psychological Perspectives* (Cambridge and New York: Cambridge University Press, 1988), 79.

3. Frank X. Barron, *Creativity and Personal Freedom* (New York: Van Nos-

trand, 1968), 7, quoted in Amy Ogata, *Designing the Creative Child* (Minneapolis: University of Minnesota Press, 2013), 19.

4. Calvin W. Taylor and Frank Barron, eds., *Scientific Creativity: Its Recognition and Development* (New York: John Wiley & Sons, 1963); Calvin W. Taylor, *Creativity: Progress and Potential* (New York: McGraw-Hill, 1964); Frank Barron, *Creativity and Psychological Health* (Princeton, NJ: D. Van Nostrand Company, Inc., 1963); E. Paul Torrance, *Guiding Creative Talent* (Englewood Cliffs, NJ: Prentice-Hall, Inc., 1962); Calvin W. Taylor, ed., *Widening Horizons in Creativity: The Proceedings of the Fifth Utah Creativity Research Conference* (New York: Wiley, 1964).

5. Taylor, *Creativity*, 10.

6. Quinn McNemar, "Lost: Our Intelligence? Why?" *American Psychologist* 19, no. 12 (1964): 876.

7. R. L. Ebel, "The Future of Measurements of Abilities II," *Educational Researcher* 2, no. 3 (1973): 2.

8. Liam Hudson, *Contrary Imaginations: A Psychological Study of the Young Student* (New York: Schocken Books, 1966).

9. McNemar, 880.

10. Ray Hyman, "Creativity," *International Science and Technology*, August 1963, 52.

11. Robert L. Thorndike, "Some Methodological Issues in the Study of Creativity," in *Testing Problems in Perspective*, ed. Anne Anastasi (Washington, DC: American Council on Education, 1966), 448.

12. McNemar, "Lost: Our Intelligence?"; Michael A. Wallach and Nathan Kogan, *Modes of Thinking in Young Children: A Study of the Creativity-Intelligence Distinction* (New York: Holt, Rinehart and Winston, 1965); Michael A. Wallach and Nathan Kogan, "A New Look at the Creativity-Intelligence Distinction," *Journal of Personality* 33 (1965): 348–69.

13. Taylor, *Creativity*, 7.

14. Unidentified persons affiliated with the Creative Education Foundation, interview with E. P. Torrance.

15. Jerome Kagan, *Creativity and Learning* (Boston: Houghton Mifflin, 1967), vii.

16. Catharine M. Cox, *The Early Mental Traits of Three Hundred Geniuses* (Stanford, CA: Stanford University Press, 1926), quoted in Robert J. Sternberg, *Wisdom, Intelligence, and Creativity Synthesized* (Cambridge: Cambridge University Press, 2003).

17. John Baer, "Domain Specificity and the Limits of Creativity Theory," *Journal of Creative Behavior* 46, no. 1 (2012): 16.

18. Baer, 16.

19. Hudson, *Contrary Imaginations*.

20. Library of Congress, Nicholas E. Golovin Papers, Box 26, NYU Creative Science Program—Book Project—Chapter drafts by Blade, Coler, and Fox, 1961–1963.

21. Stephen Cole, "Review of *Essays on Creativity in the Sciences*, by Myron A.

Coler," *Technology and Culture* 6, no. 1 (1965): 158–59, https://doi.org/10.2307/3100984.

22. Taylor, *Creativity*, 7.

23. Paul Smith, ed., *Creativity: An Examination of the Creative Process* (New York: Communication Arts Books, 1959), 54–55.

24. Mel Rhodes, "An Analysis of Creativity," *Phi Delta Kappan* 42, no.7 (1961): 305–10; Calvin Taylor and Robert L. Ellison, "Moving Toward Working Models in Creativity: Utah Experiences and Insights," in *Perspectives in Creativity*, ed. Irving A. Taylor and J. W. Getzels (Chicago: Aldine Publishing Co., 1975), 191.

25. Taylor, *Creativity*, 7.

26. Chambers, "Creative Scientists of Today."

27. Cox, *The Early Mental Traits of Three Hundred Geniuses*, quoted in Sternberg, *Wisdom, Intelligence, and Creativity Synthesized*, 95.

28. Taylor and Barron, eds., *Scientific Creativity: Its Recognition and Development*, 372.

29. Frank Barron, *Creative Person and Creative Process* (New York: Holt, Rinehart and Winston, 1969), 2.

30. This reason was suggested to me by more than one respondent, but further research would be necessary to track the extent of the decline in creativity research published in existing academic journals.

31. Rosalie Deer Heart and Doris J. Shallcross, *Celebrating the Soul of CPSI* (Buffalo, NY: Creative Education Foundation, 2004), 143–54.

32. Gruber, Terrell, and Wertheimer, *Contemporary Approaches to Creative Thinking*, x.

33. Hudson, *Contrary Imaginations*.

Chapter 8

1. Carl R. Rogers, "Toward a Theory of Creativity," in *Creativity and Its Cultivation*, ed. Harold H. Anderson (New York: Harper & Brothers, 1959).

2. "You and Creativity," *Kaiser Aluminum News* 25, no. 3 (January 1968): 17.

3. Abraham H. Maslow, "Emotional Blocks to Creativity," in *The Farther Reaches of Human Nature*, An Esalen Book (New York: Viking Press, 1971), 85.

4. Jacques Ellul, *The Technological Society* (New York: Knopf, 1964).

5. Matthew H. Wisnioski, "How the Industrial Scientist Got His Groove: Entrepreneurial Journalism and the Fashioning of Technoscientific Innovators," in *Groovy Science: Knowledge, Innovation, and American Counterculture*, ed. David Kaiser and Patrick McCray (Chicago: University of Chicago Press, 2016), 341–42.

6. William G. Maas, quoted in Wisnioski, 342.

7. Steven Shapin, *The Scientific Life: A Moral History of a Late Modern Vocation* (Chicago: University of Chicago Press, 2008), 96.

8. William Whyte, *The Organization Man* (New York: Simon and Schuster, 1956), 8.

9. "Transcript of President Dwight D. Eisenhower's Farewell Address (1961)," National Archives, accessed July 14, 2020, https://www.archives.gov/milestone-documents/president-dwight-d-eisenhowers-farewell-address.

10. Fred Turner, *From Counterculture to Cyberculture: Stewart Brand, the*

Whole Earth Network, and the Rise of Digital Utopianism (Chicago: University of Chicago Press, 2006); David Kaiser and Patrick McCray, eds., *Groovy Science: Knowledge, Innovation, and American Counterculture* (Chicago: University of Chicago Press, 2016).

11. John F. Sargent Jr., "The Office of Technology Assessment: History, Authorities, Issues, and Options," Congressional Research Service, April 14–19, 2020, https://www.everycrsreport.com/reports/R46327.html#_Toc38965552.

12. E. Finley Carter, "Creativity in Research," in *Creativity: An Examination of the Creative Process*, ed. Paul Smith (New York: Communication Arts Books, 1959), 113.

13. Carter, 119.

14. Carter, 115.

15. John E. Arnold, "Creativity in Engineering," in *Creativity: An Examination of the Creative Process*, ed. Paul Smith (New York: Communication Arts Books, 1959), 34.

16. John E. Arnold, *Creative Engineering*, ed. William J. Clancey (n.p.: William J. Clancey, 2016), 128.

17. Quoted in Wisnioski, "How the Industrial Scientist Got His Groove," 342.

18. J. J. O'Connor and E. F. Robertson, "Jacob Bronowski Biography," MacTutor, last update October 2003, accessed May 24, 2017, http://www-history.mcs.st-and.ac.uk/Biographies/Bronowski.html.

19. Saul Bass, "Creativity in Visual Communication," in *Creativity: An Examination of the Creative Process*, ed. Paul Smith (New York: Communication Arts Books, 1959), 130.

20. Jacob Bronowski, "The Creative Process," *Scientific American* 199, no. 3 (1958): 63.

21. Frank Barron, "The Psychology of Imagination," *Scientific American* 199, no. 3 (1958): 150–56.

22. Bronowski, "The Creative Process," 60.

23. David F. Noble, *America by Design: Science, Technology, and the Rise of Corporate Capitalism* (New York: Knopf, 1977), part 1; Steven Shapin, *The Scientific Life: A Moral History of a Late Modern Vocation* (Chicago: University of Chicago Press, 2008).

24. Dennis Flannagan, "Creativity in Science," in *Creativity: An Examination of the Creative Process*, ed. Paul Smith (New York: Communication Arts Books, 1959), 104.

25. Flannagan, 105.

26. Flannagan, 105.

27. Flannagan, 108.

28. American corporations have long embraced the fine arts to represent themselves and capitalism. See Roland Marchand, *Advertising the American Dream: Making Way for Modernity, 1920–1940* (Berkeley: University of California Press, 1985); Neil Harris, *Art, Design, and the Modern Corporation: The Collection of Container Corporation of America* (Washington, DC: Smithsonian Institution Press, 1985); on how art was embraced by engineers critical of military-industrial technoscience, often using the language of creativity, see Matthew H. Wisnioski,

Engineers for Change: Competing Visions of Technology in 1960s America (Cambridge, MA: MIT Press, 2012), esp. chapter 6.

29. There were more: Argonne National Laboratory: "The continuing progress of civilization and culture is the result of creativity. . . . The proper environment, availability of equipment, stimulation of other scientists, the challenge to think and the opportunity for interesting problems—these nurture the creative process"; Hughes Aircraft: "Freedom of investigation . . . unmatched laboratory facilities . . . financial support of efforts toward advanced degrees . . . these are the pillars of what the Hughes Research & Development Laboratories refer to as creative engineering"; Radio Corporation of America: "Creative Ability Distinguishes the RCA Engineer . . . Aware that engineering today's defense systems would require new and fresh approaches, RCA management has consistently placed a premium on creativity. . . . Your individual thinking is welcomed. You, in turn, will be stimulated by RCA's creative atmosphere."

Chapter 9

1. Andreas Reckwitz, *The Invention of Creativity: Modern Society and the Culture of the New* (Malden, MA: Polity, 2017).

2. Mark A. Runco and Steven R. Pritzker, *Encyclopedia of Creativity*, 2nd edition (Amsterdam: Academic Press/Elsevier, 2011), xxi.

3. Zigmunt Bauman, *Liquid Modernity* (Cambridge: Polity, 2000).

4. Luc Boltanski and Eve Chiapello, *The New Spirit of Capitalism*, trans. G. Elliot (London: Verso, 2005); Richard Sennett, *The Culture of the New Capitalism* (New Haven, CT: Yale University Press, 2006).

5. David Harvey, *The Condition of Postmodernity* (Cambridge, MA: Blackwell, 1989); Andrew Ross, *No-Collar: The Humane Workplace and Its Hidden Costs* (New York: Basic Books, 2003); Andrew Ross, *Nice Work If You Can Get It: Life and Labor in Precarious Times* (New York: NYU Press, 2009).

6. Cf. Teresa Amabile, *The Social Psychology of Creativity* (New York: Springer-Verlag, 1983). As we've seen, creativity researchers had long recognized the social and environmental aspects of creativity, which were of obvious importance to managers and educators, and creativity research was already moving in a more socially oriented direction by the late 1960s. For example, the seventh and final Utah Conference in 1966 was dedicated to the theme "Climate for Creativity." See also the work of Morris Stein.

7. Amabile, *The Social Psychology of Creativity*.

8. Charles J. Limb and Allen R. Braun, "Neural Substrates of Spontaneous Musical Performance: An FMRI Study of Jazz Improvisation," *PLOS ONE* 3, no. 2 (February 27, 2008): e1679.

9. The list of interviewees included Mortimer Adler, Ed Asner, John Hope Franklin, John Gardner (familiar from chapter 3 as the supporter and popularizer of the IPAR creativity research, and the author of the influential Rockefeller Brothers report on education), Robert Galvin (the CEO of Motorola and an Alex Osborn devotee), Steven Jay Gould, Kitty Carlisle Hart, Eugene McCarthy, Oscar Peterson, David Riesman, Jonas Salk, Ravi Shankar, Benjamin Spock, Mark Strand, E. O. Wilson, and C. Vann Woodward, among dozens of others. Mihaly Csikszent-

mihalyi, *Creativity: Flow and the Psychology of Discovery and Invention* (New York: Harper Perennial, 1997), 373–91.

10. Csikszentmihalyi, 1.

11. Csikszentmihalyi, 1–10.

12. Beth A. Hennessey and Teresa M. Amabile, "Creativity," *Annual Review of Psychology* 61, no. 1 (January 2010): 570, https://doi.org/10.1146/annurev.psych.093008.100416.

13. Csikszentmihalyi, *Creativity*, 7

14. Hennessey and Amabile, "Creativity," 590.

15. Hennessey and Amabile, 571.

16. Hennessey and Amabile, 582.

17. Bruce Nussbaum, *Creative Intelligence: Harnessing the Power to Create, Connect, and Inspire* (New York: HarperBusiness, 2013), 6–7.

18. Robert J. Sternberg and Todd I. Lubart, *Defying the Crowd* (New York: The Free Press, 1995), vii.

19. It's not just the how-to books that pull this move. Leading creativity expert Margaret Boden's book *The Creative Mind: Myths and Mechanisms* opens with the litany of geniuses: "Shakespeare, Bach, Picasso; Newton, Darwin, Babbage; Chanel, the Saatchis, Groucho Marx, the Beatles. . . . From poets and scientists to advertisers and fashion designers, creativity abounds," runs the first line, before immediately clarifying that "everyday" activities like fixing a car also entail creativity. Margaret A. Boden, *The Creative Mind: Myths & Mechanisms* (New York: Basic Books, 1991).

20. Keith Negus and Michael J. Pickering, *Creativity, Communication, and Cultural Value* (London: SAGE Publications, Inc., 2004), 49.

21. Nicholas Garnham, "From Cultural to Creative Industries," *International Journal of Cultural Policy* 11, no. 1 (2005): 16; Ross, 15–52.

22. Sean Nixon, "The Pursuit of Newness," *Cultural Studies* 20, no. 1 (2006): 89–106, https://doi.org/10.1080/09502380500494877.

23. Richard Florida, *The Rise of the Creative Class: And How It's Transforming Work, Leisure, Community and Everyday Life* (New York: Basic Books, 2002), 8.

24. Florida, 6.

25. Christopher Dreher, "Be Creative—or Die," *Salon*, June 7, 2002, https://www.salon.com/2002/06/06/florida_22/.

26. See John Hartley, *Creative Industries* (Malden, MA: Blackwell, 2005); Kate Oakley, "Not So Cool Britannia: The Role of the Creative Industries in Economic Development," *International Journal of Cultural Studies* 7, no. 1 (2004): 67–77; Geert Lovink, *My Creativity Reader: A Critique of Creative Industries* (Amsterdam: Institute of Network Cultures, 2007); Gerald Raunig, Gene Ray, and Ulf Wuggenig, *Critique of Creativity: Precarity, Subjectivity and Resistance in the "Creative Industries"* (London: MayFlyBooks, 2011); Terry Flew, *The Creative Industries: Culture and Policy* (Newbury Park, CA: Sage Publications, 2012). An example of arguments for the economic impact of the arts is New England Foundation for the Arts, "New England's Creative Economy: Nonprofit Sector Impact," September 2011, https://www.nefa.org/sites/default/files/documents/NEFANonprofitStudy_3-2010.pdf; on Soho see Sharon Zukin, *Loft Living: Culture and Capital in Urban Change*, Johns Hopkins Studies in Urban Affairs (Baltimore, MD: Johns Hopkins University Press, 1982).

27. Doug Henwood, "Behind the News," May 10, 2018, http://shout.lbo-talk.org/lbo/RadioArchive/2018/18_05_10.mp3.

28. Garnham, "From Cultural to Creative Industries," 16.

29. Johannes Novy and Claire Colomb, "Struggling for the Right to the (Creative) City in Berlin and Hamburg: New Urban Social Movements, New 'Spaces of Hope'? Debates and Developments," *International Journal of Urban and Regional Research* 37, no. 5 (September 2013): 1816–38, https://doi.org/10.1111/j.1468-2427.2012.01115.x.

30. Angela McRobbie, *Be Creative: Making a Living in the New Culture Industries* (Cambridge: Polity Press, 2016); Tyler Denmead, *The Creative Underclass: Youth, Race, and the Gentrifying City*, illustrated edition (Durham, NC: Duke University Press, 2019).

31. "Mission," *Creative Class Struggle* (blog), accessed November 7, 2011, http://creativeclassstruggle.wordpress.com/mission.

32. Samuel Franklin, "'I'm Still an Outsider': An Interview with Richard Florida," 2022, https://arcade.stanford.edu/content/im-still-outsider-interview-richard-florida.

33. Oli Mould, *Against Creativity* (London: Verso, 2018), 11–12, 16.

34. Steven Poole, "*Against Creativity* by Oli Mould Review," *Guardian*, September 28, 2018, https://www.theguardian.com/books/2018/sep/26/against-creativity-oli-mould-review.

35. The 1962 Port Huron Statement by the Students for a Democratic Society calls to "replace power rooted in possession, privilege, or circumstance by power and uniqueness rooted in love, reflectiveness, reason, and creativity."

36. Kirin Narayan, *Everyday Creativity: Singing Goddesses in the Himalayan Foothills* (Chicago: University of Chicago Press, 2016), 29; Richard H. King, *Race, Culture, and the Intellectuals, 1940–1970* (Washington, DC: Woodrow Wilson Center Press, 2004), 125, 156; see Craig Lundy, *History and Becoming: Deleuze's Philosophy of Creativity* (Edinburgh: Edinburgh University Press, 2012).

Conclusion

1. Thomas Osborne, "Against 'Creativity': A Philistine Rant," *Economy and Society* 32, no. 4 (November 1, 2003): 507–25, https://doi.org/10.1080/0308514032000141684.

2. Evgeny Morozov, *To Save Everything, Click Here: The Folly of Technological Solutionism* (New York: Public Affairs, 2013).

3. Jenny Odell, *How to Do Nothing: Resisting the Attention Economy* (Brooklyn, NY: Melville House, 2019), 25.

4. Andrew Russel and Lee Vinsel, "Innovation is Overvalued. Maintenance Often Matters More," *Aeon*, April 7, 2016, https://aeon.co/essays/innovation-is-overvalued-maintenance-often-matters-more; Andrew Russel and Lee Vinsel, *The Innovation Delusion: How Our Obsession With the New Has Disrupted the Work That Matters Most* (New York: Currency, 2020); Giorgos Kallis, Susan Paulson, Giacomo D'Alisa, and Federico Demaria, *The Case for Degrowth* (Cambridge, UK: Polity, 2020).

INDEX

Page numbers followed by "f" indicate figures.

Osborn, Alexander Faickney: beliefs of, 69–70, 72; on brainstorming, 52–60, 67, 69; as CEF founder, 163; on education, creativity in, 70–71; on government's use of creativity, 228n44; influence of, 139, 192; research on creativity and, 73–75; Torrance and, 125

Packard, Vance, 11, 134, 147
Parker, Dorothy, 7
Parnes, Bea, 192
Parnes, Sidney J.: CPSI and, 61–62, 65; Guilford on, 76; importance, 192; publications by, 156; Torrance and, 125; at University of Buffalo, 73–74
Partnership for 21st Century Skills, 2
permanent revolution, 10
persistence, importance of, 162
personal issues, creativity as solution to, 69
pessimism, optimism versus, 16
Peterson, Oscar, 190
Pickering, Michael J., 196
PKL (agency), 142
Pleuthner, Willard, 64, 65, 67–68, 69
pluralism in American schools, 126–27
Port Huron Statement (Students for a Democratic Society), 242n35
postindustrialism, 187
Pound, Ezra, 219n17
Practice of Creativity, The (Prince), 103
Prince, George, 103–7, 109–11, 113, 116
Pringles, 115
product development, 113–14
productivity, as goal of creativity, 93
progress and creativity, 166–84; art and science as acts of creation, 174–79; creativity as corporate value, 179–83; creativity as responsibility, 172–74; introduction to, 166–70; technoscience, 170–72
psychologists: concept of creativity,

construction of, 21–22; impact on fields of study, 20–21; power of, 23
psychology: on creativity, 159; as field of study, state of, 22–26; Maslow on, 82. *See also* research on creativity
psychometrics: Galton and, 28; Guilford and, 26, 27; racism and, 30–31; Taylor and, 27; Torrance and, 122

race: in creative economy, 201; psychometrics and, 30–31; in research on creativity, lack of attention to, 39
Radio Corporation of America (RCA), 240n29
RAND corporation, 68f
Razik, Taher A., 49
reason-why advertising, 140, 144, 146, 148, 152
Reckwitz, Andreas, 185
Reeves, Rosser, 236n29
reification, 21
research on creativity, 19–51; conclusions on, 48–51; creative persons, identifying, 35–38; creative persons and class, race, and gender, 38–45; creativity versus genius, 28–33; creativity versus intelligence, 26–28; criteria for creativity, 45–48; divergent thinking, 33–35; funding for, 17; introduction to, 19–22; Osborn and, 73–75; post-1970s, 189; psychology, state of, 22–26; social and environmental aspects in, 240n6
research on creativity, critiques of, 155–65; conclusions on, 163–64; introduction to, 155–60; responses to, 160–63
Rexroth, Kenneth, 19, 35
Riesman, David, 11, 12, 86, 190
Rise of the Creative Class (Florida), 197
Robinson, Kenneth, 2–3
Rockefeller Brothers Fund, 13, 126, 127